Oil Lamps

Oil Lamps

The Kerosene Era in North America

CATHERINE M. V. THURO

Photography by Ken Bell

OIL LAMPS
The Kerosene Era in North America
Copyright © 1976
Fourth Printing, 1981
Catherine M.V. Thuro

Library of Congress Catalog Card Number 75-21331
ISBN: 0-87069-121-X

Designed by Jann Williams and Catherine Thuro
Typeset in Mallard and LeGriffe
Photography by Ken Bell

Printed and bound in the United States of America

Published by
WALLACE-HOMESTEAD BOOK CO.
1912 GRAND AVENUE
DES MOINES, IOWA 50309

To my husband, Carl, who shared the enjoyment of collecting and research for this book, and to our sons, Wes, Ken and Randy for tolerating it.

FLOWER ARRANGEMENTS — Lois Wilson

SETTINGS AND ACCESSORIES — Donald McCormack
— Flavia Redelmeier
— Catherine Smith
— Kinghorn Antiques Limited

PHOTOGRAPHS FROM THE
COLLECTIONS OF
— Dr. Walter Beattie
— Marian & Peter Blundell
— Debra & David Christmas
— William Cole
— Kenneth Douglas
— Marion Kribs
— Janice Moodie
— The Sandwich Glass Museum
— Joseph Strain
— June & Mel Walton
— Kenneth Wheeler
— The Author

Table Of Contents

a. Oil on Canvas by A. Francis '94

With a background of many excellent books on glass and lighting, and at a time when a full range of kerosene lamps was available for study and photography, the idea for organizing this book became an intriguing challenge. Until recently, kerosene had not captured the imagination of those who have recorded or collected articles from the past.

"Century-old", pre-Civil War (1861), or Canada's pre-Confederation (1867) homes are generally associated with gas, whale oil, lard lamps or candles, all of which preceded kerosene. Kerosene lamps, burning essentially the same product as that of a century ago, have been and still are, a stand-by for electrical power failures. Bless the blackouts! Without them, thousands of early lamps, burners and chimneys would have been destroyed years ago. Full-time use of kerosene in many rural and remote areas is a memory of the 1940's, and, for those who recall this, the mental picture is usually one of cleaning smoky chimneys, and of the liquid pictured (b). This situation was not conducive to using kerosene lamps to re-create the lighting mood of a century ago. Candles have held this role until the recent marketing of a refined petroleum product, which permits the use of these lamps without smell or smoke. This gives a much cleaner and brighter light than candles, and a few lamps will provide an acceptable level of illumination for conversation or entertaining. A kerosene lamp can be an appropriate accessory to century-old furnishings, or in a comtemporary setting, a refreshing contrast and link with the past.

Initially, my interest in old tools and implements created an awareness of people of the past. These people were involved in the making of, and in the use of these objects which were of great importance to their existence. A study of glass lamps may not appear to be one very concerned with people, however, the human element is apparent when one reads the history of the glass industry and its personnel. The dedication of students, collectors, dealers and authors, has resulted in the compilation of an astounding wealth of material.

In every book on glass, the role of the people involved is interwoven with basic statistics of the industry. The field seems to have had a generous share of colorful personalities, and interesting family associations. A more direct association of people and product is the way in which glass quality reflects the human element in the process of manufacture. The great majority of kerosene lamps required the skill of the glass blower, whereas most glassware of this period was merely pressed. The hand operations contribute to the variations of thickness and other irregularities. These, together with the pressed, cut or engraved patterns, create light reflections and refraction, which cause delight to the collector and dismay to the photographer. Of the hundreds of photographs taken for this book, I doubt if there were five which utilized identical setups. The slightest rotation of a lamp would make the pattern detail spring forth or fade out. The challenge of providing each lamp with its own "personalized" lighting setup was so ably met by photographer Ken Bell.

When we were first married, my husband and I decided on contemporary decor, and I therefore chose only a few mementos from the very large collection of antiques my parents had gathered. An oil painting by A. Francis, and the white glass lamp (c) were among these

b. Today it is clean, perfumed, and does not smoke.

c. This 17-1/8" Acanthus Leaf lamp in opaque white glass, originally had a matching tulip shade with the leaves forming an irregular top. It is reported to have been made in pink and in yellow cased glass.

half dozen items. If in fact, I had an early interest in kerosene, it lay dormant for many years until the celebration of Canada's Centennial in 1967. Along with most other Canadians, an awareness of our past, particularly the last century, aroused a curiosity which led to exploring museums, antique shops, auctions and libraries to discover more. These sources make it possible to enjoy the sense of delight and satisfaction experienced in identifying an object. This is taken a step further and becomes more personal as material from two or more sources is combined. The final step is to combine material from several sources with a particular object to study, to form original opinions or conclusions. This is when the concept of a book takes hold and the author is at the mercy of this compulsion until it is completed.

The aim of this book is to illustrate the broad range of kerosene lamps that exist today, to place them using information currently available, as closely as possible to the period in which they were first used, and to give the area of original use, and manufacture if known. Some lamps were manufactured over a long period of time, and possibly by different companies in both the United States and Canada.

Kerosene lamp production coincided with the expansion of the glass industry in Northeastern U.S.A. and Eastern Canada, and with the introduction and popularity of hundreds of glass patterns for tableware. The late 1850's represented not only a transition from whale oil or burning fluid, to kerosene, but an equally distinctive and dramatic transition in the design of hand and stand lamps. With the many examples shown, various design trends become apparent, and whether the collector is looking for something historically accurate, or just a useful and charming reminder of the past, an example of the particular lamp or type, should be found here.

All of the examples shown, with a few noted exceptions, have been acquired or seen in Canada, and I believe were imported when manufactured, for use in Canadian homes. The vast quantity and variety of lamps produced in the United States and used throughout Eastern Canada, has presented an excellent opportunity to study American design and production of lamps, while at the same time illustrating lamps that were used in Canada. Some lamps are still in the homes or area of original use due to the late distribution of rural hydro electric power in Canada, and the recent emergence of many of these, show by their condition that they have not been regarded as treasures.

The time spent on removing the gummy or hardened oil on neglected specimens is a time of excitement and anticipation as the glass quality and true character of the lamp is revealed. One can then imagine scenes brightened by its golden glow. The age and type of the lamp will indicate the decor which may have surrounded it, and the headlines and stories which could have been read by its light. Perhaps it illuminated family gatherings, entertainment, meetings, or the making of handicrafts. A far cry from present-day standards, but a much wider gap existed between kerosene and candle.

The locale from which these lamps have recently emerged has little significance in establishing the area or country in which they were made, but it is noteworthy in that the information may have some value in future research, and for collectors or those engaged in restoration who seek a type of lamp used in their area. Until recently it was reasonably safe to assume that lamps found in Canada were used in Canadian homes from the time of manufacture, unless brought north later by immigrants. This situation has differed from the post-war selection in shops in the United States, particularly the border states. From a dealer in Canada comes the story of shipping south of the border, close to a hundred lamps a week for several months. From a dealer in the United States a story of having received as many as 1,200 lamps in a single shipment from Canada. The area of original use will be given only if there has been reasonable assurance of the source.

I would like to offer my thanks to those associated with research centers in the United States and Canada, and to the collectors, dealers and others who have been so helpful in countless ways, and whose enthusiasm has propelled this undertaking. The search for lamps and information has given my husband and me the opportunity to meet a remarkable, helpful and friendly group of interesting people. We cherish these memories and look forward to new friendships, and to renewing old ones. Among these are:

John A. Artzberger
Martin Avenhus
Mr. & Mrs. Leslie Baker
Aram Baltayan
Molly Bartram
Anita and David Bates
Dr. Walter Beattie
Ann Beaulieu
Noel Binns
James Bisback
Marian and Peter Blundell
Carleton Brown
Mr. & Mrs. Arthur Burridge
Nancy Caldwell
Catherine Christie
Sandra and Bill Caskey
William Cole
Dorothy and John Dobson
Nell and Leslie Donaldson
Kenneth Douglas
Gertrude Doyle
Joyce and Don Dunham
Elizabeth Earle
Sally Earle
Mary and Dick Francis
Vera and Allan Fraser
Mary Garden

Pat and Bill Gerbrant
Carmen Gove
Mr. & Mrs. E. Gust Hagglund
Dr. Thomas H. Hartig
Janet Holmes
Ruth and Dr. Howard Hostetler
Grace and Bob Houle
Ruth Ingram
Lowell Innes
George Johnston
Fred Jordan
Jonny Kalisch
Jack and the late Shirley Knowles
Marion Kribs
Dwight P. Lanmon
Vera and James Lee
Joyce Lees
Eva Mackie
Hugh Manning
Allan Markham
Beatrice and Mike McCormack
Mr. & Mrs. Clarence McCuaig
Mrs. Harold Mercer
Nancy Merrill
Ruth and Bob Meyer
Agnes Middleton
Beverly and Tom Mileham

Eunice and the late Frank Millard
Carol and Henry Milberg
Janice Moodie
Christine and Peter Palmer
Earl Patte
Dr. Arthur Peterson
Margaret and Mogens Philip
Mr. & Mrs. Peter Picken
Eugene Rae
Myrtle Reeve
Gay and Don Robertson
Mr. & Mrs. John Robinson
Dr. & Mrs. Loris Russell
Wolfgang Schlombs
Kay Shelley
Jean Smith
Lena Stanbury
Dennis Steep
Henry Stevenson
Barbara and John Todd
Maxine Treleaven
June and Mel Walton
Kenneth Wheeler
Margery and Norman White
Mr. & Mrs. Percy Wollacott
Leah and Peter Woloson
Margaret Zack

LIGHTING CHART 1850-1950

FUEL AND ENERGY SOURCES OF ILLUMINATION

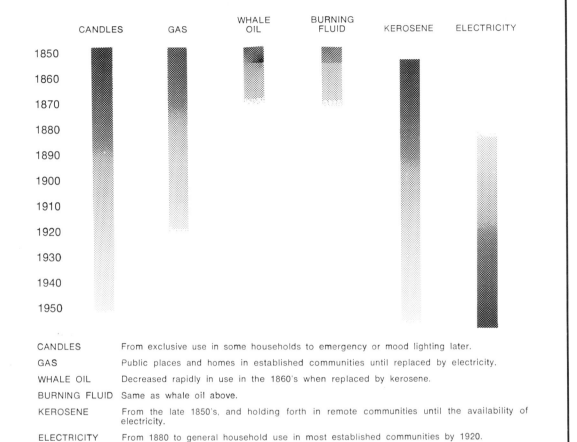

	CANDLES	GAS	WHALE OIL	BURNING FLUID	KEROSENE	ELECTRICITY
1850						
1860						
1870						
1880						
1890						
1900						
1910						
1920						
1930						
1940						
1950						

CANDLES   From exclusive use in some households to emergency or mood lighting later.

GAS   Public places and homes in established communities until replaced by electricity.

WHALE OIL   Decreased rapidly in use in the 1860's when replaced by kerosene.

BURNING FLUID   Same as whale oil above.

KEROSENE   From the late 1850's, and holding forth in remote communities until the availability of electricity.

ELECTRICITY   From 1880 to general household use in most established communities by 1920.

THE STAND OR POST LAMP

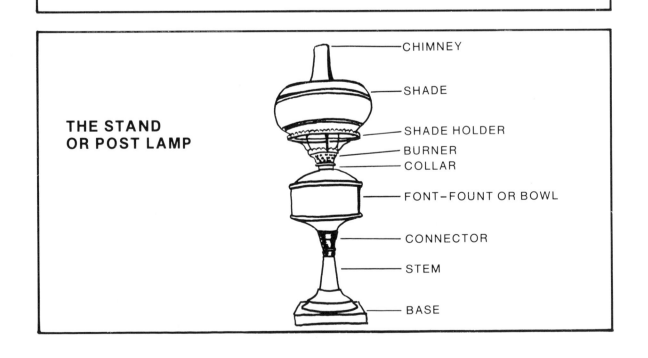

- CHIMNEY
- SHADE
- SHADE HOLDER
- BURNER
- COLLAR
- FONT-FOUNT OR BOWL
- CONNECTOR
- STEM
- BASE

History and Research

The nineteenth century in North America saw the use of ancient forms of lighting, the development of known forms, and the discovery of revolutionary new ones. No attempt will be made here to detail these forms so well chronicled in other works, but a brief outline is given to place the "kerosene era" in relationship to other lighting.

Primitive forms include splints and rushlights. Lard was used in simple saucer type holders, and in many ingenious lamps invented during the first half of the 19th century. Candles had principal use until replaced by more convenient forms of lighting, but would then, as now, be a good emergency light, particularly in a wind-proof lantern. Whale oil was used in glass or metal lamps with a single or double round wick supported in a vertical tube. In addition to these, there were a number of complex lamps made for this fuel, some of which were very handsome and ornate. The same simple lamps that were used for whale oil were also used for burning fluid, a dangerous and potentially explosive mixture of turpentine and alcohol. Burning-fluid burners do not extend down into the font, and have the distinguishing characteristic of divergent wick tubes. James Young, a Scotsman, obtained a patent in England in 1850 and in the United States in 1852, for a fuel to be used as an illuminant. He called it Paraffin Oil. This was essentially the same product patented in the U.S.A. in 1854 by Dr. Abraham Gesner, a Canadian geologist, who called his discovery Kerosene. On this side of the Atlantic, he is credited with the discovery by reason of his having given public demonstrations of this illuminant in 1846. This precedes recorded information regarding Dr. Young's work. Kerosene was to become the means to a bright, portable and inexpensive light which would be available to every home, and which would bring about a dramatic change in the habits and lives of the populace. One can reflect upon the changes in the pattern of family life as they acquired lights which allowed them to continue their tasks, or to enjoy reading or games after dark. To each person it meant an extension of time for work or enjoyment. The availability of kerosene, also known as coal oil, rock oil and lunar oil, was limited until the development of the first dug well in Ontario in 1858, and the first drilled well in Pennsylvania in 1859, produced quantities for widespread use and distribution.

Among the first advertisements for coal oil recorded in the Toronto Daily Globe are those of Parson Bros., Coal Oil and Lamp Agency. On July 28, 1858, they advertised

Petrolia or Oil Springs, Ontario circa 1870
Courtesy Ontario Archives

"THE GREAT COAL OIL LAMP
The Cheapest and most Brilliant Light ever introduced
GAS NOT EXCEPTED"

This is followed by a description which reads like the beginning of a problem in an old arithmetic book:

"This lamp will give a light equal to three burning fluid lamps of two wicks each at half the cost."

A few weeks later, on August 20, 1858, the same company's advertisement claimed:

"Pure Coal Oil gives at the same cost—

7 times as much light as Burning Fluid
6 times as much light as Sperm Oil

> 5 times as much light as Lard Oil
> 3 times as much light as Whale Oil
> 2 times as much light as Rapeseed Oil
> 2 times as much light as Rosin Oil
> 3 times as much light as Candles."

These comparisons and descriptions, if accurate, provide us with a clear picture of the economy involved and of the impression this light must have made upon those seeing it for the first time. Reports are that it was an exciting, sometimes terrifying, and certainly memorable experience.

Oil lamps, burners and promotion were all essential ingredients in the acceptance of this new means of illumination.

MORE LIGHT!

FOR SALE, THE PATENT RIGHTS

FOR

An Entirely New Light!!

WHICH HAS THE FOLLOWING CHARACTERISTICS.

1st.   It costs less than one fifth of any other practical artificial light.
2nd.   It is a perfectly steady light, so that persons with dim or weak eyes can use it without unpleasant results.
3rd.   It is capable of being adjusted to the nice lamps now in use.
4th.   It is never out of order.
5th.   There is nothing unpleasant about it.
6th.   It is perfectly safe.

All this is clear, palpable reality to the beholder; and believing that it must at once come into general use, and wishing to send it broadcast, we have adopted a simple plan and scale of disposing of the rights to the same by counties or towns, in such a way that without risk all persons of fair capacity and industrious habits can be sure of replenishing their pockets, or adding largely to an already ample treasury.

This magnificent opportunity to make money will be explained by the proprietors for the whole Canadas; persons can commence by buying territory for the amount of from $50 to $2,000. We pledge our business reputation (and we have been somewhat successful) that any person can make more money with this Patent for the next year than they have made. or would be likely to make in the next three years, with the same capital and exertion in any other business. In view of these facts, much more might be said. We earnestly invite you to call and examine the merits of this new light at the American Hotel.

WILLIS JONES & CO.

Toronto, Oct. 24, 1857   2854-tf

Courtesy Toronto Globe and Mail

The "MORE LIGHT" advertisement which first appeared October 24, 1857, ran for 28 days in January, 1858, and was most frequently displayed on the front page. The lighting fuel is not mentioned, but the Willis Jones & Co. signature suggests this might have been a promotion for the burner which was patented by Edward F. Jones of Boston, Mass., on May 4, 1858. Burner and lamp were synonymous in early kerosene days, and many patents issued under the heading lamp, were really for what we now refer to as burners. This explains the reference to the "Jones Improved Patent Lamps" on the cover of the S.E. Southland Co., of Philadelphia, catalogue of 1859. This catalogue is of immense value in the illustration, description and dating of kerosene lamps and use. Over 550 sizes and types of lamps are listed in this catalogue, and a claim that "millions have been sold" suggests that in approximately one year, the year preceding the first drilled well, kerosene illumination was successfully launched on a large scale.

Another advertisement in the Globe dated October 23, 1859, states,

"THE JONES LAMP
Manufactured in every variety and style
and sold at greatly reduced prices.
By: Tarbell & Wyan,
37 Central St., Boston.
(successors to E. Jones & Co.)

N.B. The Jones burner recently improved gives more light than any
other kerosene or coal oil burner manufactured."

This may also yield clues to the role this Jones name played in the
early promotion of kerosene lamps.

*This lamp conforms to the description "Britannia Low Side Handle Lamp" on page 11
of the S. E. Southland's Catalogue.*

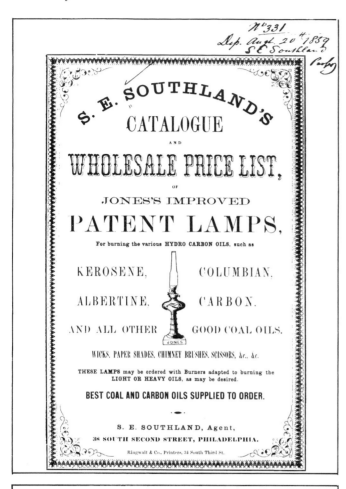

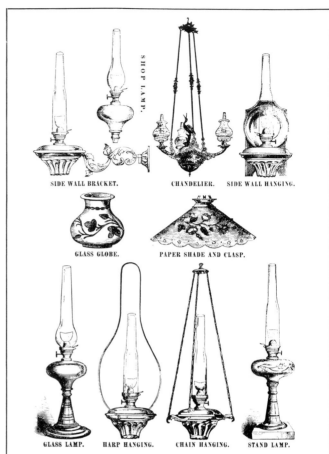

KEROSENE, COAL AND CARBON OILS, have already, in a very short time, worked their way into public favor, to an extent scarcely credited by those not conversant with the business. At first imperfect, and exceedingly disagreeable in smell, the oil has at length been **DEODORIZED** and brought to a state of perfection *hardly anticipated by the most sanguine.* It may now be obtained in any desired quantity and of superior quality. The material for its manufacture is *absolutely inexhaustible.* That it will eventually come into universal use, with all such as desire to *avoid danger,* and at the same time possess themselves of the *very best* and **MOST ECONOMICAL** artificial Light within their reach, there cannot be a doubt. To make *success certain,* two things are indispensable, viz:—**GOOD OIL AND A GOOD LAMP.** Millions of these Lamps have been sold, and wherever good oil has been used, *in Lamps of proper construction, perfect success* has invariably been the result. Wherever satisfaction has not been realized, you may be sure that you have either a *poor lamp, poor oil,* or *both.* The oils commonly called cheap or heavy oils, will *never* be burned in *any lamp* with even *ordinary satisfaction.* Good oils will eventually be sufficiently low in price to do away with the necessity of attempting to burn poor oils, for the sake of economy.

BREAKAGE AND LEAKAGE.—The goods will be thoroughly packed and marked "*Glass.*" The Oil will be put in Barrels of the very best quality, and when shipped in "*Good Order,*" the breakage and leakage must be at the risk of the purchaser. Neither will occur, except when packages are *unfairly* handled by transportation agents.

Entered according to Act of Congress, in the year 1859 by S. E. SOUTHLAND, in the Clerk's Office of the District Court, for the Eastern District of Pennsylvania.

TERMS CASH,

On Delivery, or subject to Draft at Sight.

UNDOUBTED CITY REFERENCE REQUIRED before delivering Goods ordered by Letter.

The Prices named, show the *comparative value* of the different styles, and are designed to be an **APPROXIMATE GUIDE,** for the *convenience of parties wishing to order before seeing the Goods.* The prices of manufactured goods depend so much upon the ever varying prices of material and labor, that it is, of course, impossible to continue long, without alteration, a specific price list.

No pains will be spared in making the goods *unexceptionable in style and* QUALITY, and **they will be sold at COMPETING PRICES.**

A Discount will be made from these prices on all bills amounting to $25 and upwards. (Oils invariably net cash.)

Bad Oils, *totally unfit for any satisfactory use,* have been, and will be again forced into the market, at temptingly low prices.— They have done much to injure the unprecedented popularity of Coal Oil Lamps.

Good Oils, can now be had in large quantities, therefore, prudent buyers should consult their interest by purchasing only from *reliable sources.* MY CUSTOMERS *can depend upon me for a supply of* **GOOD OIL,** at market prices for equal quality. LAMP SELLERS have a DOUBLE INCENTIVE for selling none but the best Oil.

Oil Barrels, will be charged at the cost. If not bored or otherwise injured, they may be returned, and when sold they will be credited in account at whatever they sell for, less the freight and cartage.

Order the Goods by the Numbers. You will then be sure of getting the goods you order without mistakes or confusion.

DIRECTIONS FOR USING THE LAMPS.

Remove the Cap and trim the Wick even with the Tube, replace the Cap, turn the Wick up through the opening, light it, and turn it down below the opening, adjust the Chimney, and allow it to burn low for a few moments, so as to prevent charring.— Breaking of Chimneys is avoided by turning the blaze on gradually. To use as a Night-Lamp, re-trim, as the crusted wick prevents perfect combustion.

1

JONES'S BURNERS.

No. 1, Small.—Narrow Wick and small short Chimney—for carrying about—makes a fine Night Lamp.—(will fit any of the old No. 1 Lamps.)

No. 2, Medium.—(Is the old No. 1.)
No. 3, Large.—(Is the old No. 2.)

OUTSIDE GLOBES may be attached to any Lamp in the Catalogue.

STAND LAMPS,

For the No. 2 (Medium) Burners.

The No. 1 (Small) Burners also fit these Lamps.

Glass Lamps.

Per Doz.

1.	Plain Flint Glass Lamp, *8 inches high,					$6 50
2.	Engraved	"	"	"	"	7 00
3.	Plain	"	"	"	Ring Fount,	6 50
4.	"	"	5½ "	"	low, side handle,	7 25
5.	Engraved	"	"	"	"	8 00
6.	Plain	"	Shop Lamp, with peg for socket,			6 00
7.	"	"	"	"	inverted peg,	6 00

White Marble, 3½ inch Square Base, Brass Column.

9¼ INCHES HIGH.

11.	Plain Flint Glass Fount,				$10 00
12.	Engraved	"	"		10 50
13.	White	"	"		10 00
14.	Plain Blue	"	"		10 00
15.	Ring Punty	"	"		11 00
16.	White Plated and Cut Fancy Glass Fount,				18 00
17.	Blue	"	"	"	18 00
18.	Ruby	"	"	"	18 00

‡ The prices given are for the Lamps complete, including PLAIN Chimneys. Globes and Holders must be ordered separately.

*The height given is the distance from the table to the flame.

3

White Double Marble, 5 in. Heavy Square Base, Fluted Brass Col'm.

13 INCHES HIGH.

791.	Plain Flint Glass Fount,			$26 50
792.	Engraved	"	"	27 25
793.	Plain White	"	"	26 50
794.	" Blue	"	"	26 50
795.	Ring Punty	"	"	28 00
796.	White Plated and Cut Fancy Glass Fount,			36 00
797.	Blue	"	"	"	36 00
798.	Ruby	"	"	"	36 00

No. 3 HANGING LAMPS.

Chain Hanging, with Tin Reflector.

801.	Fluted Clear Glass Fount,			$20 00
802.	" White	"	"	20 00
803.	" Blue	"	"	20 00
804.	" White Plated and Cut Fancy Glass Fount,			31 50
805.	" Blue	"	"	"	31 50
806.	" Ruby	"	"	"	31 50
807.	Brass Fount,			29 50
808.	Japanned "			25 00

‡Harp Hanging, with Tin Reflector.

811.	Fluted Clear Glass Fount,			$18 00
812.	" White	"	"	18 00
813.	" Blue	"	"	18 00
814.	" White Plated and Cut Fancy Glass Fount,			30 00
815.	" Blue	"	"	"	30 00
816.	" Ruby	"	"	"	30 00
817.	Brass Fount,			29 00
818.	Japanned "			24 00

*Side Wall Hanging, with Plated Reflector.

821.	Fluted Clear Glass Fount,			$19 50
822.	" White	"	"	19 50
823.	" Blue	"	"	19 50
824.	" White Plated and Cut Fancy Glass Fount,			31 00
825.	" Blue	"	"	"	31 00
826.	" Ruby	"	"	"	31 00
827.	Brass Fount,			29 00
828.	Japanned "			24 50

‡ Fine Hall or Entry Lamps when fitted with Globes and Holders.
* These Lamps can be furnished with a fine Glass Silvered Reflector, which never tarnishes, at an additional charge of five dollars per dozen.

No. 3 HANGING LAMPS.   28

Side Wall, Gilt 10 inch Swing Bracket.

831.	Fluted Clear Glass Fount,			$25 00
832.	" White	"	"	25 00
833.	" Blue	"	"	25 00
834.	" White Plated and Cut Fancy Glass Fount,			36 00
835.	" Blue	"	"	"	36 00
836.	" Ruby	"	"	"	36 00
837.	Brass Fount,			34 00
838.	Japanned "			30 00

Side Wall, Gilt 14 inch Swing Bracket.

841.	Fluted Clear Glass Fount,			$30 00
842.	" White	"	"	30 00
843.	" Blue	"	"	30 00
844.	" White Plated and Cut Fancy Glass Fount,			42 00
845.	" Blue	"	"	"	42 00
846.	" Ruby	"	"	"	42 00
847.	Brass Fount,			40 00
848.	Japanned "			36 00

Side Wall, Bronze 6 inch Swing Bracket.

851.	Fluted Clear Glass Fount,			$15 00
852.	" White	"	"	15 00
853.	" Blue	"	"	15 00
854.	" White Plated and Cut Fancy Glass Fount,			27 00
855.	" Blue	"	"	"	27 00
856.	" Ruby	"	"	"	27 00
857.	Brass Fount,			25 00
858.	Japanned "			21 00

Side Wall, White Painted 6 inch Swing Bracket.

861.	Fluted Clear Glass Fount,			$16 00
862.	" White	"	"	16 00
863.	" Blue	"	"	16 00
864.	" White Plated and Cut Fancy Glass Fount,			28 00
865.	" Blue	"	"	"	28 00
866.	" Ruby	"	"	"	28 00
867.	Brass Fount,			26 00
868.	Japanned "			21 00

CHIMNEYS,

For the No. 2 (Medium) Burners.

1001.	Plain, Bulb, Lip, 8 inch Chimney,				$0 87½
1002.	Ground,	"	8 "	"	1 12½
1003.	Plain,	"	9 "	" small,	87½
1004.	Ground,	"	9 "	"	1 12½
1005.	Plain,	"	5 "	" for hand Lamps,	87½
1006.	" Bulb, Slip, 8 "	"			87½
1007.	Ground,	"	8 "	"	1 12½

For the No. 3 (Large) Burners.

1021.	Plain, Bulb, Lip, 10 inch Chimney,				$1 12½
1022.	Ground,	"	10 "	"	1 37½
1023.	Plain, Straight, Lip, 9 inch	"			1 12½
1024.	Ground,	"	9 "	"	1 37½
1025.	Plain,	"	12 "	"	1 12½
1026.	Ground,	"	12 "	"	1 37½
1027.	Plain, Bulb,	"	10 "	" (Waterbury Burner),	1 12½
1028.	Ground,	"	10 "	"	1 37½
1029.	Plain,	" Slip	10 "	"	1 12½
1030.	Ground,	"	10 "	"	1 37½
1031.	Plain,	"	12 "	"	1 12½
1032.	Ground,	"	12 "	"	1 37½

For the No. 1 (Small) Burners.

1041.	Short, Plain, Chimney for Hand Lamps,		87½
1042.	" Ground,	" "	1 12½

GLASS GLOBES WITH HOLDERS.

(Not included in the price of the Lamps.)

For Lamps with No. 2 Burners.

1051.	Plain Ground,	$4 75
1052.	Ground, Cut and Engraved,	5 50

For Lamps with No. 3 Burners.

1061.	Plain Ground,	$5 50
1062.	Ground, Cut and Engraved,	6.50

PAPER SHADES WITH FRENCH CLASPS.

1071.	Plain Printed, Assorted Colors,*	$2 50
1072.	" Views, Assorted Colors,*	3 00
1073.	Transparent, Painted Flowers, Assorted Colors,*	4 00
1074.	" Views, " *	4 00
1075.	Plain Green Dome, Small, with Wire Holders	3 75
1076.	" Large	4 25
1077.	Dome, Painted Views, Assorted Colors,	4 75
1078.	" Flowers,	4 75

* These Shades with a Wire Holder will be furnished 50 cents per dozen less.

23 Jan. 1880.

The S. E. Southland's catalogue is the most important catalogue I am aware of, relating to kerosene. It presents a picture of kerosene as an accepted and popular illuminant in 1859. Statements such as "The material for its manufacture is *absolutely inexhaustible*," and the advertising copy of the day, are informative and entertaining. The list of lamps indicates that most of the lamps had marble bases, and brass or glass stems. Fonts were plain or engraved, or plated (overlay) and fancy cut. Ring Punty is a puzzling name included with almost every group. I have interpreted it as a reference to the most common early pressed glass pattern font seen with brass stem and marble bases. There is a section on these lamps and their variations on page 84.

a. Early bracket or hanging lamp font.

Although few in number, the illustrations are very important. The font (a) is similar to those in the catalogue. The fine quality white glass has brilliant orange highlights, when back-lit by the sun or strong light. Other lamps, holders, chimneys and shades, show us what was used in kerosene's earliest days.

From this beginning, kerosene had widespread use to the turn of the 20th century and then its use decreased during the next 50 years as electricity became available. Both burning fluid and whale oil disappeared, or had minimal use, as kerosene, which could also be used in the same lamps, became available. Promoting the use of burning fluid lamps for kerosene was one aspect of the broadside (opposite) advertising a kerosene burner.

Charles F. Martine of Dorchester, Mass., obtained a patent on May 20, 1862 for a burner which was basically a perforated cylinder surrounding the flame, and resting on a tall wick tube. This invention was designed to "Improve that class of lamps which are used without a chimney." Another Martine patent of Sept. 19, 1865, with similar intent, shows a perforated wick tube. Presumably, these patents were marketed, but I have not heard of an example in existence today.

Courtesy Ohio Historical Society (verbatim reprint)

HARRY. There it is again! another chimney broken this week !
No wonder we are running behind hand Sarah , when
it takes all my spare money to find Chimneys.

SARAH. Indeed Harry it was not my fault, they break without
being touched. Why cannot you get one of MARTINE'S
PATENT BURNERS, and let us fix up our old fluid lamps;
Brother George uses them and says he would not be
without them for any thing.

HARRY. Give me my hat and coat Sallie and I will go out and
get one at once and who knows but by economy we
may get to be as rich as your Brother George.

GEORGE. Emma when you see this lamp burning so beautifully,
can you imagine that we were once foolish enough, to
spend our money in Chimneys to be broken by Careless
servants?

EMMA. It does seem almost incredible George but what a
blessing it has proved, That was a lucky quarter
you expended, when you bought MARTINE'S PATENT
BURNER

GEORGE. It was so, for I date the commecment of our prosperity
from that time.

Artificial gas for lighting introduced about 1800, became available in larger centers in the 1840-1860 range. It was used for street lighting, in commercial establishments and homes which could afford it during that period and up until about 1910. The invention of the Wellsbach gas mantle in the 80's dramatically increased the light output. However, enthusiasm for its use was to be over-shadowed by electric light which emerged about 1880, and was in general use in established communities by 1920.

These dates and uses are generalizations. Availability and cost extended the use of all forms of lighting before electricity. This is evidenced by such things as patents and advertisements for certain forms of lighting which occurred long after an improved form had been introduced.

Research is a dimension added to collecting which expands the intrinsic value of objects from the past and extends one's frame of reference. There are four areas of information which are of interest in the study of lamps, and their relative importance is a personal choice. They are:

1. The first date of manufacture. This may be established by a patent date, although production may have preceded granting of the patent.
2. The location or area of manufacture.
3. The name of the manufacturer.
4. The area of original use.

Many factors are considered in endeavouring to find the answers, and a patent is probably the most positive way. Kerosene lamps and related items inspired inventive and creative instincts to the extent that as Dr. Arthur Peterson points out in his book, Glass Patterns and Patents, there was a dramatic increase in the number of patents during the early 1860's when patents in other areas declined due to the Civil War. Dating from 1861, an invention patent was in effect for 17 years, and a design patent could be applied for, for a period of 3-1/2, 7 or 14 years. Anyone was free to use the design after this period. As was expected, principals or employees of glass companies, frequently took out design or invention patents, but as would **not** be expected, they sometimes assigned these patents to other manufacturers! Between 1861 and 1876, and occasionally later, patent information was embossed on many glass lamps, possibly as protection against infringement, and possibly because it might have been considered to make the article more saleable. An aspect of patents that can be confusing is that the patent illustrations often differ from the article marked with the patent date.

Many glass catalogues are not dated, and those that are, frequently contain illustrations of articles that pre-date the catalogue by a few decades. Catalogues are valuable guides but should be used with caution. Glass company catalogues or advertisements may show products which were made by member companies before a merger. Such was the case in the merger of 18 companies to form the United States Glass Company in 1891, and of the 19 companies which formed the National Glass Company in 1899. It is possible also, that then as now, manufacturers will include in their catalogues, products supplied by other companies. In other instances, catalogues may contain illustrations of lamps produced over a long period of time. The Sears Roebuck catalogue of 1927 features a page of kerosene lamps, one of which was patented in the 1890's and another about 1880.

The several books which contain researched and catalogued glass patterns, frequently list manufacturers and dates. Sometimes the dates given are the result of the researcher having been familiar with the qualities and characteristics of other more positively dated glass. This "educated guess" method appears to have some validity in the number of times these guesses have been substantiated by subsequent research.

The most controversial research approach is that involving fragments or shards. These are the pieces of glass found by excavation at the sites of former glass companies. Some authorities claim these pieces are proof that the article was made there, while others would disregard such claims. The shard may have been a sample of another glass maker's ware, or a piece of "cullet," which is the glass industry's term for pieces of broken glass from any source, a quantity of which is added to each batch of glass being made. The quantity may be up to 1/3 or more of the batch, and was generally provided by rejects or breakage. A surplus or deficiency occasionally meant an exchange of cullet between factories. Advertisements for cullet appeared in newspapers, and scrap glass may have been used for this purpose. One should investigate the basis of authentication and then judge its validity.

The next research procedure is probably the most entertaining, and there is considerable scope for one to pursue. This is in the area of relating the shapes and pattern designs of lamps. Any interest which has required an attention to detail will be an asset in the pursuit of identifying and relating lamps. In the manufacture of glass tableware, each piece was designed to relate to the set, and while there may have been some duplication or interchanging of parts such as handles or finials, it was not practiced to the extent that it was in lamp manufacture. Perhaps this freedom developed from the early lamps, where it was standard practice to attach fonts to a base which may have been mass produced by another manufacturer.

This mixing and matching characteristic of lamps can lead to relating lamps to each other, and then, if one of these possesses a design feature of a recognized tableware pattern, or other known glass piece, it might lead to the manufacturer and date. This might not be conclusive evidence but reliable enough to warrant recording in the event that someday more positive association will be discovered.

Several examples of related patterns are shown in the sections on stand and hand lamps, and different forms are illustrated as it requires observation of many lamps to establish relationships. It is important to study plain fonts, stems and bases as well as handles. Collars and brass connectors, particularly dated ones, may be important clues. If a distinctive collar turns up on a particular lamp, it may need the support of additional examples to verify its likelihood of being original.

There are three types of brass connectors often found today which require the base and font pegs to be especially molded for their use. One is a threaded screw type patented by the Atterbury brothers in 1868 and used on lamps manufactured by Atterbury & Co. After this patent had expired, another screw socket appeared in 1891 in an

Atterbury Screw Socket

advertisement of Hobbs Glass Company, successors to Hobbs Brockunier & Company. This connector has a patent pending note, and was shown in the United States Glass Company catalogue on their "World's Fair" (1893) lamps.

The trade journal China, Glass and Lamps in 1891 notes that Thos. Evans Co. made use of a screw socket on their lamps, but they are not pictured or further described. This could be the type occasionally found with a thread cast on the peg of the font which screws into a threaded metal cup with a hole in the bottom. A nut inside the cup receives a threaded rod which passes through the stem and base to be secured by another nut. The third type of connector is a clinched-on brass cylinder which requires vertical and horizontal indentations in the glass parts. This was patented in 1870 by John H. Hobbs of Hobbs Brockunier & Company. If it can be determined that the glass base and font have been molded to correspond with the connector, it can be assumed that those parts were also a product of that particular company. The next step is to find the same part, say font, on an all-glass lamp with a different design base. This would establish that the same company also made lamps with those bases, and so on.

Some lamps are found in quantity throughout an area but this can indicate a large shipment at the time of manufacture and is not conclusive information. Another peculiarity is to find lamps of the same size and design which have a distinct difference in proportion and in the quality of the molding. These characteristics can mean different manufacturers and/or different periods of time. Glass color, if distinctive, may be a guide in identifying a manufacturer, however, this is made difficult by the scarcity of colored pattern glass available for comparison. A large variety of both related and unrelated lamps are illustrated to enable the reader to experience the joy of discovery careful observation will likely bring. There is a very good possibility one will be able to recognize new pattern combinations or design relationships. The attics, closets and cupboards, and the barns, sheds and garages must still harbour hundreds of different pattern lamps, of which many will relate to the ones pictured here.

Some paths lead to confusion and disappointment, but they are quickly forgotten with the discovery of a route that is directed towards a conclusion, which is later verified by accepted criteria.

Hobbs connector

a. Pomona

Advertisements have provided valuable information about lamps and lamp parts. Archives and attics are potential treasure houses to be explored. The lamp in illustration (a) appears to be the same as in the Thomas Evans advertisement from the trade journal China, Glass and Lamps, 1893. The trade name Pomona appears to be appropriate for this lamp. Size is 9-3/4″.

ESTABLISHED 1869

INCORPORATED 1887

THOS. EVANS CO.,
CRESCENT GLASS WORKS.
LAMP CHIMNEYS
GLASSWARE.
PITTSBURGH, PA.

POMONA

Capacity, 60,000 Chimneys Daily.

Glass and Glass Companies

The subject of glass will be dealt with only to give some basic information, and an explanation of the terms used to describe the lamps illustrated. Most lamps were made of colorless glass which will be referred to as clear. One hears the words flint, lead, crystal and lime to describe clear glass mainly, and colored glass occasionally. Crushed flint, as the silica or sand, which is the basic ingredient in glass, has been said by some writers to have been seldom used in glass produced in North America, however, in many issues of China Glass and Lamps in the 1890's, price lists of glassmakers supplies regularly include flint. The word "flint" glass has been an accepted synonym for "lead" glass, by the layman and by the glass industry, for about three hundred years, when in 1674 George Ravenscroft of England obtained a patent for glass in which flint was used. This glass was found to be subject to crissiling and decay. After many experiments, it was announced, two years later, that lead was used to correct this problem, and since then, both flint and lead have been used to describe clear brilliant glass although they each have a different role in the glass formula. Glass is basically melted silica, which can be flint or sand, and lead serves as a flux to promote the melting of the glass. Crystal, the transparent quartz-like mineral has no role in glassmaking, but the word has long been another accepted synonym for lead glass. Thus we have three accepted words to describe the same glass!

Lime glass dates from 1864 when the discovery was made of a recipe containing bicarbonate of soda and lime, which produced an inexpensive fine quality glass to compete with lead glass. Lamp bases may be tapped to see if they give the characteristic ring of lead glass, but the font will have the sound deadened by the collar. Many of the large size all-glass lamps made before 1875 have lamp fonts which appear to be of superior quality to their bases. In view of the difficulty of determining the glass ingredients, the lamps pictured have their glass quality indicated by the general appearance, as follows:

excellent quality—Brilliant, well molded, smooth to sight and touch, and with only minor flaws which will not detract from the overall impression of superiority.

good quality —Glass which also has few imperfections, but which lacks brilliancy. It is well molded.

fair quality —Glass of little brilliancy in which the imperfections such as bubbles, striations or poor molding detract from the total impression.

primitive quality—This is used to describe glass with many imperfections, when the design of the lamp is unsophisticated, and the flaws seem not only appropriate, but add to the character of the lamp.

poor quality —Describes glass with many imperfections which suggests carelessness rather than character in the total impression one has of the lamp.

Glass which is slightly colored is referred to as having a tint. Amethyst, the most common tint, depends on the proportion of manganese used in the batch to neutralize the natural green color of glass. This tint becomes more pronounced with exposure to ultra-violet rays, either artificial or sunlight. The degree to which this takes effect is a result of the predisposition of that particular piece of·glass due to its formula. For this reason, a piece of glass from 1910 may acquire a deeper tint than one from 1860. A tint of pink is found in some lamps of the seventies, and sometimes a charcoal grey tint occurs in lamps of any age. Green is seen occasionally and yellow rarely. The honey amber of the Waterfall lamp, sometimes called Coolidge Drape, is more pronounced and classed as a color. Other colors found in lamps are various shades of blue or green, amber, yellow-green vaseline, cranberry or ruby, and rarely amethyst, brown or orange.

A technique of painting a color on glass and then firing it was popular. This is referred to as stained glass and occasionally shows signs of wear. Overlay or cased glass is a glass which has one or two thin layers of another colored glass. This type of glass was sometimes engraved or "cut back" to the inside layer in geometric or floral designs, to create the spectacular lamps made by the Boston and Sandwich Glass Company and others in the late 1850's and 1860's. Other times, an overlay was left uncut, or acid etched to produce a design. Opalescent glass appears fiery orange when held against a bright light or sunlight, but opal is a word often used to describe white glass or milk glass which has no opalescence. Lamps or bases in this book are referred to as opaque glass with color and opalescence noted if present. Opaline is used to describe a translucent glass which upon close examination is seen to have tiny bubbles or flecks, and is often referred to as clambroth.

Glass manufacture in the United States evolved from the first hand-operated pressing machines in the 1820's to the fully automated machines of this century. There was a vast number of patents issued for glass manufacture during this period, many of them relating to lamps. One of these was the Joseph Magoun patent of 1847 to produce a lamp font without mold marks on the shoulder. A goblet shape was made first and then the upper part was reheated and drawn in. Another way to form the font was to blow glass inside a mold and then open the mold when the glass cooled.

Lamps blown in a mold, a method used throughout the lamp making period have an uneven surface inside, opposite to and corresponding with the pattern outside. A pressed lamp will be smooth inside the font. Free-blown lamps, which of course have no mold marks, are a rarity for kerosene, although they were commonly used for whale oil. Mold marks may be smoothed by fire polishing so it requires careful examination to determine how the font was made. A fourth method was to press mold the font or the entire lamp in sections and then fuse them together.

This is the method used in the Thomas Atterbury patent of September 29, 1876, in which the significant part is the joint between the upper and lower part of the font. Atterbury describes these joints as having "marees" or "offsets" to receive plain parts, and they appear rather like a carpenter's "V" joint or lap joint. There were a few significant aspects of this patent, one of which was a mechanical means of producing a font or piece of hollow glassware without mold marks or seams on the upper portion. While this patented lamp, with the flange or drip catcher is seen occasionally in the stand and footed hand forms, no other lamp application of this patent by the Atterbury Company has come to my attention. The revival of the expired Atterbury patent screw socket in the 1890's, by the United States Glass Company, may have had a parallel in the appearance of the many lamps of the Atterbury September 29, 1876 patent type, in the same catalogue. These lamps, several of which are illustrated in both the picture section and in the United States Glass Company catalogue illustrations, are described as extra heavy, strong, and one piece. The reference to one piece meant that the font per se was not entirely separate. These lamps are indeed very heavy, and are also of very good to excellent quality; clear and bright but not lead glass. This became the first time the weight and clarity and design of all-glass lamps approached those handsome fonts of the early 1860's. Unfortunately, United States Glass Company catalogues of this century indicate that this high level lasted less than a decade. Design quality plummeted; the brightness dulled, and the heaviness became coarseness. Some of this was obscured by finishing the lamps with frosting and painting.

The greatly diminished market for kerosene lamps, coupled with the development of automatic blowing machines, marked the end of the glass quality and design associated with the kerosene era. Mold-blown fonts were phased out around 1910-15 although in some factories this practice may have been carried on later to a limited extent. In the 1930's, some new designs were introduced with large footed glass fonts and matching chimney shades. Floral designs on these lamps were usually finished in garish red and green on a gold background.

Some of the more interesting and complex glass techniques of the 1880's and 90's were used in the manufacture of vase or parlor and miniature lamps, but there is little variety in this area in hand and stand lamps.

Another type of font made in the 1860's had a pattern pressed inside. Thomas Atterbury obtained a patent in 1861 for manufacturing a font with the pattern between two layers of glass and this lamp is shown with the Atterbury lamps. A surprising variety of lamps made by Atterbury & Co. have been found in Canada, many of which are examples of the design and invention patents of Thomas and James Atterbury. Daniel C. Ripley of Ripley & Company, also obtained a number of patents for glass and lamp manufacture, however, these are not as abundant as Atterbury lamps, and involve only three basic types. A very distinctive patented "drip-catcher" font known as the Oil-Guard lamp, was patented by George H. Lomax, and many of these are still found in Canada and the U.S. with their identifying Sept. 20, 1870 patent date.

Hobbs Brockunier and Co. (later Hobbs Glass Company) was a company associated with the brass clinch connector used on their opaque glass lamp bases. It is interesting to note the contributions of men associated with this company. William Leighton Sr. discovered the lime glass recipe in 1864, mentioned earlier, and William Leighton Jr. patented the Blackberry design in 1870. John H. Hobbs designed the brass connector and obtained patents for glass patterns.

The term "Midwest" often used with reference to glass companies, refers to those located in the Pittsburgh and nearby Ohio Valley region. Today, of course, the term suggests a more westerly area. Atterbury &

T. B. ATTERBURY.

MANUFACTURE OF

HOLLOW GLASS WARE.

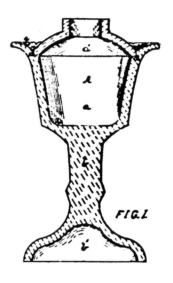

FIG.1

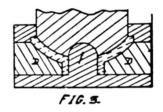

FIG.3.

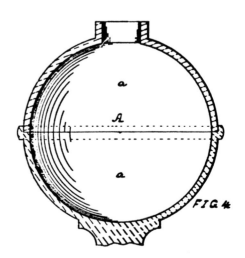

FIG.4

No. 181,618.

Patented Aug. 29, 1876.

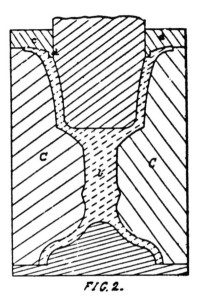

FIG. 2.

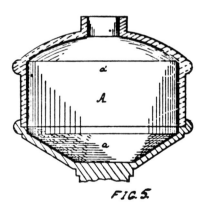

FIG. 5.

Witnesses
Paul Bakewell
R.C.W.Fenshaw

Inventor-
Thomas B. Atterbury
by Bakewell & Kerr
his Attorneys

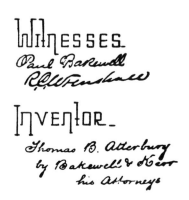

Co., the King Glass Company, Adams & Company, Bryce Walker & Company (later Bryce Brothers) all of Pittsburgh, and the Central Glass Company, and Hobbs, Brockunier & Company of Wheeling, West Virginia, The Riverside Glass Company, Wellsburgh, West Virginia, The Dalzell, Gilmore & Leighton Company, Findlay, Ohio and The La Belle Glass Company of Bridgeport, Ohio, were all glass companies of the Midwest who produced lamps found in abundance in Ontario.

Many New England companies produced glass of excellent quality, beauty, and artistic merit. Unfortunately there exists some confusion and controversy regarding attribution of articles to these companies, and since many lamps are types made by more than one company, "New England type" is used here to describe them. The Sandwich Glass Museum has a splendid display of breathtaking examples of lamps which combine fine craftsmanship with unique artistry. Another Massachusetts firm, The Union Glass Company of Somerville, manufactured the Lomax patented lamps mentioned earlier. The route to Canada for these lamps from Massachusetts would likely have been by boat to Nova Scotia, where many examples have been found.

The foregoing list is, of course, a partial one, but it includes many of the largest and most noted companies. Furthermore, lamps from all of these companies have been found in quantity in Eastern Canada, which suggests they were exported for sale at the time of manufacture, rather than an item included in the furnishings brought in by an immigrant or vacationer from the United States.

With reference to quantities, it is difficult and perhaps undesirable to predict the current supply of various lamps. If one labels an item "rare" or "scarce", the attention focused upon it will quickly draw most known specimens out of hiding, and this may involve sufficient numbers to place the article in a "common" category. For this reason, and because prices may be unreasonably and unrealistically affected, the writer makes reference to abundance and not the lack of it.

Relationships to a glass manufacturer's patterns or patents are mentioned in the description accompanying the lamps illustrated. Authors' names, where applicable, accompany these attributions. Other attributions are based on research material from resources listed in the bibliography. The study of production methods of glass lamps is basically the study of glass manufacture in general, and this information is available from books on glass, and from encyclopedias.

Glass design nomenclature is an important aspect of glass and lamps. For the inquisitive enthusiast who wishes to identify a particular glass pattern, the first perusal of a comprehensive glass book generally produces amazement at the number of patterns, and a sense of awe and respect for those whose knowledge of patterns, covers a large percentage of these. Fortunately for those concerned with the area of lamps, the range is relatively small, and fortunately it is surprising how quickly casual study and frequent consultation will accustom the eye first to basic types and then to finer distinctions. Knowledge of descriptive terms used by authorities will facilitate comprehension and communication in the study of glass designs. Many pattern names involve one or more design features, and the usual procedure an author uses in bestowing names on hitherto unnamed or multi-named patterns, is to adhere to as descriptive a name as possible. If too many of the same elements exist in several patterns, an additional name, perhaps that of the manufacturer is added. If too many different elements occur or if they are too simple, or even non-existent, a neutral unrelated name may be chosen. As with tableware patterns, relatively few lamps were given names by the manufacturer, so if a non-descriptive name is in order, the author has given the lamp a name. Heretofore unnamed flower or leaf designs have names selected by gardening author Lois Wilson, whose experienced eye and imagination give accurate or interesting labels.

The following are some of the more common descriptive terms for design characteristics:

Raised hemispheres have a variety of names which largely depend upon their size. Starting with the largest which would be perhaps 3/4" or larger, the protrusion is referred to as an eye or bullseye. On a reducing scale from about 3/8" down to the size of a pinhead, these hemispheres are called hobnail, eye, boss, pearl, jewel or dewdrop. An area of minute precise dots is referred to as lacy, or stippled if the dots are nearly flattened.

Depressions or indentations are referred to as inverted, sunken or depressed designs. These include eyes, bullseyes and thumbprints.

The pontil or punty is a rod a glassmaker uses to hold the glass while it is being finished. When this is removed and the resultant scar ground off, a circular depression remains, and a similar depression incorporated into a glass design is sometimes called a punty.

Simple geometric terms include ellipse, oval and diamond. A group of diamonds with the centre of each individual diamond raised to a point becomes a raised diamond or sawtooth pattern.

If a pattern, for example grapes, encircles a piece of glass or font, it may be called grape band, however, if the same pattern is bounded above and below by a rib or other simple design, it becomes banded grape. Cartouche, medallion or shield refer to a design in an enclosed area.

A knop is a rounded protrusion encircling a stem, and this may be a pressed design or in the case of lamps before kerosene, free-blown.

Rib describes a single or series of parallel or nearly parallel convex curves, and a flute design is a series of parallel or nearly parallel concave curves. A third pattern which like the previous two, was particularly popular in the 1860's, is the prism. This consists of a series of parallel or nearly parallel alternating raised and depressed angles. These three patterns are frequently used around the circumference of a font or around the base, hence the term rib band or prism band. Icicle is the name given when ribs or prisms are of varying lengths giving a scalloped effect to the uneven ends. The use of ribs or prisms radiating in a design suggests the names rayed, fan, or sunburst, and if at a tangent around a circle, it is a pinwheel design.

Most other terms involve common familiar names and shapes.

Collecting Lamps

Doilies for decoration and drips

For those who wish to study and collect lamps, probably the most challenging and interesting collection would consist of lamps representing each type. Cost or investment, whichever your point of view, could be pared considerably by leaving out the piano, hall and library lamps, and concentrating on the smaller table lamps. Many collections involve a variety of one type, e.g.: footed hand lamps. In one area, avid lamp collectors define their collections as having "singles" or "sets." The latter refers to as many sizes and types of one pattern as possible. With some patterns, having increments of 3/16″ in the stand lamps, a set can consist of eight to ten lamps. Embossed lettering, particularly if it involves a date, appeals to many collectors. These self-authenticating lamps provide for some, the incentive to research the patents and discover their raison d'être.

Whether the lamp is to be used with kerosene or converted to electricity, the display or setting will add immensely to its attractiveness and enjoyment. A display with incandescent backlighting will liven colors and accentuate glass quality and tints. White or a soft blue are good backgrounds for a front or side lit display, and a colored shelf can add color without detracting from tints and textures. Felt will provide an excellent cushioned base as well as a quick and easily changed source of color. For the single lamp or for a pair, a doily is an appropriate accessory. Our ancestors spent countless hours, perhaps by kerosene light, crocheting, tatting and knotting an amazing variety of runners and doilies which lost popularity and importance, but which usually had sufficient appreciation to prevent their being destroyed. Many families have boxes or trunks filled with handiwork, and many pieces have found their way to auctions or antique dealers. In addition to protecting surfaces from scratches, they were often intended to absorb oil which might drip from the lamp.

The variety of electric bulbs and adapters, and fine electric cords currently available can be put to use to approximate or increase the level of illumination in kerosene days. A multitude of lamps and early lighting devices have been destroyed by drilling or by discarding parts. Far better to secure a fine cord around the outside of a lamp with tape or nylon fishing line tied horizontally at intervals, than to damage an old lamp which can never be replaced. If parts have to be removed, they should be carefully stored, and a note regarding their location affixed to the bottom of the lamp. When having work done by others, one should understand the procedure intended, and should stress the need to avoid irrevocable damage or alteration.

From its earliest days and throughout the history of its use, kerosene was continually extolled to be improved and odorless, cleaner burning and brighter than the same product of earlier days. Today, the new refined fuel, referred to usually as lamp oil, is cleaner (no smoky chimneys), brighter, perfumed and colored. Some colors are very intense, but they may be mixed to tone down or change them. It is to be hoped that someday a colorless fuel will be available for those who wish to avoid altering or masking the glass color.

The precautions of earlier days for the use of kerosene lamps are appropriate today. The lamp and burner should be in good order, with a properly fitting collar and burner that screws in tightly. New wicks should be perfectly dry, and when first lit, should be kept low until the chimney warms up gradually. Old chimneys are more likely to break, and therefore, reproductions are a wise choice from the standpoint of safety, and to preserve the short supply of old ones. Once the chimney is warmed, the lamp may be turned up for all to enjoy its mellow light.

Before one arrives at the stage above, a thorough cleaning may be necessary. Sometimes a lamp is acquired with a thick gummy layer of oil. One should not despair, as the cleaning is usually easy and the oil will have served as a protective coating. Many a metal lamp or lamp part has been well preserved in this manner and efforts involved in cleaning are amply rewarded. Whatever method is used for cleaning, care should be taken to avoid sudden temperature changes. The broken lamp illustrated is an example of what can happen when a warm hand grasps a piece of chilled glass. The dealer who had this unhappy experience reached into his truck on a cold winter's day to lift out the lamp, and when his warm hand touched the font, it instantly snapped in two.

Old glass with its imperfections is more subject to stress and will occasionally crack while sitting undisturbed on a shelf, thus precaution should be taken to maintain an even temperature or have a gradual change in cleaning, storing and transporting. Many lamps have spent their lifetime at or near room temperature, and a trip in a car trunk in freezing weather can cause a crack. If chilled, glass should warm up gradually over a period of several hours before being cleaned.

Like refinishing furniture, cleaning lamps may involve a variety of techniques and products. For all-glass lamps, a concentrated liquid household cleaner used full strength will soften the oil, and this may be speeded up by swishing it around with a 1/2″ paint brush. The same brush can also be used to paint the cleaner around the collar and in the crevices on the outside. Metal polish will clean the collar, but care should be taken not to scratch the glass surrounding the collar.

The result of a sudden temperature change

Brass requires careful cleaning as many parts originally had a black or a dull ormolu finish, and if there is any trace of this it should not be buffed or scratched. If it is certain none of this exists, a brass cleaner may be used, but steel wool and abrasives should be avoided. A paste made with powdered ammonia and liquid household detergent is a good brass cleaner. It should be left on for a few minutes, and then rinsed off. Gilded or painted designs on glass may be damaged by a strong cleaner or detergent, thus very dilute detergent or soap, or even cold cream, is recommended. Stained glass, usually ruby colored, or acid etched frosted glass, may be damaged with abrasives, but will clean easily with liquid detergent. Marble is very porous, and over the years spilled oil will have given it a mellow ochre color, with perhaps a few stains and dirt along the edges. A marble cleaner, lemon oil or furniture polish should improve the appearance, and if the marble becomes dried out, it may be soaked in kerosene to restore its aged look.

Some metal figure stem lamps are devoid of any finish and are very attractive, while on others, the metal is dingy and splotchy and the original gold finish remains only in a few crevices. To restore this gold finish, a water soluble rub-on paste, usually available at hobby shops, will give a dull sheen closely resembling the original finish. If there is a range of shades of gold, mixing and experimentation will achieve a close match.

Metal lamps may be cleaned most easily with petroleum solvent or mineral spirits. Many nickel plated central draft lamps have been stripped and the brass body buffed, however, nickel plate with its gradations of sheen and with brass showing through the worn areas, has the charm of an antique and evokes the comfortable feeling of an honest attempt to preserve the original character.

Figure stem before   *After rub-on finish*

a. Lamp repair

If it is necessary to re-cement a collar or brass connector, only a patching plaster which can be later softened with water should be used. This may be tinted with dry powdered color used in grout for tile work, to produce a putty colored plaster with an aged look. If a good level burner and chimney are screwed in, and the lamp set on a level surface while the plaster sets, it may be taped as in the illustration (a) to compensate for an irregularly shaped font. A towel surrounding the base is a good precaution. Insoluble adhesives should never be used.

Fortunately, fakes and reproductions of kerosene lamps are not as common as in other forms of glass made at the same time, but they do exist and are, as would be expected, usually copies of very popular lamps, or of those in the higher price range. Most are described in books on the subject by Dorothy Hammond and by Ruth Webb Lee. These are listed in the bibliography. Recently made all-glass large chunky, Princess Feather pattern lamps, are easily recognized by the added flower on the font. Reproductions would be more

welcome if they had such distinguishing marks, or had an embossed date. Unfortunately, there are reproductions reported in the Princess Feather pattern, which are difficult to distinguish.

Opaque glass base or brass stem and marble base lamps occasionally have had the base or font damaged, and the good parts assembled to make new lamps. This is not a drastic measure because when these lamps were sold originally, in many instances, they were available as separate parts to be assembled by the merchant or customer.

b. Twentieth century reproduction

Engraved or cut overlay lamps with brass stems and marble bases, were made early this century. One type I have seen had an excellent quality ruby font cut to clear. It was drilled through the bottom of the font, and intended for use with electricity when manufactured. It is advisable to check the bottom of the fonts of any expensive lamp, because many old lamps have been drilled.

A lamp which should be mentioned is the example (b) which was made in blue or cranberry opalescent coin dot with matching shade. The base of this lamp has no sign of age or wear. Tom Mileham of Buffalo, N.Y. reports this lamp was advertised in the 1920's along with others which were intended to be used with electricity. Reproduced lamps of this period have attained a certain status and command prices well above recent reproductions.

Hardware and gift stores often stock new kerosene lamps but they are easily recognized, particularly by the metal parts. If there is some doubt about a lamp in an antique shop, a reputable dealer will guarantee authenticity and include a note to this effect on the bill.

Accessories—
Collars, Burners, Chimneys and Shades

For those who wish to reinforce the atmosphere of the era, a few related items may be sought. For new and burnt matches, holders of glass, tin or iron, are interesting when combined with a lamp of similar material, quality and period. They were made to be hung on a wall, set on a table or suspended from a hanging lamp.

Some had strikers in the form of a roughened or finely corrugated surface.

f. Doilies

As mentioned earlier, doilies are most appropriate, and at the same time provide a contrast in texture and material.

a. Tin Match Holder

b. Tin Match Holder

c. Cast Iron Match Holder

d. Glass Match Holder

e. Aladdin Parts and Match Holder

g. Hooks

Cast iron hooks (g) for hall or hanging lamps come in a variety of sizes and designs. The threaded screw may vary from two to six inches in length, and the very heavy cast iron lamps will require a strong and secure fastening.

h. Smoke Bell   *i. Chimney-Top Heaters*

The smoke bell (h) suspended above the chimney of a hanging fixture is often of matching glass or metal. These bells were also sold separately as new or replacement parts.

Chimney-top heaters (i) utilized the steady heat for warming food, as a vaporizer, or for heating curling tongs. There are several variations of this wire rack which was popular for years. They correspond to the description of a patent obtained on November 28, 1876, by Edwin W. Brown of Worcester, Mass., for a heating attachment for lamp chimneys. Unfortunately the patent drawing was not available for verification. The brass attachment, right, is embossed TIP TOP — PAT. OCT. 6, 91. Both heaters incorporate holders for curling tongs although the Brown patent does not mention this.

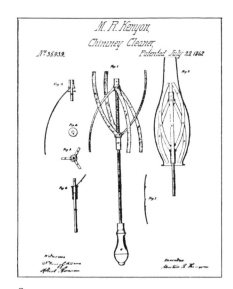

a.

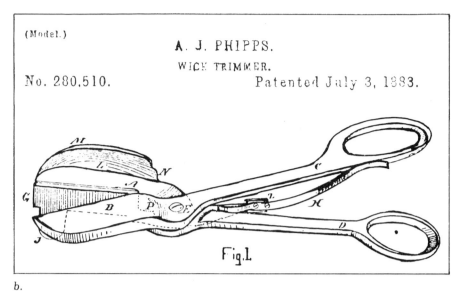

b.

Several chimney cleaners were patented, and many of these were devices for holding cloths. The one patented by M.R. Kenyon, July 22, 1862 (a), scoured the inside of the chimney with flat springs which were "A series of elastic fingers covered with worsted, cotton yarn, chamois skin, or other suitable material". Wick trimmers as shown in (b) also inspired several patents.

Wood, tole and glass containers were filled with kerosene from a barrel or drum at the store, and carried home. A piece of raw potato was a convenient plug for the spout. Several containers were patented including "The Intelligent Can" (c) with its double spout, which when emptied, will give a faint whistle—sometimes! The Intelligent Can was patented January 15, 1889, and the inverted wooden bucket (d) was patented in Canada about 1885.

A valve in the cap of the unmarked glass container (e), allows air to enter while pouring. The Queen (f) was patented February 12, 1878, and the glass liner has C R & CO., 21 embossed on the bottom.

c. The Intelligent Can

d. Kerosene Bucket

e. Glass Kerosene Container

f. Glass Lined Oil Can

Some collars indicate the age of a lamp, and others offer strong probability or positive proof of the lamp manufacturer's identity. The original collar is an important part of any lamp, and every effort should be made to preserve it. A replacement may erase important clues and sometimes will cast doubt regarding authenticity.

Quite often the glass collar portion of the lamp has settled at an angle as the glass cooled. Other times the entire font has solidified in a tipped position. If the collar is soaked off, it may be reset to compensate so that the chimney or shade will be vertical. Directions for this procedure are given in the section on collecting lamps.

In general terms, the first four illustrated are ones made prior to 1876. The first one (g) with two fine lines, is the type found on earlier whale-oil and burning-fluid lamps, which used collars of the same size and type. The next two (h) and (i), were made at the beginning of the 1860's and possibly earlier. One has a single protruding rib and an often worn design consisting of two bands of short diagonal lines on the rib and near the shoulder. The collar with two protruding ribs is otherwise plain. The collar (j) with the single base rib appears on lamps of the early seventies, including those of The Boston and Sandwich Glass Company and of the Central Glass Company of Wheeling, West Virginia.

g. Common early brass collar

h. Early brass, single rib collar

i. Early brass, double rib collar

j. Early brass, single base rib collar

The five collars on this page, are the most popular later ones. Most common is the first one (a), which is occasionally found with two patent dates stamped on the sides. These dates, April 13, 1875 and March 21, 1876, are for patents obtained by Alvin Taplin of Forestville, Conn., and George W. Brown of the same town. The method of manufacture, which involved stamped out thin sheet metal instead of the earlier use of brass tubing, and deep annular grooves to strengthen the thinner sides, represented such an economy of material and operation, that production of all earlier types appears to have ceased abruptly. The Brown patent was assigned to the Bristol Brass and Clock Company of Bristol, Conn., who probably dated the collars for a few years after the 1876 patent date. Most lamps with the dated collars have other characteristics which place them in the late 1870's, however, the I.P. Frink patented font of 1884 has this dated collar, and I have seen a lamp of the mid 90's with such a collar. The second collar (b), patented by Lewis J. Atwood of Waterbury, Conn. and assigned to the Plume & Atwood Company of the same place, is dated Oct. 31, 1876. This was also stamped from sheet metal and claimed as its improvement, the conical flange at the base which would give strength, and the stamped design on the shoulder of the collar which would create a roughened surface inside to prevent slipping. These collars with shoulder design and dated on the flange were used on lamps which appeared in the United States Glass Company catalogue c. 1893. Similar collars, such as the third one (c), without date or design were common to 1910 and probably later. These are described in an advertisement by Dalzell, Gilmore and Leighton Co. of Findlay, Ohio, as "Patent, Improved, Shrunk-on Collars" and claimed "No Plaster, No Cement, No Leaky Lamps, No Weak Lamps, No Complaints." In Findlay Pattern Glass, by Don Smith, this collar is said to have been patented by Phillip Ebling of the Dalzell, Gilmore and Leighton Company, Findlay, Ohio, and first used in May, 1894.

a. *Taplin-Brown collar*

b. *Atwood collar*

c. *Ebling collar*

The flared Riverside Clinch Collar (d), with its notch to correspond with one on the lamp font, is often found with the patent dates Sept. 19, 1882 and Dec. 4, 1883, stamped on the flat shoulder. Unfortunately, a search of these dates at the United States Patent Office failed to uncover the patents. The Riverside Glass Company of Wellsburg, West Virginia, advertised this collar as a very important exclusive feature of their many lamp designs over a period of about 25 years.

The fifth collar (e), in the picture, consists of a threaded brass insert inside the glass lamp collar. The glass is embossed Sept. 19 and Nov. 14, 1911.

d. *Riverside Clinch collar*

These collars are usually seen on one piece machine-made lamps. The chief disadvantage of this type of collar is the fact that the lamp is useless if the thread becomes stripped. This is not too serious if the lamp is very inexpensive, but it may be a consideration in the purchase of a lamp such as the Greek Key pictured on page 302. Lamps such as these should be checked with a burner to be sure the thread is in good condition. Other types of collars may be reset with patching plaster. I have seen Riverside collars which have been either re-cemented or reinforced with plaster. The Ebling collars, applied originally without plaster, occasionally have become loose and have been re-set.

e. *Brass insert collar*

f. Fluted band collar

g. Miller oval band collar

h. Hatched band collar

i. Dotted band collar

j. Patterned band collar

The first of this group of less common later collars, is the deep fluted band type (f) found on lamps which appear to be of various types, and primarily of the 1880's and 90's.

Edward Miller & Co. of Meriden, Conn., advertised the collar with the oval band (g) in the 1890's. The last three designs (h), (i) and (j) seem to range between 1880 and 1910 and are scarce, but not rare.

North American collars and burners come in three basic sizes which refer to the inside diameter of the collar and the outside diameter of the burner:

Collar size   No. 1. 7/8″   No. 2. 1-1/4″   No. 3. 1-3/4″
Burner size   No. 0. 2-1/8″   No. 1. 2-1/2″   No. 2. 3″   No. 3. 3″

Burner size 0 and 1 both fit a No. 1 collar. Measurements for chimneys with a cylindrical base are the same as burner sizes. The coronet type burner comes in a wide variety of sizes, but the thread sizes fit the 1, 2 or 3 collar.

Reproduction collars are available in the lightweight stamped type, and in a heavy type similar to the early common brass collars. These collars usually have a protective coating which should be removed by vigorous buffing with steel wool, before they are cemented in place. Adapters are available to reduce or enlarge the collar size to take a burner which is one size larger or smaller.

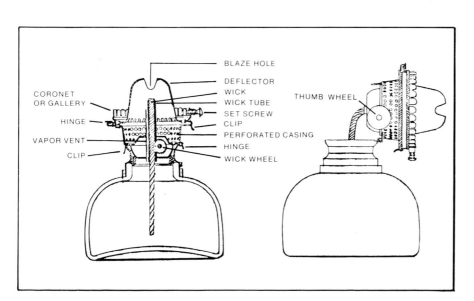

KEROSENE BURNER — The coronet burner illustrated has an additional hinge and clip to allow filling without removing the burner. The nomenclature for the prong burner is the same as for the coronet type except for the prongs.

Dr. Russell's comprehensive study of burners describes the Vienna burner (a) with a fixed deflector, as the first to be used in North America.

This burner is frequently seen on recently imported European lamps. The deflector will probably be removable, and the thread size will not be the same as on the North American burners.

a. Vienna Burner

b. Coronet and Prong Burners

The Jones Burner (b) left, patented May 4, 1858 by Edward F. Jones of Boston, launched the kerosene era in North America. Known as a coronet type, it required a flange-base chimney. Dr. Russell points out, in a letter, that the first hinged burner of this type was the Newman Burner of 1861, and that the Marcy burner patented in 1863, appears to have been the most widely used. The common prong burner (b) right, introduced about 1868, held a cylindrical straight-base chimney. Patents for burners were frequently granted under the heading lamps, so that numbers are not readily available, however, those illustrated here show a variety of attempts to "build a better burner". Patent dates on burners, particularly those on the thumbwheel, may refer to some aspect of the design which predates that particular burner by many years. The date on the thumbwheel of the prong burner is Dec. 10, 1867. This patent date occurs on a variety of burners, and the only burner patent of this date is for a coronet type. Patent dates included with the burners illustrated are for reference and research rather than for dating these particular burners.

c. *Burners Designed for Wick Trimming*

This first group of burners shows examples of designs which allow the wick to be trimmed or lit, without removing the chimney. The first has the thumbwheel inscription PAT. MAR 10/68 & MAY 6/73, and another identical burner has P & A. Mfg. Co. Aug. 1, 85. The second burner has the thumbwheel marked NOVELTY and the third, the same dates as the first. These three examples utilize a spring which is compressed to allow the wick to be trimmed. The fourth burner dated Dec. 10, 1867 and Aug. 28, 1882, has two brass pins attached to the upper part, which are guided by sleeves in the bottom. The upper part of the last burner is raised and lowered by a supporting perforated brass strip, moved by a gear which is attached to a separate thumbwheel. This is marked PATENTED JULY 29, 1884.

d. *Aids for Filling the Lamp*

This second group includes burners which permit filling without removing the chimney, and hopefully, when unlit. The first burner has a tube alongside the wick tube and a cap marked PAT. AUG. 13, 1861. The next hinged device is referred to by its inventor, G.F.J. Colbourn of Newark, N.J. as a hinged collar for lamps. Screwed into both burner and lamp collar, it allows the chimney and burner to be swung over to permit filling. Patent date on the large one is July 14, 1863, however, variations similar in appearance were also patented by T.L. Owen of Geneva, New York April 25, 1876 and by Alvin Taplin of Forestville, Conn., on March 1, 1864. Several other patents were issued for burners which incorporated similar devices.

The next burner, with the sliding trough, is dated May 9, 1893 and the following one which swings sideways is stamped G.B.N. Dow Pat. Jan. 7, 1890. The last burner is described by Russell as one patented by S.W. Lamberton of Newark, N.J., on Oct. 18, 1887. In this example, the cap of the filling tube is missing. This tube, at the side, leads through the burner and angles down alongside the wick tube. In addition to this filling arrangement, the lever at the side serves to raise a sleeve around the wick to extinguish the flame.

a. Unusual Burners

Several brass fingers and a double draft deflector allow the first burner to function without a chimney. It was made by E. Miller & Co. of Meriden, Conn.

The second burner was made by Holmes, Booth and Haydens of Waterbury, Conn., and first patented Sept. 19, 1865 by Michael Collins of Chelsea, Mass. Like the next one, a ring of curved or angled brass leaves pressed inside the chimney base and held it firmly. The third burner has the words NEW CALCIUM LIGHT and the date 1870 boldly embossed around the deflector. Having used these two burners, I would describe removing and replacing the chimney as a more convenient and single handed operation, than with any other type of burner.

Patented Feb. 11, 1868 by A.C. Arnold and E. Blackman of Norwalk, Conn., the fourth burner is described by Russell as the first of the prong type burners. The last burner embossed, THE PLUME & ATWOOD FIRESIDE, was patented by Lewis J. Atwood of Waterbury, Conn.

b. Unusual Burners

Burners in this group are of later design. The fancy pattern on the first one is typical of those in the 1890's. The thumbwheel information is P. & A. Mfg. Co. Pat. June 26, 1894. A recently reproduced Plume & Atwood Manufacturing Company catalogue c. 1900 does not show any fancy patterned burners which suggests these burners may be considered 19th Century types. The second burner, an unusual but effective type, holds the chimney on three brass toggles. The thumbwheel is stamped KING GRIP, C.A. TAPLIN PAT'D 8, 23, 93.

The third type is a relatively common one made on both sides of the border. This burner with the extra security of a wire and spring, was made by the Ontario Lantern Co. in Hamilton c. 1900. The glass deflector on the fourth burner was designed to allow more light. The word RADIANT is embossed on the glass, and the brass is stamped PAT. DEC. 19-05. R.H. MAPLE CO., DAYTON, O. A similar one found in Ontario was made by the Ontario Lantern and Lamp Co. and marked 1903.

The last burner projects two copper and zinc tubes into the font. It was patented April 27, 1897, although its purpose is not clear to me.

c. Gallery Burners

d. Ives Shade with Rectangular Burner

e. Oval Burner

Gallery type burners are those with a coronet or ring sufficiently high to hold a chimney with a cylindrical base. The examples shown in (c), include a flat wick, a folded wick and a round wick type. The first of these is a conventional flat wick burner which occasionally held two parallel wicks, or three in a triangle. The folded wick burner has a mechanism which curves a flat wick to form a circle at the top, and the third example holds a round wick between two brass tubes. The last two are referred to as center draft burners. The interesting effect of a burner wearing pantaloons was created by an honest frugal gesture. The wick had become unravelled and the hand sewn feet kept the ends from being tangled. It was a common practice to extend the life of a wick by pinning or sewing a piece of old wick or fabric to the end of the wick in use.

Rectangular and oval burners (d) and (e), were popular c. 1880. Both these burners and the two-part chimney-shades are well marked with patent dates. The rectangular burner is marked PAT'D JUNE 1, 69, SEPT. 18, 77, NOV. 18, 79, APR. 6, 80, and the lower glass portion of the chimney-shade is patent dated DEC. 16, 73, OCT. 3, 76, REIS, APR. 11, 82.

These shades are found in other shapes (f) and with other dates, but the patent that relates most closely is that of Hiram L. Ives of Troy, N.Y. granted APR. 3, 1877. By reason of Dr. Russell's account of this patent, this combination is referred to locally as the Ives shade.

Reproductions of these chimney-shades are welcome parts, which can transform old lamps into useful objects. Both parts of the Ives-type shades are available. As with all reproduction shades, they are heavier, but the difference is not as apparent as with globe shades. The reproduced lower clear glass portion is not an obvious replacement, and there is a good chance of finding an old, perhaps dated, part.

The oval burner is marked PINAFORE H. B. & H. and the chimney is embossed PAT. MAR. 30, 80. This assemblage of parts consists of the chimney and upper portion of the burner from Vermont, the lower portion from East Aurora, N.Y., the oval shade support from Buffalo, N.Y., and the shade from Ontario, Canada.

f. Flat Ives Shade

The first North American burners held the flange-base chimney (a) left. These were used into this century, although their present scarcity and limited number of advertisements in the 1880's and 1890's, suggest a greatly diminished production after the late 1860's, when the prong burners became popular. The prong and later gallery burners held a cylindrical straight-base chimney (a) right, which was first made with a plain top.

Hand-finished chimneys such as the one on the left (b), were crimped to form broad petals. The beaded or pearl top chimneys (b) right, often called "pie crust," were produced by machine.

The straight-sided chimney (c) left, was made from a glass tube which was heated in the center, drawn, cut and rather crudely finished. This type was advertised at the turn of the century as a hall light chimney, but it was also used much earlier as a regular chimney. The chimney with the round bulge (c) right, was patented June 23, 1868 by M. Sweeney of Wheeling, West Va. The patent calls for a lens to be incorporated inside the bulge, but this does not occur in this example. It is interesting that the patent drawing illustrated this chimney on a Collins burner.

The most common reproduction chimneys are shown opposite in photograph (d). Reproduction pearl or pie crust chimneys have a few annular rings and mold marks at the top, just below the beading, and like the second chimney, they usually have a small bead at the bottom. The second rather stubby chimney, has a bead at the top and bottom. The third chimney is slender and light and has virtually the same proportions as the one shown on the Collins burner patent drawing in 1865. This is a very acceptable reproduction, and its use will preserve the old chimneys for display. Reproduction flange-base chimneys with coronet burners would be a welcome combination for the owner of lamps of the 1860's and early 1870's, both for display and use. The anachronistic appearance of prong type burners and pie crust chimneys on the lamps of the 1860's is now a disturbing sight, although probably a common one from the 1870's on, as people replaced old burners with new and popular ones.

According to Peterson, Washington Beck, who was joint patentee with Thomas Atterbury on a number of patents, obtained a patent in 1881 for a lamp globe and shade. The shade (e) opposite, appears to be a product of the process described in this invention. The design is impressed and the outside surface is ground, giving good definition and sparkle to the pattern.

a. Plain-Top Chimneys

b. Crimp-Top Chimneys

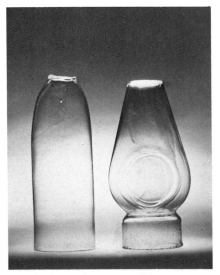

c. Cylinder and Sweeney Chimneys

d. Reproduction Chimneys

e. Pressed and Ground Shade

The shade above is very unusual. It came with a lamp from near Corning, N.Y., which is shown in the section on iron base lamps. It is heavy lead glass, and has an oval and icicle pattern cut on the lower half. The upper part has an intricate design etched on the surface.

A variety of designs was etched, silk screened or painted on the large chimneys known as "big bulge". Nine examples are shown opposite. Sometimes these designs matched one applied to the lamp, and sometimes chimneys were molded in the same pattern as the lamp. A common reproduction in the big bulge chimney has a plain or crimped top and a small bead at the bottom. These are often seen with silk screened patterns or lettering. Plain reproduction big bulge chimneys without a beaded edge closely resemble old chimneys, and are less likely to break if used.

Other shades and chimneys, some appealing and some appalling, are shown and described in the catalogue and trade journal advertisements and articles, elsewhere in this book. Most of the lamps photographed have appropriate burners and chimneys.

a. *Owl and Moon*

b. *Swan and Fruit Baskets*

c. *Adriana*

d. *Victorian Print*

e. *Torch and Wreath*

f. *God Bless Our Home*

g. *Crown*

h. *Lion*

i. *Snowflake*

Kerosene for Heat and Health

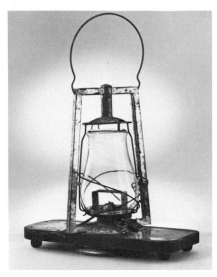

a. *Stove and heater*   b. *Stove, heater and light*   c. *Lantern footwarmer*

In addition to its function as an illuminant, the heat produced by kerosene was employed in many ways. Time and location made other fuels unsatisfactory, unavailable or inconvenient for most of the examples shown here. Furnaces were occasionally advertised, but kerosene was used more often to heat individual rooms. Kitchen stoves, and stoves for cabins and camping, are illustrated and described in many of the mail order catalogues recently reproduced.

Both stoves (a & b) would be regarded as deluxe models with the pleasant combination of brass, blue enamel and black iron. The 23-1/2″ type (a) was mainly used as a room heater, and the table model (b) 13-1/4″, primarily as a portable stove. The solid brass base bears no name or mark, but the thumbwheels, filled with a white material, have a trade mark on the end. This appears to be a modification of a German trade mark shown in Peterson's book. On each thumb wheel is fastened a small brass knob which can be rotated around the arm, and fixed in position by means of a screw. With the top tilted back, the wicks would be adjusted to an even height, and the knobs set parallel. After lighting the stove and closing the chimney, both wicks could be adjusted at any time to an equal height by observing the brass knobs. The blue enamel chimney has a mica window, and a cast iron holder above has the name embossed around the rim, Close & Co Mfgrs Woodstock Ont.

The 15-1/4″ lantern foot warmer with copper strips to conduct heat to the foot rests (c), is stamped "Patented 1908," however, other kerosene sleigh and buggy warmers were patented as far back as the 1860's. The instructions on the base are also shown (d).

THE LANTERN FOOTWARMER — DIRECTIONS

In using the "LANTERN FOOTWARMER" use it exactly as you would any other lantern. Fill the tank with oil. See that the wick is properly trimmed and that when lit it does not smoke. Keep the Copper Strip over the light clean. When driving or for outdoor use, place a foot on the Copper Plate on each side of the lantern. Draw the lap robe around and up over the knees, in the usual way, not to tightly, however, in order that there may be sufficient air for proper combustion. When the feet become sufficiently warm reverse the lantern and rest the feet on the wood side of the base, or turn the light down if necessary. Globe and burner may be removed as in ordinary lantern.

THE LANTERN FOOTWARMER CO.   (Sole Owners of Patent for Canada)   **COBOURG, ONTARIO**

d. *Footwarmer directions*

e. Portable stove

f. Brooder lamp

g. Glue pot

It is rather surprising that the type of stoves illustrated in picture (e) were seldom equipped with handles because they would have been an ideal camping stove. Both single and double burners were common, and the wicks were usually 4″ wide. This model has Tom Thumb embossed on the cast base. Overall height is 9-1/4″.

Brooder Lamps such as this 13″ one (f), are common at farm auctions today. These long burning, low temperature heaters with metal chimneys and mica windows, kept the chickens warm. Black painted steel, copper and brass, are a pleasant combination in this 5″ glue pot (g) which was probably used by a craftsman.

Schering's Formalin lamp (a), patented in 1899 is shown with its cautionary notice (b), on the bottom. This 7″ lamp, possibly English, apparently vaporized formaldehyde for disinfecting. The fuel is not mentioned, but it was likely intended to be used with kerosene. Vaporizers designed to be used with alcohol, did not require a chimney.

In addition to the chimney-top heaters shown in the section on accessories, the Wanzer Mechanical Lamp (c) has a cast iron rack for food warming or cooking. The reason this lamp did not require a chimney is that it had a motor which propelled a fan, to produce a controlled draft around the wick. Mechanical lamps are shown in the section beginning on page 68.

With the 6-1/4″ Vapo Cresoline Lamp (d) is included the original box, bottle of Cresoline with its original box, and a testimonial. According to their description, this night light warmed a strong dark liquid to "impregnate the atmosphere with remedial ingredients."

The early example (opposite) is perhaps the most interesting in appearance and operation. Patented July 28th, 1868 by William F. Rossman of Hudson, N.Y., it was described under the heading "Kerosene Lamp Boiler." Using the jacket heater principle, water was heated in the double walled upper chimney. The hot water rose through a tube to the base of the double boiler pot, and then returned to the chimney. With so many of the heaters shown, the flame was also used to illuminate, and in this instance, the light intensity was increased by the brass reflector. Behind the reflector is a wire catch, which when released allows the entire upper portion and jacket heater to be removed to light the burner. This 12-1/2″ model differs in appearance but not in principle from the patent illustration. Some of the uses proposed were as a nursery or sick-room cooking kettle, or as a glue kettle or barber's kettle.

a. Formalin lamp

b. Formalin lamp directions

d. Vapo-Cresoline

c. Wanzer lamp with heater rack

e. Rossman's Lamp Boiler ▷

Railroad Lighting and Ships' Lamps

a. Bracket lamp

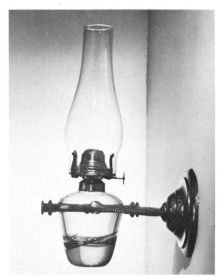

b. Bracket lamp on gimbals

*Drawing by
Richard Brown*

Kerosene lighting played a very important role on ships and trains. A wide variety of lamps and lanterns was designed to light the way, to light the interior, and for signalling. It is difficult to imagine adequate light being provided by a kerosene engine headlight, however, lenses and reflectors could concentrate a beam of light several hundred feet down the track. With so little general exterior illumination, the contrast of these train and ship lights would be more pronounced. Included here is a small selection which represents the tip of the iceberg in this area. The 4-3/4″ railroad bracket lamp (a) consists of a tin font which fits into a cast iron bracket. The early ship's lamp (b) on gimbals is not very different from those available today, except for the unusual font. The thickness (about 1-1/4″) of glass at the base provides the weight to keep the lamp vertical, and there is a rough pontil mark on the bottom. The inscription "Pat Appld For" is raised inside the font, and the only mold mark is a horizontal ring at the shoulder, above which are faint concentric rings to the collar. The collar is a type used before the mid 70's. This font demonstrates the risk involved with all old glass. The crack which encircles the lower portion of the font, appeared while the lamp was sitting undisturbed on a cabinet. Most collectors accept this risk, or the risk of accidental breakage, as a hazard inherent in glass collecting. If a piece of glass is rare and expensive, one should investigate an all-risk insurance policy which will cover these circumstances.

The large 24″ lantern (c) has two burners mounted on a single triangular font. Burners are soldered to tin cylinders rather than screwed in, and the inscription on the burner thumb wheel indicates this lantern was made by the Ontario Lantern Co., which, according to Dr. Russell, operated in Hamilton under that name from 1892 to 1905. This lamp could of course be used for other locations but was frequently used to light the station platforms.

c. Station platform lantern

So much a part of the history of the railroads are these little hand lanterns (d), which were used for light and for signalling. Most are marked with the maker's name and that of the railroad also. At a recent auction, over 200 railway lamps and lanterns were offered. Most of them were hand lanterns, and were purchased by collectors of railroad articles rather than lamp collectors. A thorough cleaning is advisable before using these lamps, either with kerosene or electricity. Wiring is simple because the font or oil pot, as they were often referred to, can be lifted out to provide ample room for a socket. The font should be saved. Many of these lamps have colored globes, and are in demand for decorating purposes.

The lantern (e) with the bullseye and colored glass sidelights was manufactured by Piper Mfg. Co. Measuring 11″ to the top of the handle, it was possibly a marine light.

Lamp (f) is a 3-1/2″ metal hand lamp marked CNR. The brass 10″ stand lamp (g) also marked CNR was used in dining cars.

d. Hand lantern

e. Bullseye lantern

f. Hand lamp

g. Brass stand lamp

Lanterns and Portable Lighting

The kerosene lantern has been a reliable and convenient portable light for over a century. During this entire period, Deitz has been the most prominent name in North American lanterns. The Deitz Driving Lamp (a) is shown in the Sears Roebuck 1897 catalogue. The ad states, "It is the only practicable and perfect Driving Lamp ever made. It will not blow out or jar out. It gives a clear white light. It looks like a locomotive headlight. It throws all the light straight ahead from 200 to 300 feet. It burns kerosene. By means of a spring on the back, the lamp can be instantly placed in front of the dash. By means of the holder, which we furnish with each lamp, it can be attached to either side of the dash. It can also be placed on the bracket of a carriage. 11″ high; 6″ in diameter; weight, 2-1/2 lbs. The price: $2.40 each." The lamp is marked, patented NOV. 25.90 and JAN. 20.97. Deitz Union Company, New York.

Lantern (b) is a Deitz Police Flash Light. The roller above the handle is pushed up and down by thumb. This rotates a tin cylinder between the glass bullseye lens and the flame to allow signalling, or to conceal the light without extinguishing the flame. These lanterns were sometimes called Dark Lanterns and were used with either kerosene or whale oil. Lamp (c) is a bicycle lamp with green and red side windows. Sizes are (a) 7-3/4″, (b) 11″ and (c) 5″.

a. Deitz Driving Lamp

b. Deitz Police Flash Light

c. Bicycle lamp

The brass plate on lantern (d) boasts "A perfect light guaranteed in any wind. PAT'D 1900." This lantern is 15-1/4″ high. The two 8-3/4″ lanterns in picture (e) are identical. One of these is provided with a candle holder and the other holds a kerosene font and burner.

Lantern (f) has embossed on the glass, Woodward's Patent April 5, 1864. This patent for an improvement in lamps was obtained by G. W. Woodward of New York, N.Y. The basic idea was to secure the glass cylinder or chimney to the metal cap and base by means of corresponding threads inside the metal, on the cap and base. The patentee describes this joint as formerly being secured by plaster. Although the glass threads are visible, this chimney is cemented at the top and bottom. Perhaps the form was more successful than the function, as its simple lines can be appreciated today. Height to the top of the metal cap is 9-1/8″.

Skaters, Cadet, Union; these are some of the names given to this small lantern (g) which came with chimneys in many colors. The more common clear ones found in Ontario may have the name "Little Bobs" in script embossed near the top. The description in the Montgomery-Ward 1894-95 catalogue states, it is "Just the thing for a lady around the house, or short journeys on dark nights." Height 6-1/4″.

The handle of the primitive lantern (h) would be hot when lit and sooty at all times. This may have been a homemade lamp, although I have seen another one like it. Many homemade lamps were made from tin cans. If a can contained a liquid, or a product which could be removed through a small aperture, a brass collar could easily be soldered on. A tin handle fastened to the side, or a wire handle such as this, would complete the lamp. Lamps from the East Coast have been found with the names of fish companies embossed on the bottom. Empty tins might have been obtained for this purpose.

d. Windproof Lantern

e. Kerosene and candle lanterns

f. Woodward's Patent Lantern

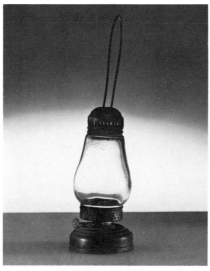

g. Skaters lantern

h. Tin lantern

a. Magic Lantern

Mail order catalogues of the 1880's proclaim the excitement and entertainment these magic lanterns (a) will provide. Glass slides with five or six scenes on each, or one long continuous picture, are moved by hand across the beam of light. The lens is mounted on a tubular sleeve which can be extended for focussing, and the brass reflector provides additional brilliance and clarity. This is 9″ to the top of the chimney.

The Parade or Campaign Torch (b), on a pole, often associated with political gatherings, was also used by lumbermen in Canada's north to light their way into the woods in darkness, and jabbed in the snow to work. More sophisticated models have been patented, some with glass or brass fonts and others on gimbals.

The pocket lamp (c) with a match receptacle and threaded cap was patented by J. Kutcher of New Haven, Conn., in 1877. This model is a variation of the one in the patent drawing but it accomplishes the basic intent of the patent.

b. Campaign Torch

c. Patented pocket light

d. *Darkroom lantern*

One aspect of early photography, often overlooked, was the dependence on kerosene for providing darkroom light. The top darkroom lantern (d) has a clear, and a ruby sheet of glass which can be raised when the tin cap is folded forward. Considerably more thought went into the design of the Premier Combination Lamp No. 1. (e). The hood is easily adjusted over the angled red window. On one side a door opens to reveal an opaque glass for negative retouching, and on the other side a sliding panel can be raised to check the flame through a clear window. On the back, a full-size sliding panel can be raised to remove and fill the font. The diminutive handle and the brass feet are absurdities which nevertheless give a distinctive character. Height is 12-1/2″ to the top of the handle.

e. *Darkroom lantern*

Metal Lamps

All-metal hand lamps were popular throughout the 19th century kerosene period. Millions of metal center draft lamps were sold in the 1880's and 90's. Many of these have been, and still are being converted to electricity. Brass was most commonly used, and it was available with a shiny finish, or treated to produce bands of dull ormolu. Nickel-plated brass was also very popular. Relatively few lamps were made of copper, bronze, pewter or Britannia metal. Tin and sheet metal with painted or galvanized finish, was protected from rusting by the oil itself.

The pair of lamps in picture (a) have air intake holes in the stem. These were a functional part of solar lamps with center-draft burners, but are superfluous here. Whale-oil, burning-fluid or kerosene burners would be appropriate with these lamps which were probably made in the 1850's.

The two lamps in photograph (b) are Canadian patented lamps which were designed to be used without chimneys. Anthony Neville of the Township of Ernest-town in the County of Lennox and Addington, Ontario, obtained two patents for improvements in lamps. These are dated Nov. 23, 1865, and May 14, 1866, and include patent drawings of kerosene lamps different from, and more complicated than the two pictured. Forty years after these lamps were made, the Planters' Hand Lamp (c) was advertised by the Plume & Atwood Manufacturing Co. It was sold as shown here, with what they describe as a "Pet Ratchet Round Wick Burner," or a "Badger Flat Wick Burner." Neither of these burners required chimneys. The badger flat wick burner had two rectangular plates which to some degree, shielded the flame and functioned as a chimney. Small brass hand lamps appear to have been made in large quantities throughout the kerosene period. It is, therefore, surprising that relatively few are in existence today.

Sizes are: (a) 8-1/8″ each, (b) left 4-1/8″ and right 3-1/4″ to the top of the burners, and (c) 3-5/8″ to the top of the burner and cap.

a. Early brass lamps

b. Neville patent lamps

c. Planters' Hand Lamp

Simple metal hand lamps were factory made, made by the local or an itinerant tinsmith, or home made. Tin cans were easily converted to kerosene lamps. Examples here are shown with a variety of old chimneys and burners. In picture (d) the left lamp is brass with a Collins burner, and the right one, without a handle, is copper. The remaining three show the variety of tin lamps available and the textures to be found in this material. A vigorous buffing will present a soft sheen resembling pewter. Any of these lamps are charming with primitive furnishings. The sizes are: (d) left 3″, right 3-1/4″, (e) 3-3/8″, (f) 3″ and (g) 2-7/8″.

d. Brass and copper lamps

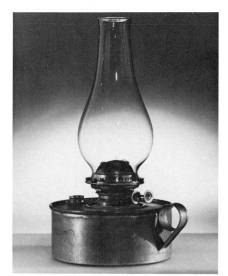

e. Tin lamp

f. Tin lamp

g. Tin lamp

a. Student lamp

In 1863 Carl Kleeman obtained a U.S. patent for an improvement in lamps of the reservoir type. Known as Student Lamps these remained popular for several decades, and a vast range of examples is in use today. Unfortunately the original condition has often been altered to accommodate electricity, however without this alternate use most would likely have been scrapped. This handsome double Student Lamp (a) has the original green shades, and has not been converted to electricity.

From China, Glass and Lamps, the following excerpt is dated December 16th, 1891:

"There is probably no article of domestic use, in the manufacture of which more remarkable progress has been made during recent years, than in the ordinary household lamp for burning kerosene or coal oil. Less than 20 years ago, the best of them was a disagreeable smoke producing and ill smelling illuminator, dispensing a poor light and always getting out of order, besides being fraught with considerable peril to the user. The contrast between these articles and the magnificent central draft lamps now produced by the manufacturers is great indeed."

The quantity of metal center-draft burner lamps produced in the 80's and 90's is staggering. The same trade journal in an 1893 article states "it will pay any jobber or jeweller to visit this city and see the line of Rochester lamps made in over 2,700 varieties, many got out expressly for the holidays with Paris shades, new in style and unique. It is claimed that no other house in the United States has such a line of banquet, piano and other shades, 25,000 dozen linen shades having been manufactured and sold by them this season." This article further states that "enterprise, push and merit are the mottos of the Rochester Lamp Co." This brass and iron creation (b) is an excellent example of a center-draft banquet lamp circa 1890.

b. Banquet lamp

a. Tin lamp

b. Piano lamp

◁ *Miller sewing lamp*

Tin was a safe and simple and inexpensive metal for lamps. This 8″ example (a) with the filler cap, has gold bands to decorate it. Tin fonts were often enclosed in the wooden lamps seen occasionally.

The piano lamp (b) standing free or incorporated with a table, and with glass or silk shades, was very much a part of the late Victorian home. This particular one is silver plated, and is topped with a frosted red Iris patterned hall lamp shade.

On the page opposite is a footed hand sewing lamp made by E. Miller & Company. The term sewing lamp was a popular designation for lamps of this size. This one is 11-1/2″ to the top of the shade.

a. Aladdin lamp

Aladdin and Rayo Lamps with a Wellsbach mantle, produced a much brighter light than the center-draft lamps without a mantle, and yet they apparently were not made until this century. Mantle lamps become very hot and should be used with caution. This is particularly true with the hanging type. Both lamps (a) an Aladdin and (b) a Rayo, have old glass shades and they measure 11-3/4″ to the top of the burner.

The New Rochester Lamp opposite has its original shade with fleur-de-lis on a frosted background. Height to the top of the burner is 18″.

b. Rayo lamp

New Rochester Lamp ▷

Mechanical Lamps

Mechanical lamps are those which provide a continuous flow of air around the wick by means of a fan or blower. The main advantage of this type of lamp is that it functions without a chimney, and perhaps the main disadvantage is the need to repair the motor occasionally. Many patents were obtained for various arrangements and refinements, but the most common lamps of this type are illustrated here, and all have basically the same construction. Some are stem winders and some are side winders. This is the patentee's description for the location of the key to wind the clock-work motor. This motor rotates a horizontally mounted propeller in the stem (d), and a draft is impelled between the font and an outer casing. The burner is covered by a snug fitting draft deflector, which has only the blaze hole opening. The surrounding rim provides support for a shade if desired.

Names associated with these lamps are De Keravenan, Jones, Hitchcock and Dyott, and Heath and Wanzer. The Ford Museum also has an example of a mechanical lamp patented May 7, 1867 by H. M. Beidler, and another stamped, "N.Y. Mays New Ideal Lamp Pat June 10, 1884." The first patent for a mechanical lamp was one obtained on October 23rd, 1860 by Francis B. De Keravenan from France who resided in New York City. On February 10th, 1863 and June 9th of the same year, De Keravenan obtained patents for improved mechanical movements for lamps, which he assigned to Joseph H. Bailey and George A. Jones, also of New York. Following this G. A. Jones patented an improvement in lamps on November 10th, 1863. In this patent Jones refers to the De Keravenan lamp as that "which has been the pattern or model of those heretofore constructed", however, thus far, the De Keravenan-Jones lamp appears to be the earliest identified mechanical lamp. The one pictured is 12″ and a smaller model has also been seen.

In the 1860 De Keravenan lamp (a), the air was impelled through tubes which passed through the font. This font was difficult to construct and the solder joints frequently leaked. To overcome these problems, the Jones patent (b) called for a separate glass inner font which allowed air to pass between the double wall. A glass inner font was patented by

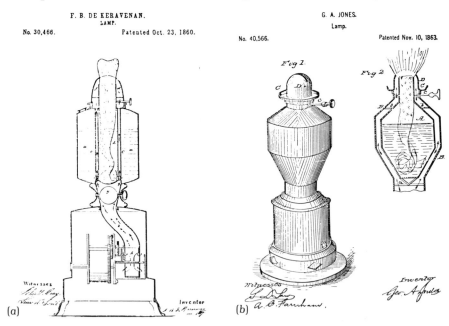

F. B. DE KERAVENAN.
LAMP.
No. 30,466.   Patented Oct. 23, 1860.

G. A. JONES.
Lamp.
No. 40,566.   Patented Nov. 10, 1863.

(a)   (b)

c. De Keravenan-Jones lamp

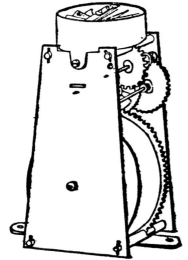

d. Hitchcock & Jones Gearing
Lamp-Train   Patented Feb. 25, 1868

Michael B. Dyott on May 7th, 1867, and this font is used in the pictured De Keravenan-Jones lamp (c). This lamp with its simple shape contrasting with the fancy key will run four and a quarter hours.

On February 25th, 1868, a patent was issued which outlined a change in the construction of the gearing of a lamp mechanism to utilize hard rubber gears. Joint patentees were George A. Jones and Robert Hitchcock. This is the first introduction into the patent records of the name which was to become the most famous name in mechanical lamps. Hitchcock, born in Ontario, Canada, obtained, in the early 1870's, a number of patents for more complicated mechanical lamps. Residence on these patents was given as Watertown, N.Y., where he set up a factory to produce mechanical lamps which were sold in great quantities in North America and abroad. These lamps, while often bearing the patent date of the early 1870 patents, do not use any of the fonts detailed in these patents, but rather a simple metal font which makes the lamp essentially the same as the De Keravenan-Jones lamp.

a. Hitchcock lamp

The 11-5/8″ Hitchcock china lamp (a) in mint condition, has a gold decorated, pink oak leaf and acorn design, above a yellow band on a cream background. The brass font and mechanism of this lamp shown in (b) sits on a brass rim which is cemented to the top of the china jacket. To wind this lamp, the metal part (b) is removed, wound, and then replaced. This mechanism was also used in hanging lamps, chandeliers and brackets. Lamp (c), the most common Hitchcock lamp, runs for over fourteen hours. This 12″ lamp is a stem winder.

In Canada, some competition to these Hitchcock lamps was offered by what is known as the Wanzer lamp, (e) opposite. According to Russell, this lamp was patented by A. G. Heath of New York in 1886. Essentially, the same as the Hitchcock lamp, it was manufactured in Canada by Richard Wanzer in Hamilton, Ontario.

b. Hitchcock lamp mechanism

c. Hitchcock lamp

This 12″ Wanzer lamp (e) which is more stable in appearance than the earlier mechanical lamps, is a side winder which will run for over thirty hours. Whether by reason of lack of evaporation, or efficiency of operation, this lamp uses very little fuel, and of course, has the decided advantage of dispensing with chimney cleaning.

The 12″ later Hitchcock lamp (d) with patent dates including December 17th, 1895, adopted the Wanzer shape and the side winding feature. Interest in and production of mechanical lamps spanned the 1860 to 1900 period, and they must have been well-known articles, however, I have not heard of a reference to them in literature. "Light the candle or the lamp," but never "wind the lamp."

d. *Hitchcock lamp*

e. *Wanzer lamp*

Hall, Hanging and Bracket Lamps

Hanging and Bracket Lamps were made for other fuels before kerosene. As with stand lamps they range from simple tin to ornate brass, and with glass fonts and shades representing a variety of types and colors. Lamp (a) has a beautiful cranberry glass shade with brass parts having an embossed water lily design. Formerly in a Maritimes home, the place of manufacture is unknown. The arrangement of chains permits the bottom brass holder to be pulled down to light a glass font, missing here.

The center draft lamp (b) is an imported harp lamp made in such a way as to allow it to be used on a table if desired. The brass plate is embossed Young's Paraffin Light and Mineral Oil Co. Ltd. This was the company founded in England by James Young. Lamp (c) is another harp lamp with a tin shade. The Aladdin Lamp (d) has an earlier shade. The cast iron frame on lamp (e) is counterbalanced by a round weight which rests on the crown. The Lomax patent date of Sept. 20th, 1870 is the earliest of seven dates in the 70's and 80's, which are found on various parts of this lamp. The original color is bronze and the hand-painted trumpet vine design is in mint condition. Another cast iron lamp (f), purchased in New York state, has a bell shade, and an early type font in a basket holder. Circa 1870.

a. Cranberry hall lamp

b. Young's hanging or table lamp

c. Harp lamp

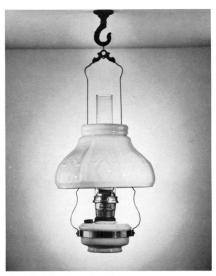

d. Aladdin hanging lamp

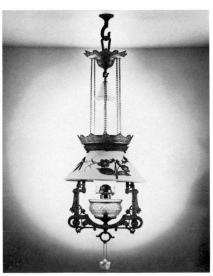

e. Lomax font hanging lamp

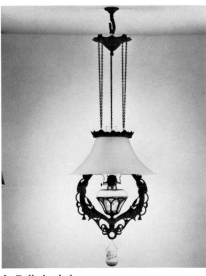

f. Bell shade lamp

g. Cast iron hanging lamp

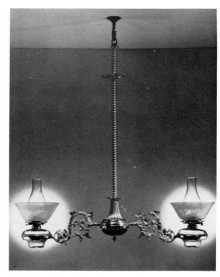

h. Brass hanging lamp

i. Combination bracket and stand lamp

Basket type holders and fancy cast iron frames were popular in the 1860's. The lamp (g) came from a church in Newcastle, Ontario. Another non-adjustable early lamp (h), probably of the 1860's, has cast brass arms with a vintage pattern. The shades are old but have been added recently.

Photographed in the standing position, lamp (i) may be adjusted above the stem to hang on a wall. The cast iron base is patent dated November 21st, 1876, August 12th, 1879, and May 18th, 1880, and the standing height is 12-1/8″.

a. Adjustable bracket

b. Angle lamp

A sampling of the wide variety of bracket lamps is illustrated on this page. The adjustable cast iron bracket lamp (a) of the 1870's has a font patented in 1875 which fits on a peg holder. The arms allow vertical and horizontal adjustment. The Angle Lamp (b) was designed to avoid a shadow below. Patented and popular in the 1890's and still popular in the 1920's, these are also found in a variety of hanging lamps having two, three or four burners attached to a single reservoir. Clear, opaque, etched and art glass shades were made for these lamps. Solid and plated brass are combined in the bracket (c). Popular in the 90's, the font is secured by a set screw.

The handsome cast iron double bracket lamp (d), boasts rectangular base Ives shades with embossed patent dates. These are described in the section on shades. Fancy cast iron brackets as in (e) were popular in the 1880's and 90's. Mirror reflectors, which were sold also with the earliest kerosene lamps, concentrate the light. The brass bracket lamp (f) has a tin font. This particular one, with the original chimney, came from a church in Welcome, Ontario, but the same lamp with a brass nameplate is reported to have been used in railway cars.

c. Bracket lamp circa 1890

d. Double bracket lamp

e. Bracket with mirrored reflector

f. Brass bracket lamp

Miniatures, Night Lamps and Novelties

The true miniature is an exact replica of a full-sized model, however the term is generally used for any small night light. Probably of the 1890's, the Cosmos pattern (a) and the Greek Key pattern (b) were popular designs. Cosmos came with pink, yellow or blue shading near the collar and at the top of the shade. Pink and possibly other colors of cased glass, and colorless glass were also made. In the photograph (c) the 2-1/4″ Improved flat hand lamp with The Little Favorite embossed on the obverse side, would be considered a miniature, and the 2-7/8″ Double Rib and Oval is either a miniature or just a small flat hand lamp. The Cosmos lamp is 8-3/8″ to the top of the chimney and the Greek Key 8-1/2″ to the top of the chimney.

a. Cosmos lamp

b. Greek Key miniature

c. Miniature and small flat hand lamps

Opposite is a full-size 10″ Crown Lamp made by the Dalzell, Gilmore & Leighton Company of Findlay, Ohio in the 1890's, standing beside its 5-1/4″ miniature.

A revival of interest in the use of candles in the 1890's probably prompted manufacture of tubular glass fonts which fit into a candlestick. The attached nickel-plated shade holder of example (a) is stamped "The Twilight", and Pat. May 22, 1894. The thumb wheel is embossed The P. & A. Mfg. Co. Acorn. A china or brass candlestick would be more appropriate than the tin holder shown here, and fabric shades were also used.

This little pig (b) likely went to market. It was probably used in a butcher shop as an advertising novelty. Glass float lights (c) had a wick held in cork which floated on a layer of oil over water. These lights hung by wires, were used on festive occasions. Another type of float lamp used as a night lamp, had one or two glass, china or metal containers hung from arms of a standard.

A cigar store was a likely location for the 9-3/4″ advertising lamp (d), and the combination cigar cutter and lighter (e) which shows signs of much use. This is 11″ to the top of the burner.

b. Pig lamp

a. Candlestick lamp

c. Float lamp

d. Cigar advertising lamp

e. Cigar lighter and cutter

◄ *Crown Lamps*

Whale-Oil and Burning-Fluid Lamps

Expense and safety were major factors in dictating the size of lamps used for liquid fuels before kerosene. On these pages are examples which clearly illustrate the general appearance of lamps produced in the 1830's, 40's and 50's. Lamp (a) incorporates several elements popular in the 1830's. The elongated free-blown font is stone engraved, and several glass wafers are used between the font and base. The stem consists of three free-blown knops which were at one time severed just below the largest one. The inside of the large knop is scarred with many minute chips or nicks, which suggest it formerly contained a coin or trinket, of sufficient value to warrant the risky operation involved in its removal. Several steps on the outside, and a pattern pressed on the underside create the fancy base which was also used on candlesticks.

Free-blown spherical fonts were often combined with finely detailed, complicated molded bases. These combinations reflect the artistic personality that is such an appealing characteristic of lamps in the 1825 to 1860 period.

The lamps in the photograph opposite illustrate the most common shapes of whale-oil or burning-fluid pressed glass lamps of the 40's and 50's. The tall narrow font of the stand lamp, or the syrup jug shape of the hand lamp, were phased out as the use of kerosene approached in the late 50's. The fact that these basic shapes were never revived is assurance that lamps of these types were not originally produced for burning kerosene. This applies also to the entirely free-blown plain lamp. A kerosene burner would now appear most inappropriate on any of these lamps, and yet with the collar size the same as that of kerosene burners, it must have been a familiar sight in the homes of the 60's to see these lamps equipped with kerosene burners and chimneys, burning the "brilliant and inexpensive new lighting fuel."

a. Lamp of the 1830's
Whale-oil and burning-fluid lamps ▷

a. Triple Flute pattern

The Triple Flute pattern (a) is one of the few earlier ones to be used in an expanded and enlarged form during the kerosene period. Triple Flute and Bar would describe the variation on the marble base. The wide bottom of the font, common to all these lamps, is a characteristic to watch for in seeking patterns made during the kerosene period and earlier. These lamps are, left 9-3/4″, center 8-3/8″ and right 10-3/8″. The left lamp in picture (b) resembles the Beehive lamp which was made by a blown and tooled technique, used at Sandwich in the 1840's, to produce open or covered dishes and lamps. Mold marks indicate that this heavy lead glass lamp is similar in appearance, but not in method of manufacture. In the center lamp, a free-blown font is attached to a separately blown stem and base. I have seen several examples of the third lamp with the pewter collar. Each of these had two continuous, slightly twisted, mold marks from collar to base. To the top of the collar, these are, left 6-1/2″, center 5-1/2″ and right 5-1/8″.

The absence of mold marks, the clarity and the weight of this simple free-blown hand lamp (c), combine to make it one of the most satisfying lamps to handle. Height is 2-1/2″. This lamp could be considered to be for whale oil, burning fluid or kerosene.

b. Free-blown and molded lamps

c. Free-blown hand lamp

Earliest Kerosene Lamps

d. *Engraved font*

e. *Engraved font*

f. *Converted solar lamp*

In the period from 1857 to 1863, kerosene went from sparse use, to widespread use. Southlands, in 1859, advertised only kerosene lamps, but the manufacturer probably produced the lamps according to demand, and without much concern regarding the fuel. These lamps had collars which allowed the use of whale-oil, burning-fluid or kerosene burners, so during the early period it was really the type of burner that determined the lamp classification.

The two free-blown fonts (d) and (e) with wheel engraved designs have the characteristic small protuberance at the base of the font which indicates an early and perhaps free-blown type. Described as turnip or pear shaped, these fonts represent a distinct design departure from the earlier glass lamps, and yet this was the popular solar lamp shape. Many of the opaque glass bases were patterned after brass and marble bases. The brass stem and marble bases were common from the late 1850's, and the opaque glass bases with brass connectors appear to have been first manufactured in the early 1860's. According to Ms. Merrill of the Sandwich Glass Museum, lamp (d) resembles a type made at Sandwich.

Towards the end of the solar lamp era, competition by kerosene resulted in factory conversion of existing stock. In the case of the ornate lamp (f), a grooved plate filled in the larger opening for a solar lamp burner, and a No. 1 collar was soldered on. Such conversions could have been made at any time, but the factory operation would probably be more precisely executed.

Most parts of this lamp influenced the design of the first kerosene lamps. The marble bases and brass stems were popular into the mid-sixties. The turnip shaped font with the annular rib to hold the prism ring, was repeated in the early glass kerosene fonts. A modified form of the frosted and engraved lead glass shade was used with many early kerosene lamps. The blue banquet lamp on the color plates illustrates the similarities noted here.

The use of prisms was carried into the kerosene period. They usually embellished very ornate lamps, and over the years most have been removed. Lamp (d) is 9-1/8″, lamp (e) is 10-1/8″, and the solar lamp (f) measures 18-1/4″ to top of the shade.

The white frosted opaline base, left, is an unusual treatment which provides a delightful contrast with the charcoal tinted, dimpled glass font. In the collection it is displayed with its counterpart, which has a shiny black base. This lamp is 7-3/4″ to the top of the collar.

The three lamps opposite, present the epitome of characteristics which would place them in the late 1850's. Marble bases, brass stems and simple squat pear shaped, or oval fonts all contribute to this conclusion. The center font is clear and free-blown, and this is flanked by fonts with pronounced bubbles and striations, which were made in two piece molds. The burners are from the early 1860's, and the chimneys are also very old. It was a happy coincidence to come upon a relatively good supply of these early burners and chimneys —250 miles apart! Sizes are left 6-7/8″, center 8-1/8″ and right 7-1/2″.

◀ *Frosted opaline base*
Early kerosene lamps ▷

Ring Punty

The name for these lamps is chosen from the S. E. Southland's catalogue of 1859. In this catalogue, all lamps are listed according to size, color and type of base except for those described as Ring Punty. There is nothing positive to connect these lamps with that description except for the fact that the pronounced rib around the center might be referred to as a ring, and the depressed ovals could be referred to as Punty. This ring design might have been inspired by the design of the solar lamps which had a ring to support the shade, and from which prisms were hung. The bases, and the glass quality and method of manufacture, place some of these lamps in the late 1850's, therefore description and time suggest the possibility these may be the lamps referred to in the catalogue. The addition of other patterns above or below the ring would be later variations.

Observation of the profiles emphasizes the wide variation in proportions, which suggests many manufacturers. Lamp (a) has a free-blown stem like those of the whale-oil and burning-fluid lamps. Lamp (b) has a stem with an additional two rings and a pressed design on the underside of the foot. This lamp has also been seen without any design pressed on the underside of the foot. Lamp (c) is the only one of the entire group which is made of non-lead glass, and a rather primitive or poor quality at that. The height of lamp (a) is 6-1/2″, (b) 7-3/4″, (c) 7-1/4″.

a. Ring Punty

b. Ring Punty

c. Ring Punty

Six Ring Punty fonts are illustrated to show the wide variety of proportions manufactured. All the lead glass fonts in this section have mold marks which disappear at the uppermost level of the pattern, which means that they were drawn into the collar in a hand finishing operation. All glass bases in this section are leaded glass. Measurements for these lamps are (d) 8-5/8″, (e) 7-1/2″, (f) 8-1/4″, (g) 9-5/8″, (h) 9-3/8″, (i) 8-3/8″.

d. Ring Punty

e. Ring Punty

f. Ring Punty

g. Ring Punty

h. Ring Punty

i. Ring Punty

a. *Ring Punty and Heart*

b. *Ring Punty and Heart*

c. *Ring Punty and Loop*

d. *Ring Punty, Sawtooth Eye and Leaf*

e. *Ring Punty, Sawtooth Eye and Leaf*

f. *Ring Punty, Sawtooth and Eye*

In this group of lamps the ring and punty design exists in the upper portion of the pattern, although the punty is now surrounded by a raised edge. Below the ring are other patterns. Lamps (a) and (b) show a considerable difference in proportion, and yet have the same pattern. Alternate hearts, have in their centers, stars or puntys. This pattern could be called Ring, Punty and Heart.

The next lamp (c) on the double step marble base, has below the ring, loops with a single rib between. Ring Punty and Loop is the name suggested.

The ribbed stem on lamp (d), has been shown on a lamp which illustrated an 1865 patented accessory. Lamps (d) (e) and (f) each have continuous sawtooth and eye band below the ring, however (d) and (e) have an additional leaf design near the bottom of the font, and in (f) a diamond exists at this point. Lamps (d) and (e) could therefore be Ring Punty, Sawtooth Eye and Leaf; and lamp (f) Ring Punty, Sawtooth and Eye. While all have excellent quality glass, that of font (e) is exceptional. These lamps measure (a) 10″, (b) 9-1/2″, (c) 10-3/4″, (d) 9-3/8″, (e) 9-3/8″, (f) 9-3/4″.

The top lamp (g) is the last in this section to include the ring punty design, and in this example the punty band is rather crowded. The pattern below the ring can be referred to as Triple Peg and Loop, thus we have Ring Punty, Triple Peg and Loop.

Lamp (h) is Triple Peg and Loop, and lamp (i) with the fancy stamped stem is Triple Peg and Loop with Scalloped Band. Sizes are (g) 9-3/8″, (h) 9-1/2″, (i) 9-1/8″.

g. Ring Punty, Triple Peg and Loop

h. Triple Peg and Loop

i. Triple Peg and Loop with Scalloped Band

Rib, Prism and Icicle Patterns

The rounded rib, the edged prism and the jagged edged icicle were used in dozens of combinations and variations in the late 1850's and 60's. With these designs, glass imperfections would have been camouflaged. This may have been a consideration in the early 60's when lead was in greater demand for wartime purposes than for glass, and before the introduction of the lime glass formula in 1864, to produce excellent quality glass without lead. The Bellflower pattern (a) and a similar Vine pattern on a fine prism background were among the earliest tableware patterns, and were manufactured by several companies. Other lamps in this section represent types which were probably made by most lamp manufacturers. A few appear to have been made by Atterbury & Company of Pittsburgh, Pa., but might easily have been products of other local companies. The Bellflower lamp is 8-3/4" and the variety of rib flat hand lamps (b) range from 2-7/8" to 3-1/2".

The group of lamps (c), having the wide rib pattern known as

b. Ribbed hand lamps

c. Melon lamps

Melon, are circa 1860 and all are leaded glass. On the left is a Melon flat hand lamp of excellent quality. A good quality more common lamp of almost identical design, is shown with the Atterbury lamps. The matching stand lamp, second from right, has the same quality and clarity. It is difficult to date the middle lamp without a handle. It may have been made around 1860, but could easily be much earlier. The fourth lamp has been seen in a slightly larger size, and the last lamp in the picture is unusual in that the melon design is carried to the bottom to create a scalloped edge. These lamps range from 2-3/4" to 7-3/8".

a. Bellflower

d. Macklin

e. Macklin Variant

Lamp (d) Macklin, is an excellent quality early lamp which has several variations. This font has a well-executed engraved pattern on a plain band; and the base is opaline. A similar larger font has been seen with a clear design on a frosted band. This was combined with a double marble base, and a blue opaline stem. Lamp (e) with the vertical rib band is a variation in ordinary glass.

The six lamps at the bottom of the page, all have ribs or prisms pressed on the underside of their bases. These are the lamps of the 1860's which would have been used in any area of a modest home, or in the bedrooms or utility rooms of carefully appointed houses. Restorations of this period often have lamps or lighting chosen from another period, or of an inappropriate character.

In recent years, these little lamps have been among the least expensive. It is not unusual to see a machine-made lamp produced early this century with a higher price tag. This fact, coupled with a curiosity about the number of variations, has led to a collection of 14 different lamps. With the exception of those linked to Atterbury & Co., there is nothing to relate any of these lamps to a specific manufacturer. Most of these fonts have been seen combined with brass stems and marble bases, or with opaque glass bases. The plain fonts in the photograph (f) are like the one on the cover of the S. E. Southland's 1859 catalogue. It is quite probable that some of these all-glass lamps were made in the late 1850's.

Lamps such as those in photograph (f) usually have a glass tint or texture to add interest to their plain fonts. The left lamp in photograph (g) is ordinary glass with an amethyst tint, and the right lamp has a lead glass base with a silvery sheen. The Prism pattern on the left lamp in photograph (h) is seen frequently, and both this font and base pattern were made by Atterbury & Company of Pittsburgh, Pa. The excellent quality right hand lamp, Rib and Flute, has been seen combined with a brass stem and marble base.

Sizes are: (d) 12″, (e) 8-1/8″, (f) both 6-1/4″, (g) L 6-3/4″, R 6-1/4″, (h) L 6-1/4″ and R 6-1/8″.

f. Prism base lamps

g. Ribbed font lamps

h. Left, prism font. Right, Rib and Flute

The font on lamp (a) Bond, has a lovely charcoal tint which contrasts with the opaline base. Lamp (b) Keele, with a medium horizontal rib has also been seen with a brass stem and marble base. Lamp (c) Essex, has an average quality broad rib font and a leaded glass base. The font on lamp (d), Waisted Broad Rib, appears also in the section on opaque glass bases. It is similar to lamp (c) except for the nipped-in part at the base of the font. This particular example has several flaws including a mold mark so pronounced that it becomes a flange. The base is slightly leaded. A rather strange profile of lamp (e) Dunn, makes one suspect that the font has been put on upside down. The prism font (f) Shaw, has a horizontal ring in the lower half. On the inside there is a distinct indented "V" at this point, and the portion below is entirely smooth. This indicates a pressed font drawn in at the top, rather than a mold blown operation.

Sizes are: (a) 7-7/8″, (b) 8-1/4″, (c) 6-1/4″, (d) 8″, (e) 7-3/4″ and (f) 9-1/2″.

a. Bond

b. Keele

c. Essex

d. Waisted Broad Rib

e. Dunn

f. Shaw

g. Blake

h. Prism

i. Bain

j. Lynd

k. Double Icicle

l. Single Icicle

Lamp (g) Blake, has a fair quality font with a wide base. Lamp (h) Prism, like lamp (d), has a font which appears to be too large in proportion to the base. The same broad prism font in lamp (i) Bain, has a better relationship with its black opaque glass base.

The rather indistinctly molded font on lamp (j), Lynd, is of fair to good quality. The opaque base, like all those in this section, is leaded. The Double Icicle pattern (k), appears in the Atterbury catalogue, 6″. The Single Icicle pattern font is combined with an Atterbury No. 40 design base.

Sizes are: (g) 7-3/4″, (h) 6-5/8″, (i) 8-1/8″, (j) 9-3/8″, (k) 6″ and (l) 8-1/8″.

Early Bullseyes

The raised or sunken circle called a bullseye, was a feature of many of the most attractive early designs. All these lamps were likely products of the 1860's, and many were made by two or more companies. All except (h) and (k) have leaded glass fonts, and all bases except the frosted opaline one on (k) are leaded.

Lamps (a), (b) and (c) are essentially the same pattern, with different proportions, and could therefore all have the name Panelled Bullseye. Font (b) is seen occasionally with gold outlining. The Double Bullseye (d) has a New England type base.

Bullseye and Fleur-de-lis fonts were made in other proportions including the nearly cylindrical whale-oil type. Both lamp (e), and lamp (f) the Bullseye Fleur-de-lis and Heart pattern were likely products of the New England area factories. Sizes are (a) 8-1/2″, (b) 13-1/2″, (c) 9-1/4″, (d) 9-3/8″, (e) 8-7/8″ and (f) 8-5/8″.

a. Panelled Bullseye

b. Panelled Bullseye

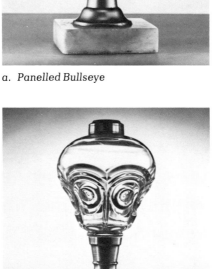

c. Panelled Bullseye

d. Double Bullseye

e. Bullseye and Fleur-de-lis

f. Bullseye, Fleur-de-lis and Heart

g. *Bullseye Band*

h. *Bullseye Band Entwined*

i. *Flame Bullseye*

j. *Flame Bullseye*

k. *Bullseye and Loop*

l. *Beaded Bullseye and Leaf*

Bullseye Band (g) is a simplified version of Bullseye Band Entwined (h). A larger leaded glass font with this pattern, and an engraved design on the shoulder, is shown in the section on iron base lamps.

In addition to the bases shown here, the lovely Flame Bullseye pattern fonts have been seen combined with blue or white opaline bases and with shiny black glass bases. An example at the Sandwich Glass Museum is combined with a Triple Dolphin base. The font is not claimed to have been made at the Sandwich factory, and the reports I have had indicate that it is not well known in the area. Many examples of this lamp have been seen in Canada, and hopefully it will someday be linked with a particular area or manufacturer. The design is frequently seen with gold outlining.

The Bullseye and Loop lamp (k) has an unsophisticated primitive quality. Its opaline base has a lavender tint. Beaded Bullseye and Leaf (l) is an attractive pattern with excellent quality glass. Additional bullseye patterns are included in other sections.

Sizes are: (g) 8-1/2″, (h) 13-1/2″, (i) 7-7/8″, (j) 11-7/8″, (k) 8-1/8″ and (l) 11-1/8″.

a. Scalloped Rib Band

Early Related Lamps— Before 1880

Any characteristic common to two or more lamps may one day be the key to pinpointing the time and place of manufacture. Several other sections include related examples which are linked to a known area or manufacturer.

Lamps (a) and (b) have bases with a continuous horizontal rib near the bottom. The base of lamp (a) is a soft blue-grey slag, and the font, with a deep thread-like mold mark, is of fair quality. Height is 11-1/4″ and a suggested name is Scalloped Rib Band. The font of lamp (b), shown here and opposite, has a loop and dart closely resembling the Loop and Dart pattern, which according to Kamm, was patented in 1869 by W. O. Davis. The addition of the heart indicates the name Loop and Dart and Heart. Lamp size is 10-3/4″.

b. Loop and Dart and Heart

c. Left, Grape Band. Right, Loop and Dart and Heart

The lamps in (c) above have had their Atterbury Prism design bases pressed by the same plunger. A flaw in this plunger has resulted in identical creased bumps in both bases above the prism band. This would suggest the Grape Band pattern on the left, and the Loop and Dart and Heart on the right, were made by the same company. The pattern, described by Lee as Grape Band, was designed and patented by John Bryce, on October 19, 1869. The cluster of grapes over the vine closely resembles the illustration in Lee, and in the patent drawing. The leaves do not cover the vine to the same extent as in the patent drawing, however they appear to be the same as in the Lee illustration. Bryce, Walker & Company of Pittsburgh made Grape Band in a number of tableware pieces. Sizes are: left 9-1/8″, right 10-1/8″.

a. Beaded Loop

This Beaded Loop pattern font (a), has nine beads between the beads above the prisms separating the loops. The similar Atterbury Shelley has eight beads, and the Ford Museum has a lamp with a Hobbs base, a regular brass connector and a green beaded loop font with 10 beads. The acid etched design on lamp (a) is the same as that on lamp (b), Beaded Bullseye, and both lamps are excellent quality without mold marks on the shoulder. Beaded Bullseye is similar to Beaded Circle in Lee's Sandwich Book. Lamp (c) Laurel, and lamp (d) Herringbone Band, have Rib and Roll bases, which appear similar to the bases on the opposite page, except that in this instance the ribs are inside and on the opposite page the bases are fluted on the outside. These lamps would be of the 60's or early 70's.

Sizes are: (a) 9-1/2″, (b) 8-1/2″, (c) 8-5/8″ and (d) 9″.

b. Beaded Bullseye

c. Laurel

d. Herringbone Band

The Diagonal Rib and Pod lamps (e) are often found in Ontario. The Rib Band lamp (f) has the same panelled stem and base. Lamp (g) I have called Gasket Band because it so closely resembles the .049 Model Airplane Motor gasket, propped beside it. The Oval Bead Band of the font in picture (h) is similar to that used with the Bakewell Pears & Company pattern Arabesque. Lamps (g) and (h) have a graceful plain trumpet shaped stem, and all four have the Flute and Roll base. Sizes are: (e) left 9″, right 3″, (f) 9″, (g) 7-1/4″, (h) 7-1/2″.

e. Diagonal Rib and Pod

f. Rib Band

g. Gasket Band

h. Oval Bead Band

a. Palmette

b. Beaded Scroll

c. Diamond Sunburst

A graceful base with six scallops is common to lamps (a), (b) and (c) of the early 1870's. Lamp (a) is the attractive and popular Palmette pattern. Lamp (b) Beaded Scroll, is similar to the Atterbury Scroll pattern except for the addition of the beads, and the design flowing in the opposite direction. The Diamond Sunburst pattern (c) was patented in 1874 by John Bryce of Bryce, Walker & Company, but variations are considered to have been made by other companies. It is interesting to speculate that if this lamp, and these bases were in fact products of Bryce, Walker & Company, it would suggest they also made Palmette and the Beaded Scroll. If other patented designs manufactured by this company, such as Grape Band, Thistle, Curled Leaf and Strawberry, were made in lamps with these bases, it would further support this theory.

Opposite are five stand lamps with the same bases, and two similar fonts. Lamps (d) and (e) can be differentiated by the names Star Loop and Cable Right (d) and Star Loop and Cable Left (e), according to the direction of flow of the cable design. Seashell (f) is a pattern which was also combined with a brass stem and marble base. Lamp (g) is Sarah and (h) is Star Oval Panel. Lamp (i) is Cord Rosette, a pattern shown on a goblet in Metz I. I would date the lamps on this page from the mid 60's. Sizes are: (d) 9″, (e) 8-1/2″, (f) left 8-3/4″ and right 3-1/4″, (g) 7″, (h) 8-1/2″, (i) 9″.

d. Star Loop and Cable Right

e. Star Loop and Cable Left

f. Seashell

g. Sarah

h. Star Oval Panel

i. Cord Rosette

On this page are three lamps with X Band bases. Panelled Fern (a) and (d), opposite, included also in the following section, was made in a goblet pictured in Metz I.

Lamp (b) has a Ribbed Band pattern made by several companies. The Sandwich Heart Variant (c) is a simple form of the beautiful pattern of vases and whale-oil lamps said by Lee to have been made at Sandwich. These lamps would be products of the 1870's. They are (a) 8-7/8″, (b) 7-1/4″ and (c) 10″.

a. Panelled Fern

b. Ribbed Band

c. Sandwich Heart Variant

Panelled Fern (d), like the other lamps on this page, is combined with a base having alternately large and small scallops. Lamp (e) is the pattern called Galaxy which is shown in Metz I on a goblet.

The strange Panelled Sawtooth pattern (f) has a three mold font with one clear, and one indistinct panel on each section. The plain font on Clifford (g), has a faintly dimpled texture. These lamps would also be from the 1870's. They measure (d) 8-1/4″, (e) 9-5/8″, (f) 9-1/4″ and (g) 7-3/4″.

d. Panelled Fern

e. Galaxy

f. Panelled Sawtooth

g. Clifford

Fern, Shields and Centennial

a. Shield

b. Diamond Band and Shield

c. Diamond Band and Fan

The lamps in this section include the above motifs, or are related to them. Two other lamps should be noted here. The Atterbury Emblem lamp is shown in this book on a prism base, and in Lindsay's American Historical Glass on another style base. Peterson shows a lamp with a Liberty Bell pedestal patented by N. L. Bradley January 11, 1876. Lamps with patriotic motifs such as an emblem or shield may have had their inspiration and production at the time of the Civil War, during the Centennial, or somewhere in between. The flat hand lamp (a) 3-1/4″, has a lightly embossed Shield pattern with dots or small beads representing stars. In the top of the shield there are 13 of these. The rather delicate handle is appropriate with the thin walled, light weight font. I think this lamp is a product of the early 1860's.

Lamps (b) and (c) have clearly defined patterns with the same design on the center band. Lamp (b), Diamond Band and Shield, with a pinwheel design on the bottom of the font, is 3-1/4″ and lamp (c), Diamond Band and Fan is 3″.

Those who have chosen names for glass patterns have referred to the arrangement of leaves or petals on these lamps as ferns. Lamp (d) with a three mold font of ordinary glass, has the Panelled Fern pattern shown on a goblet in Metz I, and in an opaque white pitcher in Belknap. She describes her goblet as being clear flint, and well-known in the Sandwich area. This font has also been seen in excellent quality clear glass without mold marks above the pattern. Blocked Fern (e) with twelve panels and diamonds beneath, has a green tint. The opaque white base is leaded glass. Fern Band (f), purchased in the U.S., has a primitive quality, and a green tint. I would place this lamp and the following two between 1865 and 70. Fern and Scalloped Rib (g) has unusual glass qualities. It is clear and bright, but with the pronounced green tint of ordinary glass. The depressed ferns are exceptionally well defined giving the appearance of having been engraved, and the strange marks visible from rib to collar, continue in some instances below the rib.

The brilliance and quality of molding give Fern and Shield (h), an excellent rating, although there are a few bubbles. Panelled Shield (i) is a handsomely embellished design, which is seen also with a figure stem. Sizes are: (d) 9-3/4″, (e) 8-3/4″, (f) 8-3/4″, (g) 10-1/4″, (h) 9-3/4″ and (i) 9-1/2″.

d. Panelled Fern

e. Blocked Fern

f. Fern Band

g. Fern and Scalloped Rib

h. Fern and Shield

i. Panelled Shield

In an article in Hobbies Magazine by Mary and Bill Wollett, this pattern (a) is called the New England Centennial pattern and described as one of the least known Centennial patterns. Their illustration includes a goblet which has the 1876 date embossed, the lamp illustrated here, and a stand lamp which has the same stem and base as the three shown on this page. The reverse side of the lamp has a ring of thirteen stars enclosed in a circle, and a scroll representing the Declaration of Independence. The glass quality is very good and the design is similar to those produced in the Midwest in the 70's. Height is 4-1/4″.

The stem and base of the three stand lamps (b), (c) and (d), may be referred to as Centennial Base. The approximate date is established by the hand lamp font, and perhaps identification of one of these patterns, or another on the same base, will give the name of the manufacturer or locale. The names suggested here are (b) Patrician, (c) Sawtooth and Swag, and (d) Woodbine. Lamp (b) is 7-3/4″ and sizes of (c) and (d) are not available as these were photographed "on location," and originally intended for reference only.

The charming pair opposite with appropriate burners would likely have been made during the Civil War. This Shield and Star pattern was also combined with a fancy opaque white glass base, which is shown with the Star, Loop and Cable Right pattern, in the Early Related Group section preceding. An all glass version has been seen with a plain stem and round base. Height to the top of the collar is left 7-1/4″, and right 7-1/8″, the difference is the result of the base thickness.

a. New England Centennial

b. *Patrician*   c. *Sawtooth and Swag*   d. *Woodbine*   *Shield and Star* ▷

Sandwich and Similar

As the uninitiated drifts into an awareness of glass, it becomes apparent that the word "Sandwich" is spoken with reverence. Curiosity about the mystique which envelopes a discussion of glass from this factory, leads one to seek out pertinent publications and examples of Sandwich glass. The suggestion that perfection is dull is emphasized in this glass, often having the contradiction of superior quality and imperfections. Distinctive design, solid colors of hue and intensity, that will sit comfortably beside each other, and color combinations of artistic merit are all important ingredients in the success of Sandwich glass. As with beauty in nature, these qualities evoke a pleasurable response in both the naive and the knowledgeable.

The quantity and variety of glass on display at the Sandwich Glass Museum reflects the character of glass made at the Sandwich and nearby factories. The closest of these other factories in distance and relationship, was the Cape Cod Glass Co. at Sandwich. Deming Jarves, who founded the Boston and Sandwich Glass Company in 1825, left to start the Cape Cod Glass Company in 1858. This Company, also located in Sandwich, was responsible for approximately one third of the glass produced in that town for nearly a decade. Cape Cod made lamps, and several other not too distant companies are also credited with the manufacture of excellent quality glass and lamps. Among these were the New England Glass Co., East Cambridge, Mass., the Phoenix Glass Works, South Boston, Mass., the Mt. Washington Glass Works, New Bedford, Mass., the Suffolk Glass Works, South Boston, and the Union Glass Company of Somerville, Mass. This company list is from Kenneth Wilson's book on New England Glass. There is also included in this book an account of the Smith Brothers company. This family, famous for glass decorating, was also associated with the Sandwich and Mt. Washington factories. The lack of catalogue and advertising material coupled with the close proximity of these companies, and the frequent exchange of personnel and ideas, makes positive attribution difficult.

The two valuable catalogue pages, shown opposite, are owned by the Sandwich Glass Museum, and are reproduced with their kind permission. In these pages, and another illustrated in Freeman, we are able to see examples of various patterns, types of cutting, descriptions of cutting, types of shades, and the size range of silvered reflectors. The lamps illustrated on the top catalogue page are certainly different in character to those on the bottom. Perhaps this is because the glass parts of these lamps are restricted in shape and importance by the metal work. The illustrations also show the types of bases and brass fittings used, and the prisms in vogue. The single, double and triple marble bases were a continuation of the types used for astral and solar lamps of the 1850's. It is, therefore, reasonable to assume that these two pages represent lamps manufactured in the early 1860's. It is difficult to say how long they would have continued production of these styles, or how long existing stocks would make such catalogue advertising valid. Marble bases appear to be combined with fonts of the early 60's, thereafter fashion and economy favored the opaque glass bases.

a. Madelaine

The figure stem shown above is second from the left on the top catalogue page opposite. The excellent quality engraved font however, has a different design. The catalogue measurement of 13-1/2″ is 2″ taller than this example. It is possible their measurement included the burner and shade holder, or that other sizes were made. The last lamp on the catalogue page is also listed as being taller than the one pictured in this section. Suggested name for the figure is Madelaine.

REFERENCE

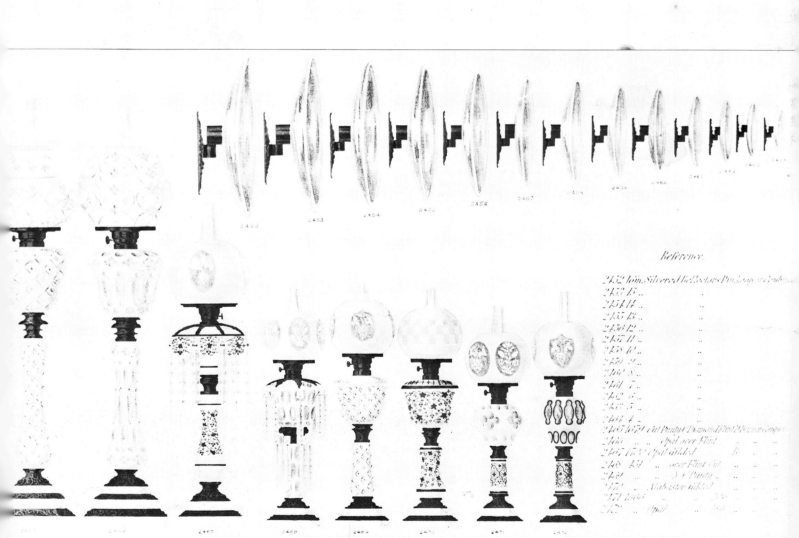

Reference.

MANUFACTURED BY THE BOSTON & SANDWICH GLASS CO.

A.S. Dowden Sandwich Mass. S.H. FESSENDEN AGENT, BOSTON U.S.A

Fragments excavated at the site of the Sandwich factory have added many more lamps to the list. Manufacture by Sandwich of these should be classified as probable in view of the discovery, at Sandwich, of fragments of patterns manufactured by other companies. The Midwest factories used the same brass fittings, and made fine quality glass of similar type and design. This makes attribution of locale extremely difficult for many of the finer lamps of the 1860's. Several examples of these are included in the section on Marble and Opaque Glass Base Lamps.

The patent dated lamps are self-authenticating, although one of these offers a contradiction to an accepted theory. The Blackberry and Onion lamps also offer interesting and puzzling relationships, both here and in the Atterbury section.

My research has uncovered information and shown new relationships which have thus far produced more questions than answers. Discussing these with Ms. Nancy Merrill, the Curator of the Sandwich Glass Museum, has been an important factor in formulating my own impressions. I am sure her visit and interest will one day add to the number of certainties in the history of lamps.

Sandwich was one of many companies which manufactured excellent quality cut and engraved lamps. The font (a) shows a finely detailed engraved vintage pattern on the shoulder, and has a white cut to green opaline stem. Other fonts have been reported to have been combined with this stem and base. This lamp is shown with other Sandwich lamps in the color section, and the stem-base combination is seen in the catalogue reproduction. Height is 13-3/8″.

a. Vintage engraving

b. Detail of Sandwich Quatrefoil font

Picture (b) is a close-up of the font of the large cranberry cut to clear lamp shown in the color section. This quatrefoil motif was frequently used on their lamps.

The design of the engraved lyre (c) is the same as on a lamp at the Sandwich Museum, however the execution is much less detailed here. The gold banded white opaline base was formerly combined with an Atterbury lamp, and replaces a white base of very small proportion. The age of the engraved chimney is uncertain. Lamp (c) is 13-1/8".

c. Engraved lyre design ▷

a. *White overlay cut to cranberry*

b. *White overlay cut to clear*

This dazzling font (a) has the white overlay cut to a brilliant cherry red cranberry. The pattern, outlined in gold, is the same as on the lamp in the color section, and shown in this section with prisms. All the brass parts including the collar have their original bronze finish. 12-3/4″.

On lamp (b), white overlay cut to clear, each clear circle becomes a lens focussing on the opposite side of the font. The far circles are reduced to give a unique quality to a simple font. Probably Sandwich, this, and lamp (a), are typical of the early 1860's. 10-7/8″.

c. *White overlay cut to green opaline*

d. *Painted white opaque glass font*

While these two bases, and the one on the following page, would all be described as blue opaline, they are each a different shade. The white cut to green opaline font (c), makes a striking combination with its blue base, and is not as compatible with the other blue bases. 13″. These two lamps are probably 1865-70.

The type of painted decoration on font (d), was frequently used on lamp shades. The lower font and shoulder are a buff color, and the band is red, white and green. The pattern is accented with gold dots. 13-1/2″. Note the collar with the tooled rib.

a. *Four Petal*

Both Four Petal (a) and Boston Bullseye (b) have deeply indented patterns, and fonts which are smooth on the inside. This indicates a pressed font which was reheated and drawn into the collar. The nearly opaque blue base does not have the opaline qualities of the other Sandwich bases.

Boston Bullseye (b) is the name I have chosen to distinguish this pattern from the many other bullseye designs. The excellent quality glass and design make these two lamps outstanding examples of their time, circa 1865. Both patterns are regarded by the Sandwich Glass Museum as products of the Boston & Sandwich Glass Company. Sizes are: (a) 10-1/2″ and (b) 10-1/8″.

b. *Boston Bullseye*

The softly frosted upper and lower parts of the font (c) provide an attractive frame for the etched landscape with the dog and birds. The blue opaline base is a stronger color than those on the previous pages.

Early Moon and Star (d) is considered to have been made by Sandwich, or in that area. I believe more examples combined with other bases will provide additional information. Another Early Moon and Star has been seen in blue, and in opaque white, and in these the moon is flattened rather than concave.

Many wooden models for the Buckle pattern (e) were found at the Sandwich factory site. It is a design considered by many to be a product of several companies in both the east and Midwest. Other examples of this font are shown in the section on iron base lamps, and these would support the theory that Buckle lamps are circa 1870. All the examples I have seen have had excellent quality glass without mold marks on the shoulder.

Sizes are: (c) 12-1/4", (d) 9-1/8" and (e) 9-7/8".

c. Bird Dog

d. Early Moon and Star

e. Buckle

a. Wolf Stem

The stem and base of lamp (a) is shown in the reproduced Sandwich catalogue pages. The stem is zinc diecast metal, and the base is soapstone. These parts may have been available to any manufacturer, so attribution to Sandwich is not positive. The font appears to be lead glass with a smooth frosting, and engraved design. Frosted fonts on most figure lamps had a pressed design on ordinary glass.

The little lamp (b) has a dark blue overlay, cut to clear. This font is combined with a brass stem and soapstone base, painted in a simulated marble design.

The catalogue pages show prisms attached to fancy cast brass rings, on cut overlay lamps. One such ring is shown in picture (c), although it is possible this small ring was originally intended to be the lower part of two tiers, and would have been attached to the top of the stem. All the overlay lamps on marble bases illustrated in the catalogue pages, unscrew between the font and the stem. Perhaps the reason for this was to accommodate the addition of a prism ring. Many lamps have had these rings removed because they obscured the glass and design of the lamp, however the Ford Museum at Dearborn, Mich., has prisms on a number of their early kerosene lamps. Sizes are: (a) 10-7/8″, (b) 7-1/2″ and (c) 10-1/4″.

b. Dark blue overlay cut to clear

c. Prism ring and prisms

Hiram Dillaway, director of the Sandwich mold department, obtained two patents for glass lamps. One granted July 18, 1871 was for a hinged, four-part mold for making "blown glass lamps, and other articles in which there are one or more depressions or recesses in the top surfaces." The Sandwich Glass Museum has a plain dated lamp without a pattern, which appears to have the same profile and drip depression as the patent drawing. The product of the mold illustrated would have two vertical mold seams from collar to peg, and one horizontal seam at the top of a flat indented band, in the middle of the font. Lamp (e) has a drip depression, with the July 18, 1871 patent date embossed around the depression, however it was blown in a three-part mold. Horizontal mold seams which are not evident, could be concealed by the pattern. Perhaps a more significant feature of this lamp is that a pressed glass pattern hitherto unidentified, can now be attributed to Sandwich. Another interesting aspect of this lamp is that the font does not appear to be lead glass, and the base of this lamp and lamp (h) are unleaded glass. It has been considered that at this time, Sandwich made only lead glass. This may be another area where lamps and patents can provide important information regarding glass production.

The second Dillaway patent for lamps was one obtained July 11, 1876 for a pressed font. This method involved pressing the font upside-down in a mold that would form a drip catcher, in the shape of a petal or stellated design on the shoulder. After removing the plunger, the open end was heated, closed in, and a peg affixed. Lamps (d), (f), (g) and (h) all appear to have been manufactured according to the July 11, 1876 patent, however, all have the July 18, 1871 date embossed on the drip depression. The habit of marking lamps with inapplicable patent dates was a common one. At the Sandwich Glass Museum a font dated July 11, 1876 has the stellated design on the shoulder. Lamps (f) and (g) have a wavy design that was made by the plunger. None of the lamps (d), (f), (g) or (h) has mold marks, indicating they were pressed into a one-piece lower portion of the mold. This was a variation suggested by Dillaway. The pontil mark on the hand lamp (d) is evident. Sizes are: (d) 2-7/8″, (e) 8-1/8″, (f) 11-1/2″, (g) 10-1/8″ and (h) 9-1/4″.

d. Dillaway patent plain lamp

e. Dillaway patent Greek Key

f. Dillaway patent Wavy Shoulder

g. Dillaway patent Wavy Shoulder

h. Dillaway patent plain lamp

The Atterbury Blackberry Sandwich mystery is illustrated and outlined here. Key lamps in this surprising relationship were discovered just weeks before the completion of this book, and with the likelihood of other lamps being recognized, explanations or speculation should await additional related examples. Lamps shown here are from (a) the Maritimes, (b) Nova Scotia, complete with what was likely its original flange-base chimney, (c) Ontario, (d) Hamburg, N. Y., (e) Ontario, (f) Quebec, (g) a Sandwich Glass Museum photograph of a lamp in their collection, and (h) from Ontario.

Blackberry lamps (a) and (b) have a pattern long associated with the Sandwich Factory. The Sandwich Glass Museum has examples of this font in clear colorless glass, in cobalt blue on a triple Dolphin base and the example (g) opposite. A private collection includes a Blackberry font in pale blue opaline, on a brass stem and marble base. This pattern should not be confused with the patented Hobbs Blackberry design which has rounded berries. Lamps (a) and (b) have different sized fonts with a slight variation in the angle of the berries along the mold seams, and with fair to good quality glass and molding.

The Atterbury Ribbed Loop font (c) and Gem base have threaded pegs which screw into the Atterbury patent dated brass screw socket. This clearly establishes manufacture by Atterbury & Company, although the loop pattern was not in the Atterbury catalogues examined. Lamp (d) has the same loop pattern on a smaller and more rounded font, and this is combined with the Nine Panel base. Lamp (e) Rib

a. Sandwich Blackberry

b. Sandwich Blackberry

Banded Panel is also combined with this base. Both (d) and (e) have fonts which match their bases in clarity or tint, which would indicate that the component parts of each lamp were from the same batch of glass. The Rib Banded Panel lamp (e) has a grey-pink tint.

The Nine Panel base of the cobalt blue Blackberry lamp (f) is the same in size and detail as (d) and (e), and all three bases have a ring when tapped, which would indicate some lead content. The collar of the Blackberry lamp is the same type as seen on the Dillaway 1871, patent dated lamps, made at Sandwich, and on the 1870 patented Lomax lamps, made near Sandwich, by the Union Glass Company, Somerville, Mass. Ms. Nancy Merrill, curator of The Sandwich Glass Museum, sent me the photograph (g) of an 8″ cobalt blue Blackberry lamp in their collection. In this example the round base is the same as that on lamp (h) with the Owl and Shield pattern. This has the curious appearance of an owl's face with a shield in the middle. These shields have alternately stripes, or an embossed center which appears to be an indistinct star. This font is shown on an opaque base with a brass connector, in a line drawing illustrating an 1865 patented hinged collar. The drawing looks less like an owl than the lamp, and unfortunately someone has scribbled in the center, obscuring the area where the star might have been.

Hopefully other lamps will emerge to shed light on the mystery created by these coincidences. Sizes are: (a) 9-7/8″, (b) 9″, (c) 10-7/8″, (d) 8-1/4″, (e) 8-1/2″, (f) 8-1/2″, (g) 8″ and (h) 8″.

c. Atterbury Ribbed Loop

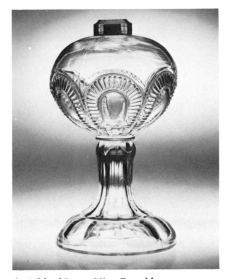

d. Ribbed Loop, Nine Panel base

e. Rib Banded Panel, Nine Panel base

f. Blackberry, Nine Panel base

g. Blackberry, Round base

h. Owl and Shield, Round base

The Onion and The Illuminator

These lamps are most appropriately placed between the Sandwich and Atterbury lamps. This illustration, from the Atterbury 1874 catalogue, appears to be the same lamp displayed at the Sandwich Museum, and on the cover of their collection book. They call it their Onion Lamp. The Curator, Nancy Merrill, showed me several fragments of this lamp in different colors of opaline glass. She mentioned also that fragments of other glassware pieces were found at Sandwich in the same type of glass and pattern.

The screw socket of the lamp at Sandwich, is not that of the familiar Atterbury 1868 patent, and examples at the museum are not marked with a patent date. This brass connection, cemented to the font and base pegs, is threaded, and screws together just below the font.

NO. 45 SCREW SOCKET

Fig. 1 The Onion

a. The Illuminator

The 9-3/4″ lamp in the photograph appears to be a modified version having a similar base, and a font with a plain shoulder. This font, called the Illuminator, is shown in the same Atterbury catalogue on all-glass lamps with a tulip pattern base. The glass is very good quality but not leaded. The coincidences here provide intriguing material for speculation.

Atterbury and Similar

4½ In. Octagon
Nº 2 Cottage Peg

Fig. 1 Cottage

5 In. Octagon Nº 2 Burner
Nº 3 Cottage Peg

Fig. 2 Cottage with Fleur-de-lis

Atterbury should head the list of names associated with kerosene lamps in North America. In his book, Glass Patents and Patterns, Dr. Arthur Peterson gives a comprehensive account of Atterbury & Co., Pittsburgh, Pa., and its President, Thomas B. Atterbury. The life span of this firm, generally associated with white glass, coincided with the pressed glass and the kerosene period, and the Atterbury brothers were clearly interested in both. Over 100 patents for glass, and lamp design and production bore the Thomas Atterbury name, as sole or joint patentee.

The variety of lamps discovered in New York State and Ontario, Canada, represents a large portion of those illustrated in the 1872, 1874 and 1881 Atterbury & Company catalogues. This section on Atterbury includes photographs of lamps which appear in these catalogues, lamps which have similar design characteristics, and catalogue illustrations of those not available for photographing.

As one builds a collection, the usual development is for each piece to contribute numerically, and to add to the comprehensiveness and understanding of the group. In this Atterbury collection, the pieces became pieces of a puzzle. Enquiries, discussion and research have added more puzzle pieces, and these are all presented in the hope that they will contribute to the final picture. The great majority of Atterbury lamps seen today range from fair to good quality, and a few could be considered very good. The puzzle is whether they also produced very fine lamps of the type we associate with the Sandwich or New England factories. In the 1872 and 1874 catalogues, there are two similar fonts whose pattern is called "Cottage".

These Cottage fonts are attached to Octagon bases with Atterbury 1868 patent screw sockets. The variations which may be noted here are the diamond pointed loop compared with the flattened diamond, and the more obvious difference of the fleur-de-lis between the loops on the font with the flattened diamond. For convenience, I will refer to this as "Cottage with Fleur-de-lis". The 1874 catalogue also shows the Cottage with Fleur-de-lis font connected to an octagonal Panel clear glass base. There isn't any reference to the variations or to the quality of glass, and for these reasons we have the beginning of the mystery. All examples I have observed with the fleur-de-lis are of excellent quality and without mold marks above the pattern. The brilliancy ranks with the best, and several have evidence of finely detailed gold loops above the top band of bullseyes. Examples of the other fonts with the pointed diamonds are all of fair to good quality with three mold seams which continue to the collar.

The Chieftain font combined with the figure stem on the following pages, is also excellent quality glass, drawn into the collar. It may be that these fonts were made prior to 1868, and the design could have appeared later on blown three-mold fonts with threaded pegs. The success of their patented lamps after that time may have led to mass production, with quality sacrificed for quantity. Other Atterbury patterns may be discovered on lamps with fair, and with excellent quality.

Cottage, Hero & Heritage

The top three lamps (a), (b) and (c) opposite, are all of excellent quality with the fleur-de-lis detail. The first two have lead glass opaque white bases with gold accent. The second font has evidence of gold loops over the bullseyes. The third lamp, with a green opaline stem, has brass fittings seen also on lamps made at Sandwich. The figure stem lamp (d), with the pointed diamonds in the loops, has good quality glass with mold marks visible on the shoulder. Measurements are 13", 12", 13-1/4" and 14-1/4" respectively.

The next lamp (e), is called Hero in the 1874 catalogue, and is shown on a base with the screw socket. This lamp with the square lead glass opaque white base, has an excellent quality font which was drawn into the collar in a hand finishing operation. The pattern below the rib is almost the same as the lower portion of the Cottage with Fleur-de-lis. There is a slight difference in the bullseyes, and Hero has two small leaves below the bullseyes.

The last lamp which is not seen in the catalogues examined, combines details of the other fonts. Shown here on the Atterbury Lace base, the pattern below the rib is essentially that of the Hero pattern except for the pointed diamond of the Cottage pattern. Combining the pattern names would suggest calling this pattern "Heritage". Height is 9" for both Hero and Heritage.

This lamp has fair quality glass with mold marks which continue to the top of the font. Another example in the author's collection has a slightly taller stem, and a No. 1 collar. It has an amethyst tint, and many flecks of white glass suspended throughout the font and base. It is understandable that a company known for making huge quantities of both clear and white glass, would occasionally have pieces of white glass in their cullet. This has been observed in several examples of Atterbury lamps, and has not been seen in other lamps.

A Heritage font with very good quality glass has been seen combined with an Atterbury No. 40 Base in opaque white glass. The common type of brass connector was used. It would be interesting to know if this font was ever made with a threaded peg to be used with the Atterbury patented threaded connector.

a. Cottage with Fleur-de-lis

b. Cottage with Fleur-de-lis

c. Cottage with Fleur-de-lis

d. Cottage

e. Hero

f. Heritage

Chieftain is the Atterbury catalogue name for the patterned fonts on this page. The 13-3/4″ figure stem lamp (a) has excellent quality glass, possibly leaded and appears to have been hand finished at the shoulder. The figure stem is one seen with overlay fonts, and with good quality, stained ruby Bohemian fonts. These facts would suggest a date of about 1865.

The leaded glass base of lamp (b) is a translucent medium blue with a few streaks of dark blue. The fonts of both these glass base lamps are good quality with marks of a three-piece mold visible on the shoulder. Height of this lamp is 10-5/8″.

The third Chieftain lamp (c) is 10-3/4″. Both this base and that of (b) appear in the Atterbury catalogue with the designation No. 40 base. Inasmuch as they are dissimilar, differentiation may be aided by calling this one No. 40 base with rib stem. The off-white leaded base has a slight greyish marbling, which closely resembles the glass of the Prism lamp base following.

a. Chieftain

Opposite. A pair of Cottage lamps with Lace bases. The glass has an amethyst tint, with many bubbles and flecks of white glass. Probably early seventies. These measure 11-1/2″ to the top of the collar.

b. Chieftain

c. Chieftain

Good to excellent quality Prism fonts (a & b) show three mold marks to the collar. Both No. 40 bases are as described with the Chieftain font. The glass of the off-white base appears to be so similar to the preceding Chieftain base that one would suggest manufacture from the same batch of glass, however, when held to the light, the base of the Prism lamp is fiery opalescent, and the other is opaque. The medium green base lamp (b) was purchased in the U.S. Attribution to Atterbury of the Prism and Chieftain lamps is based on the observations noted.

Similar to Atterbury is the only safe designation for the lamps on the opposite page. The qualities which relate them are noted, and the reader is left to ponder the possibilities. No. 40 bases of (c), (d) and (h) are cased or layered, and have little if any, lead content. Base (c) is opalescent, slightly translucent, and has the cream and blue-grey tones of a pearl button. Bases (d) and (h) are lavender, and like (c) are slightly translucent and fiery opalescent when held up to the light. It has been suggested that the unusual quality of these bases, are the result of a heat sensitive mix, rather than a separate layer of glass.

The very good quality turnip shaped Prism font (c) is a design shown in the Atterbury catalogues, and probably manufactured by many companies. The good quality Tulip font (d) is the same design as the primitive quality font on the Atterbury Lace base lamp (g), and closely resembles that of the Atterbury patent lamp with the tulip design. The ribbed Tulip font on lamp (e) is another variation in very good quality glass.

The charming Hearts and Stars primitive quality fonts (f) and (h), show mold whittle marks or pronounced striations. The jowly oval profile, the crudely applied peg, and the amethyst or green tint create a distinct personality. The watery opaline base (f) is not leaded and appears to be the type of glass used in some of the Atterbury Swan lamp bases. Base (e) is leaded, and essentially that shown with the Hero font. Lamp heights are as follows: (a) 10″, (b) 9-5/8″, (c) 9″, (d) 9-1/2″, (e) 9-1/2″, (f) 9-1/4″, (g) 8-3/4″, (h) 9-3/8″.

a. *Prism font No. 40 Rib base*   b. *Prism font No. 40 base*

c. *Turnip shaped Prism font*

d. *Plain Tulip*

h. *Hearts and Stars*

e. *Ribbed Tulip*

f. *Hearts and Stars*

g. *Plain Tulip*

Atterbury Patent Lamps

Patent dates marked on lamps are not always accurate, and the lamp does not always conform to, or even relate to patent drawings or description. These points are illustrated in some of the Atterbury lamps.

The first patented lamp manufactured by Atterbury, was one patented by Jacob Reighard of Birmingham, Pa., and assigned to Hale, Atterbury & Company of Pittsburgh, Pa. This was the firm name before being changed to Atterbury & Company. Reighard describes the nature of his invention as a "glass lamp which has two distinct openings in its top—one in the center for the introduction of the wick into the lamp and the other at one side of the center for filling in the oil or other burning fluid." This would be a cleaner and safer method for adding lighting fuel. The good quality, mammoth sized font (a) 8″ diameter, came with the Jones burner.

a. Reighard Patent font

The font with the shell pattern illustrated in the first patent issued to Thomas Atterbury on February 11th, 1862, appears to be the one on lamp (c) although it is not the double layer the patent calls for. In this case, the pattern is impressed inside, and the outside is free of mold marks. It would appear that the patent was further developed from a mold with this pattern.

The little flat hand lamp (b) has the dates February 11th and June 4th, 1862 embossed on the bottom. The lamp does conform to the February 11th patent, however, the June 4th date is an error. It is possible the reference is to the March 4th or June 3rd, 1862 Atterbury patents although the design does not relate to these patents. The handsome blue and clear Tulip and Star font (f), opposite, has these latter two 1862 dates embossed on the outside, and the number 2 on the inside. This font has been seen also on a single pedestal marble base with a fancy tooled stem. The March 4th patent was for a means of pressing articles of glassware in bas-relief and for uniting the clear or colored bas-relief glasswork to the outer surface of blown glassware. The June 3rd patent they describe as "A new manufacture consisting of glassware with its open illuminated relief work on the surface." The first patent seems to be the one most relative to the lamp.

b. Patented flat hand lamp

Lamps (d) and (e) are both embossed on the underside "Patd Feb 11th & June 3rd 1862 REISSUED July 20th 1869". These lamps do not in any way relate to the patents inscribed! The measurements to the top of the collars are as follows: (a) 4-3/4″, (b) 2-5/8″, (c) 8-1/8″, (d) 4-3/4″, (e) 7-3/4″, (f) 11-1/4″.

c. Atterbury Shell 1862

d. *Filley hand lamp*

e. *Dated lamp*

f. *Tulip and Star*

The flat hand lamps shown on this page are all manufactured using the process described in the Atterbury June 30th, 1868 patent. This patent called for a four-part mold, although the Filley pattern lamp with the ribbed band (b) used a five-piece mold. The lower portions of the mold below the shoulder included the handle matrix and font. Molten glass was first poured into the handle matrix. The glassmaker would then introduce a gather of glass into the font, close the upper parts of the mold, and the glass blown would then complete the font and handle. The point at which the blown portion of the handle meets the poured part usually leaves a bump or bulge on the handle.

The Atterbury Icicle flat hand lamps in picture (a), are 2-7/8" and 3-1/4". Atterbury Filley (b) is 2-7/8". Atterbury's Log Cabin lamp (c) is 3-3/8". The Smiths mentioned this lamp is also found in amber, blue, white opaline, and milk glass. The Shell hand lamp (d) is 2-3/4". The Ribbed Shoulder (e) and the Rib and Plain Band lamp (f) are 3-1/8" and 3-1/4" respectively. All except the Log Cabin lamp have the patent date embossed on the bottom.

There is also a plain hand lamp in two sizes, and others in patterns such as Atterbury Buckle, Slipper and Head, with the 1868 patent date.

J. S. & T. B. Atterbury.
Mold for Glass Ware.
Nº 79.298.   *Patented June 30, 1868.*

Fig: 1.

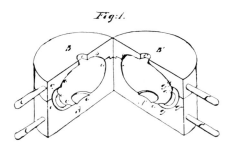

a. *1868 Icicle*

b. *1868 Filley*

c. *Log Cabin*

d. *1868 Shell*

e. *1868 Ribbed Shoulder*

f. *1868 Rib and Plain Band*

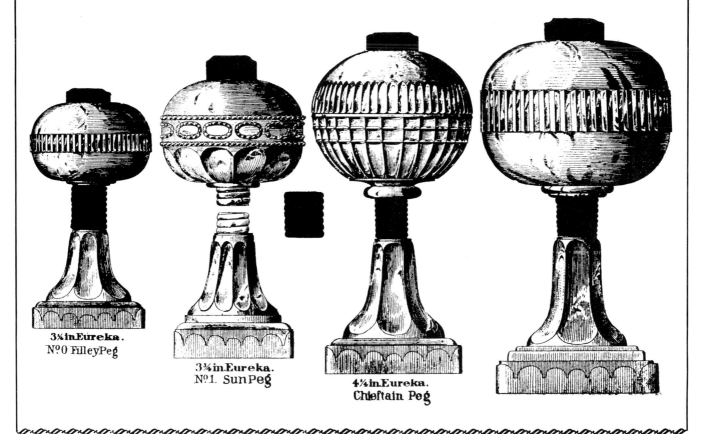

EUREKA!

The Best Improvement yet out in the Lamp Trade.

ATTERBURY'S PATENT SCREW SOCKET---PATENTED SEPT. 29, 1868.

No Plaster or Cement required to unite the Pegs to the Bases, and the labor & trouble in fitting up Lamps saved.

3¼ in. Eureka.
Nº 0 Filley Peg

3¾ in. Eureka.
Nº 1. Sun Peg

4¼ in. Eureka.
Chieftain Peg

Atterbury's Patent Screw Socket appears to have enjoyed tremendous success judging from the numbers seen today. After the expiration of the patent in 1885, the Hobbs Glass Co. and later The United States Glass Company, made lamps using a similar connector. Ease of assembly and replacement were the important features of this patent. Although interchangeability was simple, Atterbury sold lamps by a single number which referred to specific combinations.

The Bracket Lamp illustrates a patent obtained by Thomas Atterbury and his brother James, on November 22nd, 1870, for a font or other hollow ground glassware with a recessed peg for safer and better support. Also, on the same 1870 date, the Atterbury brothers obtained a patent to "produce screw-threads on the pegs of lamp-bowls and other articles of glass or vitreous ware, without leaving the joint-marks of the molds on the pegs."

Both octagonal bases pictured are dated PATD OCT 7TH 1873 & JUNE 22ND 1875 and the octagonal font is lightly embossed SEPT 16 1873 on one of the panels. The June 22nd, 1875 patent is an invention patent obtained by James and Thomas Atterbury. The nature of the patent is described as "a new manufacture, viz., a glass lamp or other glass article having its bowl made of clear or transparent glass, and its foot of pressed opal, white, or coloured glass, and the foot and bowl held together by the union of glass of the bowl with the glass of the foot." The patent further states "heretofore, opal or white or colored glass feet or stems have been united with bowls by means of a metallic socket, and by means of cement. Transparent or clear glass stands and similar glass bowls, have been made; but we are not aware that a lamp with an opal or white glass stand and clear glass bowl has ever been made and united together without a brass socket or cement." The patent claims this manufacture represents a 30% saving over a lamp made with a brass socket or cement joint. A base with a convex molded top was the key to overcome the "inconveniences resulting from unequal expansion or contraction of the foot or bowl."

The Sept. 16, 1873 and October 7th, 1873 patents are for a lamp foot and bowl respectively. These were design patents obtained by James and Thomas Atterbury for a term of seven years. The patent illustration of the octagonal font is shown with a threaded peg, and is illustrated in their 1881 catalogue with the brass patent screw socket and octagonal base. They called this their Panel lamp.

The six-sided stem has one corner which lines up with one corner of the eight-sided base. The white base lamp (a) with the Cottage font is 11-1/4", and the clear glass Panel lamp opposite is 11". Both lamps are good quality.

The logical question here is "If this method did in fact represent a 30% saving, why is there not evidence of this lamp having offered competition to brass connector types, including their own?"

a. Cottage font Panel Base

Panel lamp ▷

Two 1876 Atterbury patents are illustrated here. According to Revi, February 29, 1876 was the date of the design patent for the opaque white glass, figure base lamp (a). The outer surface of the white glass is slightly transparent about the head and hair, and the frosted Flower Band font relates well to the base. The brass screw socket with the wide section in the center, is the same as the one in the patent drawing for this lamp. This variation has the same Sept. 29, 1868 patent date as their more common screw socket. This lamp is 11-1/4″.

Lamp (b) and those on the opposite page are examples of the lamps manufactured by the process described in the Thomas Atterbury patent of August 29th, 1876. The details of this patent are outlined in the section on History and Research. Basically, a goblet shape is pressed in a two piece mold, and the shoulder of the font or vessel is a pre-molded part fused in place. This method allows an entirely pressed lamp to be made without a horizontal joint from shoulder to base, and without seams on the shoulder. Called Pressed Boss lamps in the 1881 catalogue, this pattern resembles the Dewdrop and Star pattern which was, according to Revi, patented by Jenkins Jones of Campbell Jones & Company, Pittsburgh, Pa. on July 17th, 1877. The pattern also appears on a base in the Mix-and-Match section. Shown also in the 1881 catalogue is one other size of the Boss Dewdrop lamp (b) and two other sizes of the Boss Fluted stand lamp opposite. The white shoulder is described in the catalogue as Opal. All lamps are very good quality, and all are patent dated. Lamp (b) is 8-3/4″, and the lamps opposite are from left to right 4-3/4″, 4″ and 8-1/4″ to the top of the collars.

a. Figure Stem with Flower Band font

b. Pressed Boss lamp

Pressed Boss patent lamps ▷

The clear glass stand lamp opposite is shown in the 1874 Atterbury catalogue with the same Lace foot. See the catalogue illustrations for a variation with a scroll. All the other ribbed font lamps are grouped here by reason of their similarity. These may be called Rand Rib.

The flat hand lamp (a) is the same as the one shown with the group. It appears to be an inverted font of the same design as the one on the lace foot, but careful examination reveals a surprising difference. All the fonts on the stand lamps have a ribbed pattern on the inside, opposite to, and corresponding with, the outside ribbing. This is the expected characteristic of a mold-blown lamp. The flat hand lamp (a) however, is smooth inside, indicating a pressed technique. If a plunger were used it would have to be pressed into the bottom, and the protrusion at the shoulder would be filled in. Unfortunately for this theory, the protrusion is indented on the inside. Both hand lamps sit on a ring 1/16″ high and 1/4″ wide which has been ground and which could have been fused on later. I have only my memory to rely on for attribution of (b), the Curved Ribbed Panel lamp. I believe it to be from one of the Atterbury catalogues and one I neglected to copy. Hopefully the future will provide an explanation and more positive attribution of these lamps.

In the group photograph, the square opaque opalescent white leaded base appears with other Atterbury fonts. On this base the top half inch of the stem is panelled rather than smooth. The all opaque white lamp has an old base which was substituted for the original cracked one. The quality of this substitute base closely resembles that of the font, and surprisingly the original base was the same size and design, but of leaded opaline glass with gold decoration. It may be seen in the Sandwich section with the engraved lyre font.

All lamps are of good quality. The curved ribbed hand lamp measures 3-1/2″, and in the group photograph, they are, left to right 3″, 9″, 7-1/2″ and 12-5/8″. All measurements are to the top of the collar.

On lamp (a), the collar with the single rib and tooled design on the rib and above, is seen on a number of Atterbury lamps including the example of the February 11th, 1861 patent.

a. Rand Rib

b. Curved Rib Panel

Rand Rib lamps

a. & d.
Atterbury Buckle will distinguish these lamps from the other well known Buckle pattern. This pattern appears on their 1868 patented flat hand lamp in the 1872 catalogue, and the bases shown suggest a range of 1865 to 1875. The iron base lamp is 8-1/4″, and the marble base, purchased in the U.S. is 7-7/8″.

b.
That's O.K.! In the 1872 catalogue, the all glass No. 1 O.K. Lamp with a Prism base sold for $1.45 a dozen. This one is 8-1/8″.

c.
This Atterbury Loop font was also combined with a Prism foot in the 1874 catalogue. Measuring 7-3/4″ to the top of the collar, this size has also been seen in clear green on a marble base. U.S. purchase.

a. Atterbury Buckle

b. O.K.

c. Atterbury Loop

d. Atterbury Buckle

All three lamps on the Prism foot or base, have fonts of primitive quality. The two plain fonts with striations and chisel or whittle marks transferred from the mold, are good examples of the character which resulted from lack of quality control.

Lamp (e) Atterbury Plain Oval has two mold seams. Lamp (f) with the Funnel font is shown in the 1874 catalogue. The range of popularity of these lamps was probably from the mid- to late 60's and throughout the 70's.

Drapery (g) is shown and named in the 1874 catalogue. This is an interesting name choice because there has been some confusion in attribution of another pattern known as Drapery. Swags, stipples and many tassels characterize the other Drapery pattern which was also designed by Atterbury. A patent was obtained by Thomas Atterbury on February 22nd, 1870 and he assigned this to another glassmaker, William Doyle, of Birmingham, Pa. Peterson notes that this patent which was originally called Lace, was obtained for three and a half years, and may have been produced by other glassmakers later. With the great number of factories and tremendous output, it is difficult to know which designs were duplicated by one or several manufacturers. Included in the Rib, Prism and Flute section, are several lamps which might well be products of the Atterbury factory, and conversely some of those included in this section could have been made by others. The Atterbury Catalogues also show Double Prism and Double Lace bases. Sizes are: (e) 6-5/8″, (f) 6-3/4″ and (g) 6-1/2″.

e. Atterbury Plain Oval with Prism base

f. Atterbury Funnel font

g. Atterbury Drapery

a. Atterbury Melon

b. Gem font

c. Atterbury Melon

d. Gem font

e. Star Lamp

f. Atterbury Scroll, Beaded Bar base

The stand Melon Lamp pictured in the 1874 catalogue is the same as in picture (c). While not shown in the catalogue, the matching flat hand lamp (a) is the same design and quality, and both lamps have a pink tint.

Lamps (b) and (d) are illustrated in the 1874 catalogue. The stand lamp shown on an amber Prism base is called No. O Gem. They have also named two other lamps Gem, obviously a favourite that year. One is a font which appears to have eight or nine shields or emblems and a Prism base. In order to differentiate I would suggest referring to that one as Atterbury Emblem, and would adhere to the manufacturer's names with this Gem font, and the Gem base (j) opposite in opaque white.

Lamp (e) called the Star lamp is shown in three sizes in the Atterbury 1874 catalogue, with amber bases as pictured here. The Atterbury Scroll font (f) was one of their most popular designs. It is shown here on the amber Beaded Bar base. There is a possibility that the texture produced by the design on the stem was intended to serve as a match striker. Sizes are: (a) 3-1/8″, (b) 4-3/8″, (c) 7-7/8″, (d) 6-1/2″, (e) 8-1/4″, (f) 7-5/8″.

The design of these melon lamps, differs only slightly from those pictured with Rib, Prism and Icicle Patterns on page 88. The quality however, is quite different. The other melon lamps are noticeably lighter and thinner leaded glass, with the sparkle of excellent quality glass. Many of the heavier Atterbury Melon lamps have been seen in Canada. The applied handle would suggest they were made before the 1868 patent handles.

g. *Turnip Prism, No. 40, base*

h. *James, No. 40, base*

i. *Plain font, No. 40, base*

To support the theory that the lamp with the Turnip Prism font (g) and shown earlier in this section, is an Atterbury product, it is shown here with two other No. 40 design bases which have a marbelized mix of opalescent and clear glass. Base (g) is almost opaque, (h) is semi-opaque and (i) has a greater proportion of clear glass. Lamp (h), with the pattern named James, after one of the Atterbury brothers, is also included in the catalogue illustrations. These two may be compared to show the advantage of a good photograph over a line drawing in identifying lamps. Sizes are, (g) 9″, (h) 8-5/8″ and (i) 8-1/4″.

Below are lamps which are described in the Sandwich section. Lamp (j), with a Ribbed Loop font on a Gem base, is certainly an Atterbury product. Lamp (k) with the same design font on a Nine Panel base, and (l) with a Rib Banded Panel font on a Nine Panel base, appear also to have been manufactured by Atterbury. Sizes are, (j) 10-7/8″, (k) 8-1/4″ and (l) 8-1/2″.

j. *Ribbed Loop, Gem base*

k. *Ribbed Loop, Nine Panel base*

l. *Rib Banded Panel, Nine Panel base*

Twelve Atterbury all-glass lamps are shown here with notations regarding their appearance in catalogues, or with different combinations. Most of these fonts are found on the opaque white bases with brass screw socket connectors. Lamps in the top row have bases made with 15 scallops. These were called Lace bases in the Atterbury catalogues. The middle row has Panel bases, and the bottom row Tulip bases. Lamp quality ranges from fair to good.

a. No. 30 is the only name given to this same base and font combination in the 1874 catalogue. Atterbury Fine Rib is the name suggested for the font. 6-3/8″.

b. Shown in the 1874 catalogue on this base, and on a Gem opaque white base with a screw socket, this lamp is called Ex'. This would appear to be an abbreviation, but will serve as identification until the proper name is discovered. 8-1/4″.

c. Atterbury Loop. 8-3/4″.

d. Suggested name for this lamp shown in the 1874 catalogue is Thumb-print and Feather Band. 9-1/4″.

e. This Wave font is shown in the 1881 catalogue on amber Beaded Bar bases. 9-1/4″.

f. In the 1872 catalogue, this Chapman font is shown with an opaque white Tulip base and brass screw socket. The Panel base is the one for which a design patent was obtained in 1873. 8-1/4″.

g. This Wreath font was shown in four sizes combined with Panel bases and Octagon bases in opaque white in the 1872 catalogue. They were joined with threaded connectors. 7-1/2″.

h. Scroll font is in both the 1872 and 1874 catalogues. 11-1/8″.

i. Wave. 8-1/4″.

j. Chapman. 9-1/4″.

k. The Plain Band font is shown in the 1881 catalogue on a Panel opaque white base with a screw socket. 9-1/8″.

l. Flower Band font. 9-1/8″.

All names may be prefixed with "Atterbury" for more accurate identification.

a. *Atterbury Fine Rib*

e. *Wave*

i. *Wave*

b. Ex

c. Atterbury Loop

d. Thumbprint and Feather Band

f. Chapman

g. Wreath

h. Scroll

j. Chapman

k. Plain Band

l. Flower Band

The Atterbury Screw Socket patented Sept. 29, 1868 was so successful, it is difficult to imagine their manufacture of other types of opaque glass bases after this date. The other bases shown suggest an earlier date or later replacement.

a. Ohio. The 1874 catalogue shows this font pattern on a footed hand lamp with an applied handle. The base is leaded glass. 9-3/8".

b. The font peg is not threaded, nor is the pattern in the catalogues examined. Suggested name is Olympic. The attractive red and blue slag Gem base has a threaded peg. 7-3/4".

c. This Wheeler font is shown in the 1874 catalogue on opaque white Gem bases with screw sockets. The No. 40 base has a regular peg. 8-5/8".

d. Semi-circle Rib and Jewel is the suggested name for this font shown in the 1874 catalogue on a Lace base. This is the only Atterbury font I have seen on this base. 8-1/2".

e. Ribbed Belt is the suggested name for this untitled font illustrated in the 1874 catalogue on a Prism base. 9-7/8".

f. The Flower Band font on the Octagon base has a screw socket with a different profile. It is nevertheless patent dated. 10-1/4".

g. Prism and Loop on a Tulip base. This is called Prism in 1872 catalogue. 9-1/4".

h. In the 1872 catalogue this Shelley Peg is shown with six or nine loops on Octagon bases. 9-1/4".

i. The Scroll font and Octagon base as illustrated in the 1872 catalogue. 12-1/8".

j. Wave font and Octagon base. 8-1/4".

k. Atterbury Bullseye is shown in the 1874 catalogue on a Lace base. 9-1/2".

l. Atterbury Icicle and Rib is the name suggested for this font with a threaded peg. 9-1/4".

a. Ohio

e. Ribbed Belt

i. Scroll

b. Olympic

c. Wheeler

d. Semi-circle Rib and Jewel

f. Flower Band

g. Prism and Loop

h. Shelley

j. Wave

k. Atterbury Bullseye

l. Atterbury Icicle and Rib

a. Shelley

b. Filley

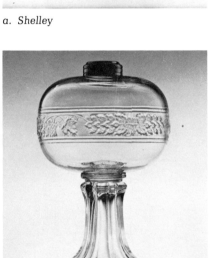

c. Grape Leaf Band

d. Atterbury Plain font

e. Diamond Band and Cable

f. Chain

The Shelley font (a) is shown in the 1872 catalogue with a white Octagon base and screw socket, and in the 1874 catalogue with this Lace base, and with their Prism base. The 1872 prices ranged from $3.00 to $8.00 per dozen depending on size. 11".

In the 1872 catalogue the Filley font (b) is shown on flat and footed hand lamps. In the 1874 catalogue it is combined with screw socket No. 40, and Eureka bases. 8-1/2". Grape Leaf Band (c) is a pattern similar to the Panelled Grape Band in Metz I, and Lee V. The Lace base and font shape are similar to the Filley lamp (b), however there is no other information to positively attribute it to Atterbury. 10-1/4". Lamp (d) has an Atterbury Plain font on a Lace base. 9-1/4". The Diamond Band and Cable lamp (e) has the Double Prism base shown in the Atterbury catalogues. 11". Another base used by Atterbury was the Stepped Prism base shown here with a Chain font (f). It is also shown in Lindsey with the Atterbury Emblem font, and in the Rib Prism and Icicle section with other lamps of probable Atterbury manufacture. 6-3/4".

All lamps illustrated in this Atterbury section have fifteen or eighteen scallops on their Lace bases. This base design may have been used by other manufacturers, although (a) and (b) are known Atterbury patterns. Elsewhere in the book are bases with six, eight or twelve scallops.

As previously illustrated, the Hearts and Stars pattern is seen combined with bases of Atterbury design and probable manufacture. These three lamps are on bases not previously identified with Atterbury fonts. Font (g) is a different shape, font (h) is slightly different, and on font (i) the stars are proportionately larger. Perhaps this was a popular pattern of the mid-sixties, manufactured by other Pittsburgh area factories. The design and glass quality have a primitive character which would be attractive with unsophisticated furnishings.

Measurements to the top of the collars are (g) 10-1/4″, (h) 7-3/4″, (i) 8-1/4″.

g. *Hearts and Stars*

h. *Hearts and Stars*

i. *Hearts and Stars*

WHITE HOUSE FACTORY.

ILLUSTRATED CATALOGUE AND PRICES

OF

FLINT GLASSWARE,

MANUFACTURED BY

ATTERBURY & Co.

PITTSBURGH. PA.

1872

"ALL ENGRAVINGS HALF SIZE OF ORIGINALS."

Seaman

4 1/2 in. Octagon

Saucer Hand Lamp Flint

Patent Hand
Human Head

Atterbury Composite

Access to the 1872, 1874 and 1881 Atterbury catalogues has provided identification of many lamps and patterns. Those shown here are the ones not available for photographing. In these catalogues, the words peg and foot, are used to describe the font and base.

On this page, the two screw socket lamps and the saucer hand lamp are from the 1872 catalogue, and the black iron-base composite lamp, and the Head Lamp are from the 1881 catalogue. All lamps on the opposite page are from the 1874 catalogue.

The following names are given to unnamed Atterbury lamps. Seaman, Human Head, Atterbury Composite, Joseph, Atterbury Buckle, Rib and Leaf Band, James, Chinquapin Oak, Atterbury Icicle, Scroll and Rib Band, and Thomas. Other names and numbers are from the catalogues. The footed hand lamp in the top row opposite may be the one pictured with the Atterbury patent lamps, however, the dates on that lamp are for a font patent unlike either of these lamps. This lamp resembles a single handled Ripley lamp.

In the second row opposite, the No. 18 Patent has an applied handle clearly not their famous patent handle. As mentioned earlier the fourth lamp in the third row would be better identified by the name Atterbury Emblem. The Gem name was also given to another font and base.

Other known Atterbury lamps not illustrated in these catalogues are the screw socket Swan Lamp, and the Slipper flat hand lamp.

Joseph

No. 2 Tucker Fount

No. 2 Grant

No. 14 Patent Hand
Atterbury Buckle

Amber Foot Lamps

No. 15 Patent   Lamp

No. 1 Reed Lamp

Sherman

Ohio

Shell

No. 18 Patent
Filley

Rib and Leaf Band

James

12. Prism Oil
Filler Lamp

Chinquapin Oak

Atterbury
Emblem

7
Atterbury Icicle

Lace Foot 21
Scroll and Rib Band

Illuminator Font
Tulip Base

No. 55

Thomas

4$\frac{1}{2}$" Octagon
No. 2 Octagon Peg

No. 40 5 in.
No. 3 Filley Peg
No. 2 Burner

Patterns Under Glass

Strictly speaking these patterns are pressed inside the font, leaving the outside smooth. A pattern on a plunger was pressed into the glass in a smooth mold. The font was then removed from the mold and skillfully drawn into the collar. Such lamps are particularly handsome although they must have been difficult to clean. Other than the Hobbs lamp following, none embody characteristics which relate them to manufacturer or locale, however they all appear to be products of the 1860's.

Lamp (a) Bethesda is 9-1/2″. Lamp (b), Dumbarton is 9-3/8″, and lamp (c) Prism Under Glass is 10″. The handsome 10-3/8″ lamp (d) opposite, is Tulip and Prism.

a. Bethesda

b. Dumbarton

c. Prism Under Glass

d. Tulip and Prism ▷

a. Hearts Under Glass

All the lamps in this category appear to be of glass with a lead content. The Hearts Under Glass (a), has the same 16 scalloped base as the Bullseye and Fleur-de-lis and Heart lamp. These were made in a three-part mold with two parts having 6 scallops each, and the third part with 4 scallops. This lamp is 8-7/8″.

Panelled Spears (b) is an unusual pattern which has been seen combined with an opaque white glass base. 8-1/2″. Lamp (c) I have called Veronica, a name close to the Victoria pattern it resembles. This particular 8″ example has a translucent blue base. Numerous examples with fonts in a variety of sizes and proportions, have been seen combined with opaque white glass bases, with marble bases, and with the Hobbs base opposite.

b. Panelled Spears

c. Veronica

Hobbs, Brockunier & Company

The history of Hobbs, Brockunier & Company is well chronicled by Revi. This Company, which at one time was the largest in the United States, included many men who made significant contributions in glass production, techniques, and design. One of the most noteworthy was the formula developed by William Leighton in 1864, which allowed excellent quality glass to be produced without lead. This offered competition to European imported lead glassware. It was the only company which produced large quantities of first quality lamps in both the earlier period of the 1860's and 70's and in the art glass decade of the 80's. Production was continued for a time after their merger with the United States Glass Company in 1891.

The brass clinch connector, patented by John L. Hobbs May 24th, 1870, is an important factor in the attribution of many lamps to the Hobbs Company. In all examples the connector is clinched onto corresponding horizontal and vertical grooves on the base, and in some examples the font is also held without cement in the same manner.

Those fonts without the corresponding indentations and which are cemented in, may only be deemed to be a product of this Company if they are found in significant numbers combined with Hobbs bases. The all-glass lamps also offer clues to products of this Company. Unfortunately at the present time, lamps produced before 1870 are not identified, however, there is a good possibility links may be found to connect lamps produced in the 1860's to Hobbs, Brockunier & Company. The Veronica pattern font (a) shown here is clinched on the Clover Leaf base. Height is 11-1/4″.

◁ a. Veronica

The stunning Cranberry Coin Dot lamps on the cover and color page are shown in a Hobbs Glass Co. catalogue belonging to the Oglebay Institute at Wheeling, West Va. Two sizes of stand lamps, and a night lamp, with matching shade, were made in blue opalescent and the clear opalescent shown here in a flat and a footed hand lamp (a) and (b). The catalogue also shows stand lamps with plain fonts described as clear, sapphire or old gold. A variety of colored opalescent shades and globes is included in this catalogue.

The stand lamp in picture (b) is the Snowflake pattern shown in ruby or cranberry opalescent in the color section. The nickel plated brass screw socket is covered by a ribbed glass sleeve. This lamp and screw socket was advertised by Hobbs Glass Co. in

a. Hobbs Coin Dot

b. Hobbs Snowflake and Coin Dot

c. Engraved font

the trade journal China Glass and Lamps in 1891, and by United States Glass Company after the merger. Both lamps in picture (b) have a fine ribbing on the bottom of the base. Lamp (a) is 2-7/8″ and in picture (b) the left lamp is 8″ and the right 4-5/8″.

Lamp (c) illustrates a font cemented onto a Hobbs base. The center band, and dotted rings above and below are stained a soft rose color. The design and quality of the engraving is fine and delicate. 11-3/4″.

d. *Pink Satin font*

With the exception of a quarter inch band at the shoulder, this pink font (d) has a satin or frosted finish, and the surface is decorated with a colored and gold painted design. This lovely Cloverleaf base has also been seen in a solid brown color. At the moment Hobbs' manufacture of the font can only be considered probable. In the color section, the lamp Chenoa with the red background, is a font which also comes in the same shape as lamp (d), and has also been seen on a Hobbs base. Another pink font such as this one, has a different design painted on the surface, and is combined with a Lady with Urn metal figure stem.

One of the most significant roles the study of lamps may play, will be that of supplying authentication regarding attribution of not only glass patterns, but of types of glass produced as well. Many examples of fonts combined with Hobbs bases will have to be observed and recorded before attribution can be considered possible. The following lamp (e) is a good example of parts from two different companies, combined many years ago. The dealer from whom I purchased this lamp, said it was entirely covered with red paint when she first saw it in a home. The lamp has an Atterbury Loop font with characteristic flecks of white glass, combined with a Hobbs Base. The font peg is without indentation, and the brass connection hasn't any horizontal indentations in the upper part. 10-1/4″. The Hobbs Double Diamond Cluster font (f) is clinched on. This pattern very closely resembles the Central Glass pattern made in lime glass. Here the top of the plain panel has a downward curve, and the tops of the two flutes between the panels are flattened. The reverse applies to the Central Glass product. This 14″ lamp is exceptionally large.

The Hobbs Star (g) is an attractive pattern with a clinched-on font. At the Ford Museum, the same base with a regular connection is combined with a green beaded loop font. There are ten beads between the beads above the flutes, dividing the loops. Lamp (g) is 8″.

e. *Atterbury Loop font*

f. *Hobbs Double Diamond Cluster font*

g. *Hobbs Star*

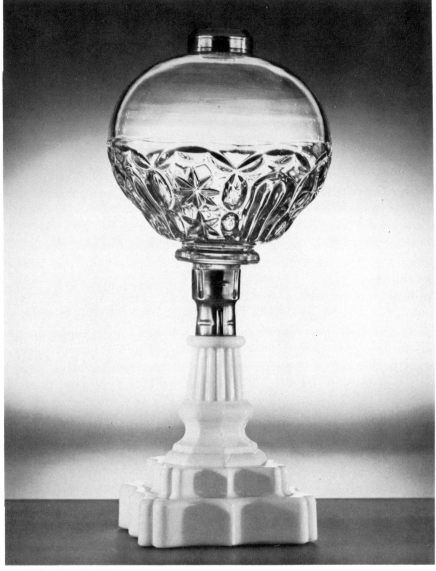

a. Hobbs Star Panel

Hobbs Star Panel (a) and opposite, left, is a beautiful lamp with a clinched-on font. The shade resting on the chimney was discovered with this application, although it may have been originally intended to be used with another holder. Height is 13″.

The Quad Loop pattern (b) and opposite, right, is a simple bold design, thus far seen only in excellent quality brilliant glass. This font has been seen with at least four other Hobbs bases, although never clinched on. In a private collection a blue opaline base is combined with an engraved font of this design. If this is a Hobbs font, the bases of all-glass lamps (b) and (c) would also be a Hobbs product, and the Teasel font (c) could be attributed to this Company. I think this is all probable, and look forward to further examples which will add information to this theory. Goblets in this pattern in Millard show a variation. The pattern he calls Teasel is described as being a product of the 70's manufactured by Bryce Brothers of Pittsburgh, Pa. The other pattern he calls Short Teasel, also of the 70's. A later 1906 version called Long Leaf Teasel is illustrated in Peterson. Lamp (b) is 10-7/8″, (c) 11-1/4″ and the right lamp opposite is 13″.

b. Quad Loop

c. Teasel font

left—Hobbs Star Panel;
right—Quad Loop ▷

a. Hobbs Blackberry

Hobbs Loop and Rib Band, and Hobbs Blackberry fonts are each shown clinched onto opaque white bases, and with an attractive Diamond stem-base. According to Revi the Blackberry pattern which was made in many pieces of tableware, was patented by William Leighton Jr. Feb. 1, 1870. This pattern and font shape closely resembles the Sandwich Blackberry, however the long pointed berry of the Sandwich pattern presents a simple distinction. The base (d) has clusters of blackberries at the corners. Several pieces of Blackberry in opaque white glass are shown in Belknap, and Lee lists many pieces in clear, and in white glass. Sizes are (a) 8-5/8″, (b) 9-7/8″, (c) 10-1/4″ and (d) 10″.

b. Hobbs Loop and Rib Band

c. Hobbs Loop and Rib Band

d. Hobbs Blackberry

Another group of connections and coincidences is presented here. My reference file of photographs includes an all-glass lamp with font (g), on a base like that of lamp (e). This simple base is almost exactly like that used by the Central Glass Company and possibly others. The distinctive difference here is the convex lower portion of the stem. Fonts (h) and (i) have the same bases and the same 11-1/4″ overall height, but the plain band font is recessed in (h) and raised in (i). Fonts (e) and (f) are basically the same shape but have a different surface treatment. Given the name Wheeling, font (e) would be Wheeling Panelled, font (f) would be Wheeling Frosted Grape Leaf and (i), Wheeling Plain. (h) suggests Wheeling Reversed, and (g) simply Hobbs Plain Band. Sizes are: (e) 6-7/8″, (f) 10″, (g) 10″, (h) and (i) as mentioned 11-1/4″ each.

Lamp (f) has a base with the same design as the white blackberry base with the exception that the raised fruit design is a bunch of grapes. Peterson illustrates a pattern known as Grape with Overlapping Foliage which was designed by J. H. Hobbs, Feb. 1, 1870. This is the same date as the blackberry design patent. It may be that a font having this Grape with Overlapping Foliage, was intended to be combined with this grape base. Another Hobbs font that would be appropriate with this base has a Fruit Medallion pattern. This pattern was seen on a large lamp, clinched onto a Hobbs base. Six oval medallions approximately 1-3/4″ wide by 2″ high contain embossed fruit designs. Two have apples, two have pears, and the other two medallions have bunches of grapes. These are arranged around the lower half of the font. The surrounding area, and that above a narrow indentation in the middle of the font is plain. Three mold marks are visible from the center indentation to the peg. This lamp was not available for photographing.

The brass connector on this lamp still retains horizontal dark bands, and traces of an original ormolu finish. It is remarkable that any of this original finish remains because it is easily removed by liquid brass cleaners, and of course, any abrasives.

e. Wheeling Panelled

f. Wheeling Frosted Grape Leaf

g. Hobbs Plain Band

h. Wheeling Reversed

i. Wheeling Plain

Marble and Opaque Glass Base

a. Ashburton

The lamps in this section are individuals. They bear no positive relationship to each other or to a particular manufacturer. The popular period of the marble base lamps was before 1865, and it would seem that their popularity dwindled after that time. The glass base lamps of the type shown here would have been popular from 1865 or earlier, to 1875, and with diminished popularity and production to 1885. It is to be hoped that future research will direct many of these to specific manufacturers and that present names will neither conflict nor confuse future attributions.

Ashburton (a) resembles most closely the Creased Ashburton pattern in Metz I. Lamp (b), Early Almond Thumbprint, is also shown with an engraved font and opaque white glass base in this section.

The blue cut to clear overlay lamp (c) has the appearance of European design. The green opaline font opposite originally had a gold band and leaf design around the middle. The chimney and burner would be appropriate with all of these lamps of the early 1860's. Sizes are: (a) 9-1/4″, (b) 8″, (c) 8-7/8″ and opposite 8-1/4″.

b. Early Almond Thumbprint

c. Blue overlay cut to clear

Green opaline font ▷

a. Triple Peg and Loop

Triple Peg and Loop (a), included also in the Ring Punty section, is a graceful pattern in excellent quality glass. All brass stems on this and the opposite page are unusually fancy and seem to have been made in the 1860 to 1865 period.

Triple Diamond Medallion (b) was used in an illustration of an 1865 patent. Triple Flute and Bar (c) is shown also with the Early Related Lamps. Here it has an interesting stem with a spiral design.

The left lamp opposite has another Triple Flute with Bar font, with gold banding. The metal parts of the stem and base, of this and the middle lamp, retain their original ormolu and black finish. The engraved font of the middle lamp has two mold marks on the shoulder and none below. It was perhaps pressed upside down and drawn into the base of the font. The Marble Base is black with gold streaks, and is referred to as Gold Marble. The right lamp with the Giant Prism Band has a slate base painted black. The outside lamps were probably products of the early 60's and the center one may have been made earlier. Sizes are: (a) 8-3/4″, (b) 11″, (c) 9″ and opposite from left to right 12-1/4″, 11″ and 10-1/2″. All these lamps appear to have lead glass fonts.

b. Triple Diamond Medallion

c. Triple Flute and Bar

left—Triple Flute and Bar, ▷
middle—early engraved font,
right—Giant Prism

a. White opaline font

b. Blue opaline font

c. Ribbed Cup

d. Plain mold-blown font

e. Early Peacock Feather

f. Early crown lamp

Lamps (a) and (b) both have opaline fonts and fancy bases. Lamp (a) is white and (b) is light blue, and both have Greek Key designs in gold, although they are facing the opposite direction. Lamps (c), (d), (e), and (f) are all ordinary glass. Lamp (c), Ribbed Cup is mold blown with a primitive quality, and a slate base painted to resemble marble. Lamp (d), also mold blown, has good quality glass.

Early Peacock Feather lamps are shown in (e). This pattern is one of the few distinctive pressed glass lamp patterns in ordinary glass made in the 1860's. The Early Crown lamp (f) has fair to good quality glass.

The Ruby glass font in the photograph opposite is shown in a period setting with furniture, and most accessories pre-dating 1870. The chimney is patent dated 1868. Sizes for these lamps are (a) 10-1/2″, (b) 11-3/8″, (c) 8-3/8″, (d) 9-1/2″, (e) the pair are 8″, (f) 13″, and the lamp opposite is 8-3/8″.

Ruby glass font ▷

a. Amethyst overlay cut to clear

b. Petal and Rib

c. Pauline

d. Divided Heart

e. Eyes and Ties

f. Prisms and Diamond Point

A variety of fonts and bases is shown here. Lamp (a) has a beautiful amethyst cut to clear font. It has a primitive quality with many bubbles, and appears to have been free blown. The opaline base is the same design as the one combined with the Sandwich Four Petal font. The excellent quality Petal and Rib font (b) has another design opaline base. Lamp (c) Pauline was purchased in the United States. Divided Hearts (d) combined here with a graceful base has been seen with other bases. This is a Sandwich area pattern. Lamps (b), (c) and (d) are all excellent quality without mold marks on the shoulder.

Eyes and Ties (e) with blown three-mold font is on an unusual, slightly marbleized base. Prisms and Diamond Point (f) has a blown three-mold font of only fair quality, The wide base of the font suggests this pattern may have been made in an earlier cylindrical whale-oil form. These lamps would have been made from 1865 to 1875. Sizes are: (a) 10-1/2″, (b) 10-1/8″, (c) 10-7/8″, (d) 9-5/8″, (e) 10-1/4″, (f) 10-1/2″.

The finely ribbed font (g) with white threading has recently been combined with an old base which was probably made by Atterbury & Company. The original was a square black glass base. The excellent quality Scallop and Fan lamp (h) has a reproduction base. This offers a good solution to the problem of surplus fonts, but unfortunately reproduction brass connectors do not seem to be available.

Cherry Ripe (i) is a busy pattern with bands of four different designs. Glass quality is excellent, and the shoulder is free of mold marks. Harlequin (j) is another busy but cheerful pattern of good to excellent quality glass. There are faintly visible mold marks on the shoulder.

Waving Wheat (k) is a graceful delicate pattern, although the No. 2 collar seems to be rather large. Sawtooth (l) is simple, bold and beautiful. This excellent quality font has also been seen in a smaller size. Lamp sizes are (g) 8-1/4″, (h) 10-3/4″, (i) 9-1/4″, (j) 9-5/8″, (k) 10″ and (l) 13-1/8″.

g. Yellow font with white threading

h. Scallop and Fan

i. Cherry Ripe

j. Harlequin

k. Waving Wheat

l. Sawtooth

a. Early Almond Thumbprint

b. Scalloped Medallion

c. Thumbprint

d. Honeycomb

e. Wedding Ring

f. Lotus

Early Almond Thumbprint (a) like the Thumbprint (c) shown below, is an excellent quality font, with a clearly defined pattern indented in thick glass. The stone engraved design fills the upper part of the font, and the chimney and burner are appropriate with this lamp of the mid 60's. Illustrations in Lee E.A.P.G. show a catalogue page from Bakewell Pierce & Co. with the Thumbprint or Argus pattern and Millard credits this company with Almond Thumbprint. Probably made in the 70's, the Scalloped Medallion Panel font (b), has an engraved pattern with heart shaped leaves and berries on the shoulder. The shade holder and shade were in use on this lamp for many years and are perhaps the original ones. A repair or reinforcement has been made to the brass connection.

Honeycomb, New York, and Vernon are three names given to the pattern on font (d). This very popular pattern was made in tableware pieces by both New England and Midwest companies over a long period of time, although fonts appear to have been made in the 1865 to 1875 period. The Wedding Ring pattern (e) in Lee's Victorian Glass book is described as a pattern of the 60's. She does not list a lamp, although this one fits the description and time of the pattern. The old base is a recent replacement. Lotus (f) is another pattern of the 60's, and like all others on this page is without mold marks on the shoulder. Sizes are (a) 10-1/4″, (b) 10-3/4″, (c) 9-3/8″, (d) 9-1/2″, (e) 10-1/4″ and (f) 10-3/4″.

Heart Top Panel (g) is a strange pattern with the upper and lower portions seemingly divided, and bearing no relationship to each other. Filley or Notched Bullseye (h) is a pattern dated 1875-1880 in Kamm, and said to have been made by Bryce Brothers. She refers to a goblet in Lee's E.A.P.G. as having a different shape, so perhaps this pattern was made by others. I would place this lamp circa 1870, and have seen it combined also with a Hobbs base. The pattern was re-issued later by the United States Glass Company.

The engraved turnip-shaped font (i) is stained ruby, however, the color has been worn thin near the base of the font. Font (j) is both stained and frosted, with only slight traces of frosting on the middle part. The ruby stained part is in excellent condition although gold outlining of the design is almost completely worn off. These two stained lamps would be circa 1870. Lamp (k) Panelled Block and Bar deserves the adjectives excellent and superior because it has one of the best quality fonts in the book. The Diamond Bead and Rib stem is an unusual design although the base is the same as that of the base on the Divided Heart lamp. This pattern and the next would be made in the 60's. Small Flowered Tulip with Ribs (l) is the name of this pattern in Metz II. The font which was mounted on a rough block of wood has been combined with an old base. Sizes are (g) 10-7/8″, (h) 10-7/8″, (i) 12-1/2″, (j) 11-3/4″, (k) 10-1/8″ and (l) 9-7/8″.

g. Heart Top Panel

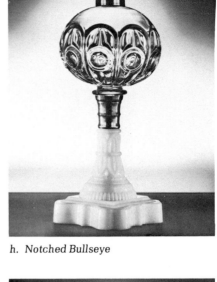

h. Notched Bullseye

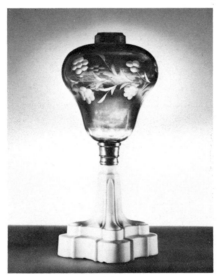

i. Engraved stained font

j. Frosted and stained font

k. Panelled Block and Bar

l. Small Flowered Tulip

a. Diamond Band and Loop

b. Diamond and Loop Panel

c. Opaline melon font

d. Panelled Arches

e. Waisted Broad Rib

f. Dexter

Diamond Band and Loop (a) has excellent quality glass except for the single inperfection that looks like a small bird flying across the font. Diamond and Loop Panel (b) has an excellent quality font and is combined with the same design base as (a).

Lamp (c) has a white opaline melon font and black glass base with gold trim. Panelled Arches (d) was also made in a smaller size. Waisted Broad Rib (e) on a dark blue glass base is shown in all glass in the section Rib, Prism & Icicle Patterns. In picture (f) a similar base in white has an unusual brass connector. The font pattern is Dexter.

Lamps (a), (b), (c) and (d) would be of the 1860's, and (e) is circa 1870. The stamped collar and font design suggest lamp (f) was made in the late 70's. Sizes are (a) 10-5/8″, (b) 10-7/8″, (c) 9″, (d) 9-3/8″, (e) 9-5/8″ and (f) 9-3/8″.

The lamp opposite has a frosted and ruby stained font. The pattern was outlined in gold, but only a few traces remain. Height to the top of the collar is 9-1/8″. Circa 1870.

Frosted and stained font ▷

◆ Iron Stem-Base

a. Triple Scallop and Rib Swag

b. Sawtooth Band and Panel

c. Green opaline font

If price is an indication, iron-base lamps are not as popular as opaque glass-base or marble-base lamps. One reason for this is that they are frequently rusty, and in need of cleaning. The original finish on these bases was black, or a metallic gold, copper or bronze finish. Any of these finishes may be easily restored with paint, or the rub-on paste finishes. If it is desirable to retain an old or antique appearance, a thin coat of wax over the remnants of the original finish is all that is necessary. Some iron bases, particularly well detailed pieces, are attractive if buffed with fine steel wool, and protected with a coat of thinned satin finish urethane.

The distinctive base of lamp (a) may be European. The Triple Scallop and Ribbed Swag font has been seen on an American opaque white base. The Ford Museum has an unmounted font of the same design, with the exception of a sawtooth swag, rather than the ribbed swag.

Lamp (b) Sawtooth Band and Panel is one of those fonts with a wide base that suggests the design may also have been used on the narrow whale-oil type fonts. These attractive black bases are shown elsewhere in the book, and they are generally combined with excellent quality early fonts. The quality of the lovely simple green opaline font (c) appears to be too fine for its more ordinary base. Sizes are: (a) 9-7/8″, (b) 9-1/2″ and (c) 10-1/2″.

The collars, patent dates, and the fonts they are combined with, place these lamps in the 1865 to 1880 period. The attractive Bullseye Band Entwined font (d) is shown also in the Early Bullseye section. The leaded glass shade was on this lamp when it was purchased at an auction near Corning, N. Y. It has a finely detailed etched pattern and deeply cut icicle band.

The Buckle font (e) has the same engraved pattern on the shoulder as the Bullseye Band Entwined. This would make the manufacture of the Buckle fonts (e), (f) and (g), by the same company, a distinct possibility. Models for goblets in this pattern are on display at the Sandwich Glass Museum. Revi links this pattern with the Union Glass Co., Somerville, Mass., and Gillander & Sons of Philadelphia, Pa. The clear trim lines of bases (f) with the brass stem, and (g) all iron, are a good combination with this fine pattern, which is exceptionally well suited to fonts. Sizes are: (d) 13-1/8", (f) 10-3/4", and (g) 9-7/8".

d. Bullseye Band Entwined

e. Buckle

f. Buckle

g. Buckle

a. *Frosted with Clear Bar*

b. *Frosted with Clear Bar*

c. *Frosted with Clear Bar*

d. *Dexter*

e. *Keyhole*

f. *Elder Eight Panel*

Each of the Frosted with Clear Bar fonts (a), (b) and (c) has a different shape. The font on lamp (a) has "Patent Applied For" embossed around the peg. This could apply to the font, or to the unusual stem with the hand holding a torch. The traces of silver paint are probably from a later application. Definition of the patterns on iron stems and bases varies considerably, and the more common base (b) is an example of a well molded one. The more elaborate design of base (c) is well molded, and the metal surface is very smooth. Nothing has been added or removed, as the unpainted finish was clean and almost rust-free.

The iron bases on these two pages were made in one piece, or in two, three or four pieces bolted together. Lamp (d), Dexter, has a two-part base, with the same design as the 1876 patent dated base (k) opposite. The bases of lamp (e) Keyhole, and (f) Elder Eight Panel, are also made in two pieces. The damage to the inside surface of lamp (f) has not responded to treatment with vinegar or muriatic acid. After this photograph was taken, a temporary but effective method was used to hide these marks. Clear silicone on absorbent cotton, rubbed on the inside, visually removed the horizontal streaks and shading. Sizes are: (a) 9-1/8", (b) 8-1/2", (c) 12", (d) 9-3/4", (e) 9-3/8", and (f) 8-3/4".

The attractive stippled Birch Leaf pattern (g) was used on a goblet shown in Metz II. It also appears to be like the leaf on an opaque white syrup jug in Belknap, where it is described as a rose leaf. Grape Band (h), another pattern made in goblets and in tableware, is shown and described in the Early Related Lamps section.

Diamond Sunburst (i) was a tableware pattern for which a design patent was obtained by John Bryce of Bryce, Walker & Company, in 1874. It was later manufactured by other companies with several variations. This font is reported to have been seen combined with an opaque white glass base, and is also included in the Early Related Lamps section.

Feather Duster with Sawtooth Band (j) is combined here with a short one-piece metal base. This attractive pattern was often used with composite lamps, and is included in the Mix and Match section. The base of Tassel (k) has four sections. The bottom section, and the cross-bar attached inside it to hold the bolt, are both marked Pat. Mar. 7, 1876. The collar is patent dated August 21st, 67 and June 17th, 73. Lamp (l), Honeycomb and Cable, is similar to lamps in the Early Related Lamps section. Sizes are: (g) 8-5/8″, (h) 9″, (i) 9-1/2″, (j) 8″, (k) 11-3/8″, and (l) 10-1/8″.

g. Birch Leaf

h. Grape Band

i. Diamond Sunburst

j. Feather Duster with Sawtooth Band

k. Tassel

l. Honeycomb and Cable

Figure Stem

Figure-stem lamps, like the metal-base lamps appear to have been most popular during the 1865-1880 period. It is possible that the range was greater, but it is very difficult to say how much beyond it would have been extended. The quality and design of these lamps varies greatly. Originally, most of them had a gilt, bronze or black finish. Figures now devoid of any finish sometimes have the appearance of iron or pewter and may be left this way, while others are drab and dingy and may be restored with a

b. front, Mary and Her Little Lamb   *c. back, Mary and Her Little Lamb*

paste, gilt or bronze finish. Many beautiful engraved overlay or Bohemian glass fonts were mounted on figure stems, although frosted fonts were the most common. The figure on lamp (a) has had the gilt finish restored. This is a relatively common base, which is seen combined with cut overlay or excellent quality glass. The font, in mint condition, is ruby stained, frosted, and has clear shamrocks outlined in gold. Two other parts might be original. One is the shade holder attached to a ring which fits snuggly over the collar, and the other is the early patent Rising Sun burner stamped PAT. AUG. 3, 1858, Re-issued SEPT. 13, 1859. This refers to a patent obtained by William Fulton of Cranberry, New Jersey. The thumb wheel is marked Benedict & Burnham Mfg. Co. PAT. SEPT. 16, 1862. It is quite possible that this lamp was made before 1865. The original shade was probably round.

Mary and Her Little Lamb is another of the early figure stems. Front and back views show the exceptionally fine detailing. Like many of the figure-stem lamps in the Sandwich catalogue, this one required the font to be molded specifically for the brass parts. In this case, the bottom of the glass font is flat although it appears to follow the shape of the supporting brass cup. In peering into the font, one can see at the bottom, a number of embossed letters. These are difficult to decipher, but could read, J. Fiden. Hopefully another example will be more legible. Sizes are: (a) 13-1/2″ and (b) 14″.

a. Lady with Urn

Another gilded lady, restored with gold paste. This paste is water soluble and easily removed. The section on collecting glass shows a "before" picture of this lady. The collar is patent dated Aug. 21-67 and June 17-73.

Like the Atterbury figure stem, this base has been referred to as Jenny Lind, or as the Goddess of Liberty. The only photograph I have seen of Jenny Lind, bears no likeness to this lady, and as mentioned earlier, the garland of flowers in the hair suggests the liberty cap, and is consistent with other similar figure stems. This base is metal, and the bases of (a) and (b) are soapstone painted black, indicating they were made earlier. 13".

d. Helen font

a. Eugenie

The name Eugenie embossed on the figure stem leaves no doubt as to its representation. Empress Eugenie (1826-1920) was the wife of Napoleon III. After 1870 she was forced to live in exile, and it is difficult to judge whether this lamp was made before or after this date. The soapstone base and stem may have been made before 1870, and the font may have been made after that date. Both the frosted Greek Key and stem are very good quality. 10-3/8″.

John and Peter (b) and (c), are carefully detailed figures which were likely designed by the same person. The relaxed stance, faces that reflect personality and the detail of cloth and clothing give a distinctive character to these lamps. John (b) has a frosted and engraved font, and Peter (c) has a font of the same shape with dull surfaced cut circles. John has a metal base and Peter's is soapstone.

Dairymaid (d) is supporting the font which is known as Honeycomb, New York, or Vernon. On lamp (e), Grape Harvest, the chubby boy, or girl, sampling a bucket of grapes is well detailed. The Britannia metal on this and one of the Atterbury lamps resembles pewter, and neither has any indication of a former finish. A variety of composite lamps have this Webster font in clear or colored glass. Compared with others in this section, the Peace stem (f) is poorly defined. The Doily font which is a similar shape to the font (g), has a primitive quality with a distinct texture from the mold chisel marks.

Farm Boy (g) has his sickle, and bundles of grain at his feet, and dog at his side. This figure has the natural relaxed attitude of John and Peter above. Link Belt is a good quality pressed and frosted font. Sizes are: (b) 9-1/8″, (c) 8-1/4″, (d) 11″, (e) 10-1/2″, (f) 10-3/4″, and (g) 10-1/2″.

b. John

c. Peter

d. Dairymaid stem—Honeycomb font

e. Grape Harvest stem—Webster font

f. Peace Stem—Doily font

g. Farm Boy stem—Link Belt font

Lomax

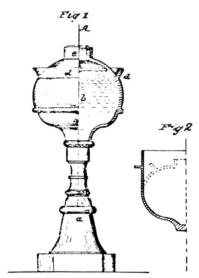

a. *Lomax Plain, all glass.*

Frequent overflow of kerosene "with the disagreeable consequences now so constantly experienced," was the concern of George Henry Lomax of Somerville, Mass. His patent of September 20th, 1870 further states "the purpose of my invention is to arrest this flowage of fluid over the exterior of the lamp." He also made reference to the Michael B. Dyott patent of September 29th, 1863 for a mold-blown method of producing an annular drip depression surrounding the collar. In the Lomax patent for a pressed font, he describes, "Fig. 2, is a section of a part of the lamp as it comes from the mold." In hand finishing, the upper portion is drawn inward to form the collar, and the flange tilted upwards. In addition to its function as a drip catcher, Lomax suggests this ring might also serve as a shade holder.

The 9″ all-glass lamp (a) has the date September 30, 1870 embossed inside the font around the stem. The Union Glass Company of Somerville, Mass., made the Lomax lamps, and the pressed stem and base of this lamp may be the key to identifying other lamps made by this company. The font of the 9-1/2″ brass stem and iron base lamp (b) has been fire polished to eliminate the mold marks. The dates boldly embossed on the inside of these fonts were made by the plunger which forced the glass against the inside surface of the mold.

Dr. Loris Russell in Heritage of Light, refers to a Union Glass Company catalogue, which illustrates and names several patterns in Lomax lamps. The simple distinctive stand lamp in the group photograph was called the "Plain Lomax Kitchen." Two sizes in the author's collection are 7-7/8″ and 6-1/4″. In the same photograph is a 5-1/2″ high footed hand lamp, and a 4″ low footed hand lamp that was called the "Globe Lomax hand lamp." In his 1870 patent, Lomax claims his invention is produced in a "pressure-mold," by means of a metallic plunger in a powerful press, because a mold-blown operation would not properly force the glass into the narrow cavity to form the flange. A patent was obtained on October 14th, 1873 by Lomax, for a mold in which handles could be produced on mold-blown glassware. The handle on this low lamp appears to be that of this patent. This along with the drip-catcher flange, suggests this lamp relates to both the 1870 and the 1873 patents.

Most Lomax lamps seen today have the date embossed inside the font, outside the font just above the peg on the thumbprints or petals, or on the base. Additional wording such as "Lomax," "Oil Guard Lamp," or "Trade Mark" might also be found. As shown in Arthur Peterson's book on trademarks on glass, the "Oil Guard Lamp" trademark was registered in 1871 by George Lomax. In 1885, the Henry & Nathan Russell catalogue shows lamps from Adams & Company and from Sandwich, and describes them as "Oil Guard Lamps." One wonders if any action resulted from this "coincidence."

b. *Lomax Plain, Iron base.*

Lomax Kitchen and Globe hand lamps. ▷

a. Utah.

Illustrations from the Union Glass catalogue reproduced in Revi, show the pattern name for the 8-1/2″ lamp (a) is Utah. An unusual feature of the Utah lamp is the shape of the thumbprints which makes them alternately obscure and transparent. Lamps (b) and (c) are 11-1/2″ and 10-1/4″ respectively, and their pattern is called Vienna. The shape and definition of pattern vary greatly in these two examples, and a frequently overlooked patent date is found outside the base of the font, embossed on the "petals." Vienna lamps have been seen combined with opaque glass bases having other designs. This particular base is the same as that combined with the lamp Chenoa in the color section.

On August 3rd, 1880, Lomax obtained a patent for molding glassware on metallic thimbles, and an example of a font incorporating this invention is shown on a hanging lamp in that section. The thimble recessed in the bottom of the font is seated on a peg in the center of the flat disk

b. Vienna.

c. Vienna.

d. Frosted Star font.

holder. This font is dated September 20, 1870 for the drip-catcher flange; August 31, 1875 and August 3, 1880 for the metallic thimble. August 31, 1875 is the date on the Star hanging or bracket lamp font (d) which also has a metallic thimble. The technique described in the 1880 patent may have been used much earlier. This type of font, without the metal thimble in the socket, was made with a frosted beaver design. Fonts have also been seen with a pressed and frosted geometric pattern. These fonts are most frequently seen with cast iron hanging lamps. Other Lomax hanging and bracket lamp fonts have a low foot which is held by screws in a cup type holder. One of these is shown on the hanging lamp in the color section.

The four hand lamps no doubt also have a name in the Union Glass catalogue, and are therefore unnamed here. They all have the stamped brass collars which came into use in 1876.

Sizes are (e) 5-1/2″, (f) 4-3/8″, (g) 4″, and (h) 4″.

e. Lomax hand lamp.

f. Lomax hand lamp.

g. Lomax hand lamp.

h. Lomax hand lamp.

In the words of the patentee Daniel C. Ripley, "I prefer to construct my lamps in this manner, for convenience in handling them, and passing them from one person to another. By having two handles, it will, under no circumstances, be necessary to grasp the lamp by its bowl or conical base, as the lamp can be taken from a person's hand by the handle which is opposite that held by such person; consequently, lamps of this kind, viz., with two handles, will not be liable to fall from the hand, and it will not be necessary to soil the fingers with oil, which is usually on the bowls of lamps."

Ripley patent hand lamps

The preceding photographs illustrate the most common examples of the Ripley patents pertaining to lamps, and the one illustrated in his patent of January 7th, 1868. This patent called for a pressed base having one or two handles, and a font "blown thereon". The opaline lamp being passed from hand to hand, and the left lamp pictured opposite are embossed on the underside, to be read through the glass, Ripley & Co. Pat Jan 7th, July 14th, Aug 11th, 1868. According to Peterson the second two dates were to correct defects of the preceding patent. Another clear lamp of this design simply has Patented on one side of the base and JAN 7th 1868 on the other.

The middle lamp, with the stippled web stem, appears also to incorporate Ripley's Sept. 20, 1870 patent, which is that used to produce the stem of the double font of the Marriage lamp, and described therewith. The base of this lamp has the number two embossed in the center on the underside. This is encircled by concentric bands. The first of these is stippled, the second a clear band with the same embossed dates and company name as the lamp on its left. Radiating ribs form the next band, and the outside is clear. The third lamp, with the square stippled stem, is undated, and has a rough pontil on the underside below the stem. There is an indistinct 1 in the center of this. The author also has this lamp dated, with a base identical to that of the middle lamp, except for the number 1 on the underside. Mold marks are indistinct or non-existent on the upper portions of the fonts of the middle and right hand lamps. This would indicate that rather than being blown as described in the January 7th, 1868 patent, these bases and fonts were pressed in one operation, and then drawn into the collar. This theory is further supported by the fact that there are straw marks, or pressed imperfections on the inside of some of these fonts, and by the rough pontil marks on many examples.

Old chimneys shown with the Ripley lamps, predate the lamps themselves, and are appropriate. Sizes for these two-handled lamps are: for the opaline lamp 4-5/8", and in the group picture, left to right 4-1/2", 5-1/2" and 5".

a. Ripley Hollow-Stem lamp

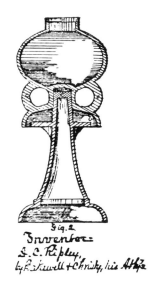

b.

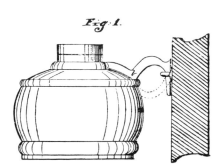

c.

Peterson states that Daniel C. Ripley and his son Daniel C. Ripley Jr. are credited solely or jointly with over sixty patents relating to glass making. Kamm 6 has a detailed account of this firm which was established in 1866, and joined the United States Glass Co. merger in 1891. She describes the firm as principally a lamp-house. Relatively little is known of the tableware patterns of this company which was one of the leading glass manufacturers, and only their patented lamps are credited to them.

Russell has an illustration of lamp (a), the Ripley Hollow Stem lamp with an artificial flower and twig inside. This is held in by a wafer of cork with patent dates of 1881 and 1882 on a paper cover. The many varieties of lamps with hollow stems, suggest this patent was for the design of the mold rather than the idea of a hollow stem for the purpose of enclosed decoration. This lamp is 10-3/4″ and has been seen in other sizes.

A patent obtained by Daniel C. Ripley, March 2nd, 1869 was for a footed hand lamp furnished with a detachable pedestal. The patent illustration (b) shows a two handled lamp with a socket in the base, resting on a separate pedestal. The patent illustration (c) is from the patent issued to Daniel C. Ripley Jr. April 5, 1870. His invention claim was for "attaching a metallic handle to a glass lamp by passing the eye of the handle over the neck of the lamp, and cementing the burner-fastening to the extremity of the neck," and for "a metallic handle of a glass lamp, having an outer hook end, suitable for use with a clip or socket, as a device for hanging the lamp." The examples I have seen of lamps with this patent date embossed on the side, however, had a one-piece iron handle and ring, which girded the font in an indentation. It was not cemented, and must have been included in the glass molding process.

The well-known and distinctive lamp (d) has become known in recent years as the Marriage or Wedding Lamp. This lamp combines an example of two invention patents (e) of June 14, 1870 and Sept. 20, 1870, (the date of the famous Lomax lamp patent), and a design patent of Feb. 1, 1870, all granted to Daniel C. Ripley. The first patent is for the mold, and the second for the method of manufacture for double or triple-font lamps. For the font patent he claims as his invention "a glass lamp, having two or more bowls blown into a center-piece, stock or bifurcated stem." He describes this lamp as having a pressed glass center-piece in which "I make if so desired by pressing in the usual way, a match box, to which I fit a cover." This center-piece was then placed inside a mold having cavities for blowing two or more bowls or fonts. Ripley's description of the final operation is "I then blow in each of the bowl-cavities a lamp bowl in such a way that each bowl will be blown onto, or against the center-piece, and form a firm union therewith." The unusual part of the manufacturing process was the requirement for the fonts to be blown simultaneously, by two glass blowers.

The design patent (f) applies to bases of any shape, with two side stems and a thin web of glass between. Ripley claimed that his patent would facilitate manufacture in that the article could be removed from the mold much sooner. The thin web would solidify almost immediately and support the semi-plastic side stems while they solidified.

Wedding lamps were made in clear glass, white, blue or green opaline, or in combinations of these colors. They are combined with the 1870 patented bases, or with opaque white or colored glass bases. Frosted, engraved or colored chimneys were often used with these lamps. I believe the flattened chimneys and burners with the thumb wheels stamped, TAPLINS PAT. MAR. 4, 1864 HINGE, are original. Height to the top of the burners is 13-1/2″.

The lack of glass patterns on the patented Ripley lamps, and the lack of catalogue or advertising material regarding this company, makes attribution of other lamps very difficult. The two Wedding lamps I have seen with opaque glass bases, are the one in Russell's book, which is unlike any I have found on other lamps, and one with an Atterbury base. The latter would likely be a replacement. If Ripley did make opaque glass bases, which were used with wedding lamps, several examples would have to be found to see if distinctive patterns were frequently used.

d. Marriage or Wedding lamp

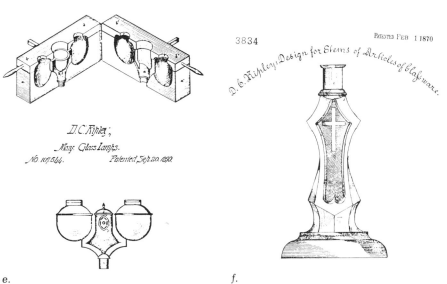

e.

f.

Patented Lamps

Patented lamps are included with their known manufacturers in other sections throughout the book. In this section there is an assortment of lamps which have been marked with a patent date, or simply marked patented. Some have been researched without success and others are recent acquisitions awaiting research. Detailed description of some of the patents in other sections, reveals how often the patent date refers to patents or improvements unrelated to the dated lamp. Some lamp patents were concerned with the function of the lamp, some with safety, some with convenience and many with glass manufacturing techniques which may or may not have had an effect on the appearance of the lamp. Many patents were obtained for lamps which were designed to contain, at the shoulder, any overflow of oil. Most of these patents were for manufacturing techniques rather than for the idea of a drip depression or catcher. In some instances the dates of two of these patents are embossed on the lamp.

Michael B. Dyott of Philadelphia, Pa., obtained many patents for lamps, and his inventive talents covered various aspects. In 1842 he designed a burner for a lamp for burning what he described as "pine oil, which oil is purified spirits of turpentine or other similar oil." On January 6, 1863 he designed a burner with slotted spiral arms which enabled the upper portion with the chimney to be raised to permit wick trimming and lighting. This was the same principle as used later on the New Rochester lamp. His other inventions included an 1856 patent for a lamp shade holder for metal or paper shades, and the 1867 patent for the glass font used in the De Keravenan-Jones lamp. In 1863 he designed a small flat hand lamp which he described as "a lamp made with a drip-trough depression, at its neck, and a handle depression or indentation, at its side, with attached handle therein."

Lamp (a) has embossed in the drip depression, the Sept. 29, 1863 date of the Dyott patent, and the July 23, 1872 date of the John Bridges patent. The Bridges patent was for a mold to produce a drip depression on blown lamps. On this page lamps (a) and (b), and on the opposite page lamps (e), (f), (g), (h), and (i), have the date of the Bridges patent. The footed hand lamp (c) has the Sept. 29, 1863 date of the Dyott patent, and another date of January 9, 1877 which has not been researched. In addition to drip catchers at the top of the font, there is also in this section, one with a saucer at the bottom of the font, and in other sections, undated ones with saucers at the base. Lamp (a) Inverted Teardrop Band is 12". Lamp (b) 10-3/4", Bridges Band, has a beige pottery stem with pink and blue flowers, and (c) which is 4-1/2" will await the name of the 1877 patentee.

This lamp was also made in a stand lamp with a round base, and a plain solid glass stem which widens slightly at the bottom. The stem was molded in two parts, and fused onto a base without mold marks. This lamp may be important for relating and identifying other lamps.

a. Bridges Inverted Teardrop Band

b. Bridges Band

c. 1863 & 1877 Patent hand lamp

Lamp (d) Bridges Bowl, is the only dated Bridges lamp with the full and correct July 23rd, 1872 date, and the shape is that of the mold in the patent illustration. Lamp (b) opposite, has July 2nd, 1872, a mistake, and the other dated lamps on this page have only July 1872 embossed in the drip depression. One rewarding aspect of researching patents is the discovery that the patent has been assigned to a particular manufacturer. In this case the Bridges patent was assigned to Adams & Company, who at that time, were located in Birmingham, Pa. This, of course, means these lamps and patterns may now be attributed to Adams & Company.

Lamp (e) Adams Plain Band, has been seen with frosted oval or star designs. It does not have a drip catcher, but it otherwise resembles Bridges Plain Band (f). Lamp (g) is Bridges Serene, and the stems of Double Bar Panel (h) and Frosted Panel (i) are the same. Other patterns may be attributed to Adams if any of these bases are to be found with other lamps or tableware pieces. Bridges Double Bar Panel (h) has a grey amethyst tint, in very good quality glass. The font of Bridges Frosted Panel (i) has a similar shape. All but lamps (d) and (f) have stamped collars made after 1876. Sizes are: (d) 10-3/4″, (e) 9-1/2″, (f) 7-3/4″, (g) 7-3/4″, (h) 10-1/4″, and (i) 9-1/8″. Most of these lamps were made in several sizes.

d. Bridges Bowl

e. Adams Plain Band

f. Bridges Plain Band

g. Bridges Serene

h. Bridges Double Bar Panel

i. Bridges Frosted Panel

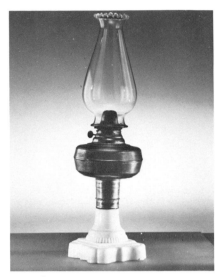

a. Perkins & House's Lamp 1860's

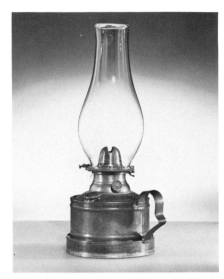

b. Perkins & House's Lamp 1890's

Perkins and House's "Non-explosive" lamps were sold for several decades. They appear in mail order catalogues, and in 1891 in the trade journal China Glass and Lamps, an advertisement of the Lane Manufacturing Co. states they were manufacturers of these lamps. Lamps (a), (b), and (h) opposite beside the clock, are Perkins and House lamps. The one opposite has the following information stamped on the font and filler cap: Perkins & House Safety Lamp, Clev'd. Non-Explosive Lamp Co. Cleveland & New York. Pat'd Dec. 11, 1866, Nov. 24th, 1857, Nov. 18, 1871 and on the filler cap, Patent Nov. 24, 1857 Extended. Nov. 24, 1871. The 1857 patent did not apply to kerosene lamps, and the 1866 patent (g) describes the non-explosive features of the lamp. These lamps consist basically of an outer reservoir, and inner tubular font with a diameter slightly greater than the wick. Between these is an air space which provides by convection, the only air supply to the flame. This 1866 patent was issued to John M. Perkins and Mark W. House of Cleveland, Ohio. I could

c. Hoyt Lamp, Extended Diamond font

d. Hoyt Lamp, Plain Panel

e. Barrie Lamp

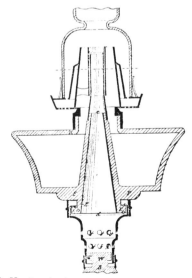

f. Hoyt patent

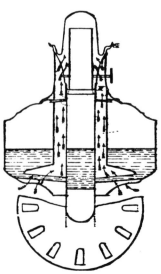

g. Perkins & House patent

not locate the 1871 patent referred to, but a July 23rd, 1872 patent issued to William J. Gordon and Mark W. House both of Cleveland, Ohio would appear to apply to the lamp (h) with the iron base. Lamp (a) is an early Perkins and House lamp, probably of the 1860's. Lamp (b) is the type shown in the 1891 advertisement, and the lamp (h) would be of the early 70's.

Although lamp (c) is dated both on the font and on the brass connection, only the connection is part of the July 23rd, 1872 patent of Jonathan J. Hoyt of Chelmsford, Mass.

An example (d) of this patent is shown with a broken tube. The patent illustration (f) shows how the glass tube provides a center draft. A round wick fits over this tube. The Ford Museum at Dearborn has two examples of this lamp. These examples are all-glass lamps, although the patent states other materials could be used. One of the witnesses to Hoyt's patent was Edwin W. Brown. This was quite possibly the Edwin W. Brown who obtained a patent in October 1876 for a wire heating attachment for lamp chimneys.

Lamp (e) has Barries Patent August 24, 1875 embossed on the underside of the font. This was the second of two patents issued to Samuel S. Barrie of New York, N.Y. for methods of attaching lamp fonts, and other glass articles to their stands. This lamp has been drilled and wired and there is no evidence of the metallic shell, button and bolt arrangement of the patent. Sizes for these lamps are: (a) 9-7/8″ to the top of the burner, (b) 5-1/4″, (c) 8-3/4″, (d) approximately 9″, (e) 8-3/4″, and (h) 10-3/4″.

h. Perkins & House's Lamp 1870's

a.. Match Holder Lamp

b. 1895 Patent Font

c. Patented Safety Handle

d. I.P. Frink Font

e. Saucer Stem

f. July 26, 1870 Patent

The patent date on lamp (a), and on other examples I have seen of this lamp, is too indistinct to decipher. This lamp could be the Perkins and House counterpart, the explosive lamp. Assuming the cylindrical container between the font and handle was for holding matches, it would become a good detonator if a spark were to ignite a bundle of matches. The font (b) dated July 9th, 1895 was likely for a lantern or hall fixture. The handle of (c) is embossed, Patent Safety Handle. This type of handle which is part of the base, is fused to the font, and provides a holder for the font.

The font (d) with the filler cap is embossed I.P. Frink, New York 1884. Tom Mileham, a Buffalo, N.Y. antique dealer, says he has had this font in many hanging lamps, particularly the iron types with slant shades. The patent date on lamp (e) is indistinct but it appears to be July 24th, 1883. Patents were usually granted once a week, on Tuesdays, and that date in 1883 was a Tuesday. The saucer-like drip catcher is part of the base, and the font is fused to the thick cylindrical wafer, which does not have any mold marks. The plain lamp (f) has the date July 26, 1870 embossed on the base. The only patents I have been able to locate for that date are the one issued to David Challinor of the glass company Challinor Taylor & Company, Limited, Birmingham, Pa. This was for a combination metal handle and reflector which attached to the lamp collar. The illustration shows this on a flat hand lamp. The other patent of that date was issued to George W. Thompson of Buffalo, N.Y. for a metal lamp.

The three-part lamp (g) and (h) has locally been named the Applesauce lamp, however nobody seems to be certain why. When the font is removed from the scalloped ring, the four pillar base may be removed and inverted to form an elevated bowl. The cup could be a match holder. Several examples of this lamp in this rib pattern, and in another leaf pattern, have been reported in Ontario. The July 25th, 1882 and March 20th, 1883 patent dates may provide additional information. Odds are that United States patents are involved because both dates were Tuesdays, the usual weekly day for issuing U. S. Patents. Canadian patents were granted on any day. In Washington, my husband and I spent a considerable time trying to locate these patents, and the Riverside clinch collar patents of September 19th, 1882 and December 4th, 1883. It is surprising that a double check of both micro film and gazettes failed to reveal any of these patents. Sizes are: (a) 3-1/8″, (b) 3-1/8″, (c) 5″, (d) 4″, (e) 7-1/4″, (f) 7-7/8″, (g) is approximately 14″.

h. *Applesauce Lamp*

g. *Applesauce base inverted*

Lamp (c) is a treasure in disguise. At the back of a shelf in a dimly-lit basement sat this absurdity, exactly as photographed here. My eyes focused on the slotted flange above the collar, and recognized it as part of W. H. Harvey's patent. I had to scan the lamp from top to bottom several times before I could believe that this was in fact, another example of the lamp shown in picture (d). Fortunately only minor damage was incurred in conversion of this lamp to electricity. William Henry Harvey of Meaford, Ontario, was granted a patent on April 2nd, 1885 for an improvement in lamps, (a) and (b). This involved a tubular unit which could be inserted into a metal or glass font. The idea was to provide a center draft to the flame without the usual arrangement of having the air intake pass through the bottom of the font. To date, this lamp can be considered the most important Canadian patented lamp. It is significant, not only because thus far only two lamps patented by Canadians have turned up, but also because the font was of necessity custom-molded to accommodate the extra-large tube, and to include a filler cap. The tube is larger than that of the largest number three size collar, and it is cemented on. Shards or fragments of lamps with this base, named in recent years Canadian Drape, have been found at the site of the Burlington Glass Works, Hamilton, Ontario. This would have been a logical company for Harvey to contact to arrange for his custom font. In my opinion this presents reliable evidence that the Canadian Drape, also shown in the Lamps 1880-1900 section was made at Burlington, about 1885. The variations found in this lamp suggest that it was also made elsewhere.

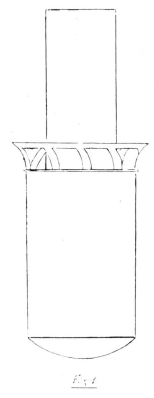

a.   *Perspective View*

Although the patent states that any center-draft burner may be used, there is no thread provided for this. Lamp (d) has had the base plate of an ordinary flat-wick burner soldered on, and the prongs are soldered to this. This arrangement has been seen on another Harvey lamp, and on the electrified lamp (c), this appears to have been removed. The wick wheel is on lamp (c). but the thumb wheel and rod are missing. They are both missing from example (d), and a button type flame spreader is missing from both examples.

It is remarkable that examples of this lamp exist today. Lamp (c) served a purpose as a support for an electric light bulb. As a means of enhancing this object, the red and gold paint carefully applied was an exercise in futility. Without a wick wheel, and with a flimsy chimney support, the past use, and potential future of lamp (d) would be minimal. Whatever the reasons for preservation, it is fortunate they were saved for historical record. These lamps are 13-5/8″ to the top of the collar.

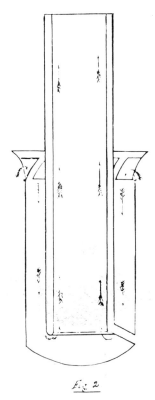

b.   *Vertical Section*

W.H. Harvey patent

c. Harvey Lamp, painted and wired.

d. Harvey Lamp with typical burner adaptation.

Glass Lamps Before 1880

Several lamps in this section may have been made in the 1880's and later. The early heavy brass collars are a good indication of lamps made before 1876. Those with the later stamped collars are included in this section if they are characteristic of lamps made during the late 70's, or if they have patterns regarded to have been made at this time. Some of these lamps may have been made by manufacturers to whom a section in this book has been devoted.

Frequently when comparing lamps of the same pattern with applied handles, it appears most likely that the same glass maker has been responsible for both handles. Their deft motions repeated thousands of times must have developed a rhythm, and a particular "twist of the wrist" would give an individual charac-

ter to the output of each person. Perhaps certain types of applied handles were characteristic of particular glass houses. The handles of the two Plain Ring Base lamps (a) and (b) are very similar, but certainly they were from different batches of glass. Lamp (a) is clear, heavier and has less sparkle. It also has mold chisel marks, a charcoal tint and a tooled single ribbed collar. The glass lamp (b), does not have the sparkle but does have the chisel marks and a faint pink tint. Most of the examples I have seen of the Cup and Saucer lamp (c) have had the stamped dated 1875 and 1876 collar. A pontil mark on the bottom suggests this lamp was pressed upside down.

The total absence of any mold marks on the very lightweight lamp Gloria (d) is a puzzle, and I think other examples should be

examined before formulating any theories regarding the method of manufacture. The lamp has also been seen in opaque white glass. The brilliant blue Ten Panel lamp (e) has also been seen in green. Two-Directional Rib (f) is another lamp usually seen with a dated collar. Sizes are: (a) 3″, (b) 3-1/8″, (c) 3-1/8″, (d) 3-1/2″, (e) 3-1/2″, and (f) 3-5/8″.

a. Plain Ring Base

b. Plain Ring Base

c. Cup and Saucer

d. Gloria

e. Ten Panel

f. Two Directional Rib

In Hayward, there is an illustration of an 1861 patent for what appears to be a combination whale-oil burner, collar and metal handle. This patented combination is mounted on a lamp of the same design as Berkshire (g), only without a handle. This lamp and the variation (h) with ovals, were made during the period when the differentiation as to type, depended upon the burner and fuel chosen for the lamp. The tulip design on lamp (i) does not include the sawtooth or rib, or appear to relate to any other tulip pattern. This charming lamp circa 1865 has an attractive handle, and the design of the tool mark is unusual, and adds to the appeal of this lamp.

There are relatively few distinctive and interesting patterns found in flat hand lamps which appear to have been made in the 1860's. The fact that applied handles are susceptible to damage, may account for the lack of variety seen today.

Milton With Flower Band (j) was also made without the flowers. This lamp has a charcoal tint, primitive quality and appears to be of the late 70's. The Interlocking Diamond Band (k) is a good quality lamp with a three-mold font. Circa 1870. Melvin (l) has an attractive trim shape with a fancy applied handle. Sizes are: (g) 2-3/4″, (h) 3-1/4″, (i) 3-1/4″, (j) 3-1/4″, (k) 2-7/8″, and (l) 3-1/8″.

g. Berkshire

h. Berkshire Variant

i. Tulip

j. Milton with Flower Band

k. Interlocking Diamond Band

l. Melvin

Diamond Sunburst (a) was a popular flat hand lamp. A design patent for this pattern was obtained in 1874 by John Bryce of Bryce Walker & Co. This lamp without dots in the diamonds as shown in the patent is probably a later variation. An all-glass stand lamp and an iron-base lamp in the Diamond Sunburst pattern are shown in other sections of this book. The flat hand lamps often have a pink or green or charcoal tint, and were made in blue and green, and possibly other colors. The very attractive Leaf and Dart pattern (b) is listed in Lee as being a product of the Richards & Hartley Flint Glass Company of Tarentum, Pa. Circa 1870. A tableware pattern made in colorless glass, it was originally called Pride. Chain With Star (c) was another pattern made in table-ware. Lee lists it as a pattern of the 1880's and Kamm states a butter dish made in the pattern was shown in a trade catalogue of Bryce Bros. This catalogue she judged to be of the 1890's, although she describes her example of a cream pitcher as having a handle typical of those of the mid-eighties. I have included it in this section because the rather primitive glass quality, shape, and applied handle are more typical of the lamps of the 1870's. Additional examples may alter this opinion.

The three plain lamps at the bottom of the page are difficult to date and could be of later manufacture, although as a general rule, the plain mass-produced lamps of the 80's and particularly of the 90's have molded handles. Lamp (d) is Six Point Star Base. Lamp (e) Ribbed Circle Base, has an interesting shape, and (f), Eight Point Star Base, has the number 142 inside. Sizes are: (a) 3-3/8″, (b) 3-1/2″, (c) 3-7/8″, (d) 2-3/4″, (e) 2-7/8″, and (f) 2-5/8″.

a. *Diamond Sunburst*

b. *Leaf and Dart*

c. *Chain with Star*

d. *Six Point Star Base*

e. *Ribbed Circle Base*

f. *Eight Point Star Base*

g. *Saucer Base*

The three lamps on this page illustrate a good variety of applied handles. Saucer Base lamp (g) has a simple shape. On this, a pattern would only detract from its appearance. The stem base appears to have been pressed upside down in a seamless mold, and the wear around the bottom indicates considerable use. The preceding description applies also to Aries (h). The extravagant handle is well suited to the flattened spherical font. The initial M scratched on the base, was the sort of identification used for lamps which were taken to community gatherings for additional illumination.

The seamless handle on the Footed Ten Panel lamp (i) is 1-1/4″ across the top. This lamp which also shows considerable wear, utilizes the base to add to its fuel capacity. Sizes are: (g) 5-1/8″, (h) 5-3/8″, and (i) 5″.

h. *Aries*

i. *Footed Ten Panel*

a. Amity

b. Beryl

c. Dulcia

d. Bridget

e. Stacked Thumbprints

f. Brewster

Amity (a) and Beryl (b) were probably mass-produced utilitarian lamps of the 1870's. Central Glass used a stem base like that of lamp (b), but it was also used by other Midwest companies. The most unusual aspects of this lamp are the thin glass font, and its exceptionally light weight. There is a good possibility that lamp (c) Dulcia was made by Atterbury & Company. The inconsistent thickness of glass gives interesting shading to this plain font.

The font Bridget (d) is like those made by Central Glass, but the base with twenty-six scallops does not show any similarity to their other lamps. This base appears to be an updated version of that of lamp (c). The fifteen scallop Atterbury type base on lamp (c) does not have the sound of leaded glass, however the fifteen scallop base on Stacked Thumbprints (e) has a ring. There is a faint streak of white glass in the base, which was another characteristic of Atterbury glass. The pattern of course is a variation of a handsome thumbprint design made in lead glass in the 60's. Brewster (f) is another utilitarian type with a little design interest created by the ribbing at the bottom of the font. Sizes are: (a) 8″, (b) 9-1/4″, (c) 6-1/4″, (d) 7-5/8″, (e) 7″, and (f) 7″.

g. Brockton

h. Harris

i. Armour

j. Beaded Chain Variant

k. Sawtooth Loop

l. Stippled Daisy and Leaf Band

Brockton (g) is similar to other utilitarian lamps of the 70's shown in this section. The many horizontal lines on Harris (h) from the lower font down, provide an interesting base for the plain font. The font is well dimpled from the chisel marks in the mold. More chisel marks and striations give interest to Armour (i), a lamp of the late 1870's.

The Beaded Chain of pattern (j) is similar to the Beaded Chain illustrated in Metz I and Lee V. This variant lacks the single bead in the center of the circle of beads, and the detail at the base of the font is different. Sawtooth Loop (k) is an attractive font, of what appears to be lead glass. It is excellent quality, and without any mold marks above the pattern. The base has eight scallops. The narrow band with overlapping leaves of Stippled Daisy and Leaf Band (l) is similar to other patterns circa 1870. Sizes are: (g) 6-3/4", (h) 7-1/4", (i) 7", (j) 7-5/8", (k) 9", and (l) 8".

a. Rib and Petal

b. Minerva

c. Pleat and Panel

d. Minerva

Rib and Petal (a) is one of those patterns where the font of the stand lamp was turned upside down to become a flat hand lamp, or vice versa. The glass is clear, and of very good quality, and the applied handle is interesting. The heavy brass collar of the stand lamp, and the later stamped collar of the footed hand lamp place these examples between 1875 and 1880.

The Minerva cake plate (b) has the same stem and base as the lamp (d) below. It is a pity they didn't use the dainty beaded and stippled pattern on the font. Attribution of this pattern to a particular glass company in the books on patterns, is speculative, but it is regarded as a pattern of the 1870's. Pleat and Panel (c) has the stem and base of the well-known tableware pattern. According to Lee this pattern was made by Bryce Bros. in the 70's, and originally called Darby. This lamp has been seen in a much larger size also. Sizes are: (a) left 3-3/8″ and right 8″, (c) 7-1/8″ and (d) 7-5/8″.

e. Beaded Diamond Band

f. Cross In Diamond

Beaded Diamond Band (e) is the pattern found on many Lomax patented fonts used in hanging lamps. Lomax lamps were made by the Union Glass Company of Somerville, Mass., and perhaps they also made this lamp. It has a stamped collar with the 1875 and 76 patent dates, and the lamp, seen also in blue, was possibly made in other colors. Cross In Diamond (f) is an attractive well-molded design with a base having twelve scallops. This lamp has a charcoal tint.

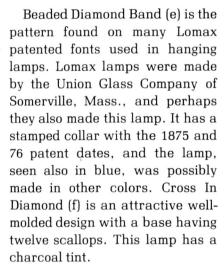

g. Chester

h. Scroll and Rib Band

Chester (g) is a busy combination of patterns, and has a font with an unusual shape. Scroll and Rib Band (h) has good to excellent quality very clear glass with mold marks well concealed along the corners of the stem and base. The fine precise base is more sophisticated than the font design. The collar has the 1875 and 76 patent dates. Crossbones (i) is an unusual pattern combined with a well-proportioned trim base. Beaded Eye Band (j) has a three-mold font with many chisel marks on the lower part. It also has the dated stamped 1875 and 76 collar. Sizes are: (e) 7-7/8", (f) 7-1/2", (g) 7-5/8", (h) 7-7/8", (i) 7-1/8", and (j) 7-1/2".

i. Crossbones

j. Beaded Eye Band

La Belle and Central Glass

a. La Belle and Corn

Belle Glass Company, and those opposite were made by the Central Glass Company.

The two lamps in photograph (a) have identical bases; and fonts which are similar to the stand lamp opposite. La Belle, left, has its name embossed on the font in Old English letters. My copy of the Daniel Ashworth design patent of February 11, 1873, shows a photograph of the handsome bold-patterned Corn lamp on the right. This is the only patent illustration I have come across with a photograph rather than a drawing. Because the bases of these lamps are the same I think there is no doubt as to the manufacturer. The hand lamp (b) has the patent date embossed on the underside.

b. Corn

ling on October 17, 1871, and was used on glass tableware as well as lamps. The primitive glass quality and design, combine to make these lamps among the most charming produced in the seventies. Sizes are: (a) left 8″, right 8-1/4″, (b) 3-1/4″, (c) 9″, and opposite left to right 8″, 3-1/4″, 5″.

c. La Belle's Ruby

These two companies are included in the same section because of links in design and personnel. According to Revi, John Oesterling and Andrew Baggs, were two of the founding members of the Central Glass Company of Wheeling, West Va. Oesterling was the company president from its beginning in 1863, until his death in 1887. The company continued and became a member of the United States Glass Company merger in 1891. Revi has a detailed account of the activities of this company after that time, but lamps in this section appear to be lamps of the 1870's. Peterson notes Andrew Baggs left Central Glass in 1872 to become manager of the La Belle Glass Company across the river at Bridgeport, Ohio. The lamps on this page are products of the La

The central motif of La Belle's Ruby (c) appears insignificant, but it was copied on later lamps. This design was named, and patented, on June 4th, 1878 by Andrew Baggs. The base has a fine embossed design on the underside of the stem, but it is otherwise the shape of one also used by Central Glass.

Peterson notes that John Oesterling's patent for the Oval Band base on the lamp opposite, showed the base combined with this font. The Wheat In Shield design was patented by Oester-

Wheat In Shield ▷

a. *Corn In Shield with Oval Band Base*

b. *Corn In Shield with Cable Base*

Corn In Shield with Oval Band Base (a) is a variation of the lamps on the preceding page. This combination with the patented base made by Central Glass, is the link which identifies the lamp below with the same manufacturer. Corn In Shield with Cable Base (b) has been reported with the colorless font, and a dark blue base. Both fonts here are well dimpled.

Metz I shows a goblet with the Mountain Laurel pattern (c), and the lamp here has the Oval Band Base. In picture (d), Mountain Laurel is combined with a Beaded Diamond Base. The stems of lamps (d) and (e) are a similar shape, and both are fluted inside. This indicates lamp (e), Beaded Diamond and Rib Bands with the Beaded Square Base, was probably made by the Central Glass Company. It has been seen also in a flat hand lamp. Sizes for these lamps are: (a) 8″, (b) 7-3/4″, (c) 7-3/4″, (d) 9″, and (e) 7-7/8″.

An undated catalogue of the Central Glass Company belonging to the Oglebay Institute of Wheeling, West Va., has been of great value in identifying the lamps photographed. In addition to this, the catalogue illustrations of other Central Glass lamps are reproduced here with their permission. I believe this catalogue was from the late 1870's, with lamps of the early seventies included.

In The Spinning Wheel's Complete Book of Antiques, Revi shows glassware pieces in the Picture Window pattern (f). His illustrations are from a Central Glass catalogue which he dates circa 1880. The footed hand lamps here, appear to have a ribbed ring embossed on the underside. This was used on their stand lamp bases. Lamp (g) is Rope Band, (h) and (k) Central Plain Panel, and (i) is Central Rounds. Central Rib Band (j) was a common pattern made by several companies. I have named (l) Oesterling after the president of the company. Pride Plain (m), and Pride (n) are the forerunners of the banquet lamp called Pride which is illustrated in the United States Glass Company catalogue circa 1893.

c. *Mountain Laurel with Oval Band Base*

d. *Mountain Laurel with Beaded Diamond Base*

e. *Beaded Diamond and Rib Bands with Beaded Square Base*

f. *Picture Window*

g. *Rope Band*

h. *Central Plain Panel*

i. *Central Rounds*

j. *Central Rib Band*

k. *Central Plain Panel*

l. *Oesterling*

m. *Pride Plain*

n. *Pride*

Catalogue illustrations courtesy The Oglebay Institute, Wheeling, West Virginia.

a. Cord and Tassel

b. Cord and Tassel

On July 23rd, 1872 Andrew Baggs was granted a design patent for the attractive pattern he named Cord and Tassel. This was the same year, according to Peterson, that he left the Central Glass Company to become manager of the La Belle Glass Company. It is uncertain which company first produced this pattern. Although the patent gives Baggs' address as Wheeling, where Central Glass was located, he would not necessarily assign it to that company. This pattern does not appear in the catalogue pages at the Oglebay Institute, although it does include lamps with the Rib Band font on the same bases as those on lamps (a) and (b). According to Peterson the design was patented for only three and one-half years, and after that time anyone was free to use it. He also states that he received a report from Mr. C. Revi that this pattern was shown in a Central Glass catalogue, which he judged to have been from about the year 1879.

The two examples of Cord and Tassel lamps (a) and (b) illustrated here, are about the same size. The bases are the same, and the collars are the type made before 1876. The detailing of the pattern, and proportions however, are vastly different. The fine proportion and detailing of (a) are like other glassware pieces of this pattern I have seen, and more closely resemble the patent drawing. It was probably made by the first producer of this pattern, whoever that was.

c. *Central Bullseye*

d. *Central Double Diamond Cluster*

The Central Bullseye (c) is the only lamp positively attributed to Central Glass, with an excellent quality, apparently lead glass font, without mold seams above the pattern. This font and Diamond Band base is exactly as shown in the catalogue.

In the Hobbs Glass section there is a font definitely made by Hobbs which is almost exactly the same as the Central Double Diamond Cluster (d). This font is shown in the Central catalogue combined with a base having eight scallops. The bases of the next three lamps are the only link with Central Glass. The link is a weak one, and they can only be considered as possibly made by Central Glass. All these fonts are of excellent quality without mold seams above the pattern. Feline Fancy (e) is a sophisticated pattern suggestive of the later Art Nouveau period. Loop and X Band (f) and Large Prism (g) are typical patterns of the 1865 to 1870 period. Lamp (h) Central Beaded Panel is shown in the catalogue. The saucered base has a ribbed ring pressed on the underside, and the glass has a good sheen and primitive quality. Sizes are: (a) 7-1/4″, (b) 7-3/8″, (c) 11″, (d) 10-1/4″, (e) 11-3/4″, (f) 11-3/4″, (g) 10-1/8″, and (h) 9-1/8″.

e. *Feline Fancy*

f. *Loop and X Band*

g. *Large Prism*

h. *Central Beaded Panel*

a. Cable Base

One detail common to all but one of the lamps illustrated on this and the opposite page, is the indented cable design on the underside of the base, as shown in photograph (a). The exception is lamp (d). The cable added a little sparkle when viewed from above, and is of course a great asset now in identifying the lamps. Lamp (d) is illustrated in the Central Glass catalogue, and the fonts of (h), (j) and (k) are shown combined with the same base as in (d). The Star bases are not illustrated.

Rib and Star Bands (b) is a busy lamp with a patriotic motif and fine detail often seen in the 1860's

b. Rib and Star Bands

c. Shelby with Cable Base

d. Elson Fourteen

e. Elson Eighteen with Star and Cable Base

and 70's. The glass quality is quite primitive. Proportion and glass quality give interest to the plain lamp Shelby (c). As mentioned, lamp (d), Elson Fourteen, is illustrated in the Central Glass catalogue. The fourteen small panels at the base of the font, and the overall shape of the font is the same. Elson Eighteen with Star and Cable Base (e) has eighteen small panels, and a font with different proportions from Elson Fourteen. Both have two-mold fonts. These are all assigned names as the catalogue has only numbers.

Central Melon with Star and Cable Base (f) has an unusually thick dimpled font. This, and the charcoal tint, combine to make it an interesting small lamp. The Central Rib with Star and Cable Base (g) has a good quality three-mold font. The design of Central Buckle with Scalloped Cable Base (h) is a simple horizontal treatment of the well known Buckle pattern.

Grape and Festoon with Stippled Leaf (i) combined here with the Scalloped Cable Base, is a pattern shown in Metz I on a goblet. She also describes other tableware pieces in this pattern. Central Sawtooth Panel, with Star and Cable Base (j) has a dark amethyst tint, and Central Sawtooth Panel and Scalloped Cable Base (k) is quite clear. With the exception of (b) 7-3/8″, all lamps are from 6-1/2″ to 6-3/4″.

f. Central Melon with Star and Cable Base

g. Central Rib with Star and Cable Base

h. Central Buckle with Scalloped Cable Base

i. Grape and Festoon with Scalloped Cable Base

j. Central Sawtooth Panel with Star and Cable Base

k. Central Sawtooth Panel with Scalloped Cable Base

Ripple (a) is a pattern said by Revi to have been produced by Doyle & Co., and by Central Glass circa 1870. These lamps, which would be of that period, could be Central Glass products. The reasons for including lamp (b) Tudor, in this section are rather complicated. In the Spinning Wheel's Antiques Book, Revi shows this pattern, which he calls Tudor, was produced by the Central Glass Company. A comport is shown but it does not have the same base as the lamp.

a. Ripple

In the book, Lamps & Other Lighting Devices, 1850-1906, catalogue pages are introduced under the heading of Bellaire Goblet Co. The pages are said to be from an 1891 catalogue supplement of the United States Glass Company, the title page of which is said to refer to the Bellaire Goblet Co., whose address was given as Findlay, Ohio. They also describe this catalogue as having the words U. S. Glass Co. M rubber stamped on the cover, and say the catalogue was obviously prepared before the merger. The detailed account of the Bellaire Goblet Co. in Findlay Pattern Glass, by Don Smith, states this company was incorporated at Bellaire, Ohio in 1876, and moved to Findlay, Ohio in 1888.

The Bellaire catalogue referred to has (not counting hanging lamp fonts) eleven pages showing lamps definitely attributed to Central Glass in the 1870's, many of which are in this section. Many sizes and forms and combinations are included. There are fourteen pages of other lamps which are related to each other, and one of them, their number 772, has the base and reversed stem of the Coin Blank lamp (e) opposite. The patterned footed hand lamp form of number 772 is the same as the footed hand form of lamp (b), which is their number 810. This I believe strongly suggests the lamp Tudor was made by the Central Glass Company.

In Nova Scotia Glass by George MacLaren, the Tudor lamp is pictured and called Nova Scotia Diamond. Shards or fragments of dozens of patterns known to have been made in the United States, have been found at the sites of Canadian glass factories. Some of these are prefixed with "Canadian," or have Canadian names.

b. Tudor

c. Patience Band

d. Rope Band

The collars on the majority of lamps on the preceding pages are almost entirely of the type manufactured before 1876, and many of the stamped ones are patent dated. These signs indicate that the examples here all seem to have been made in the 1870's. In addition to the Bellaire catalogue, some of these Central Glass lamps were also in a later U. S. Glass Company catalogue circa 1893. It is difficult to say how many of these lamps were made at the later date of the Bellaire and U. S. Glass Co. catalogues, or why they were included in the Bellaire catalogue. None of these examples from Ontario and Quebec suggest later manufacture, perhaps some U. S. examples will. Lamp (c) Patience Band is not in the catalogues, however the stem and base are Central Glass design. Rope Band (d) is a pattern shown in the catalogues.

Lamp (e) I have called Coin Blank with Owen Base because the font is the same design as the U. S. Coin lamp (f). The importance of its relationship in establishing the attribution of lamp (b) has just been described.

Kamm in Book 7 notes the pattern of lamp (f), which features facsimiles of U. S. coins, was originally called "The Silver Age" and that it was first made by the Central Glass Company shortly before this company joined the United States Glass Company merger in 1891. After the merger production was stepped up and member companies, Central Glass and Hobbs Glass, manufactured the line. Kamm also states the order to cease production was given by the government in May 1892, because reproduction of the coins was illegal. Lindsay notes the 1892 date was one hundred years after the U. S. Mint was established, and the Columbian Coin dated 1492 and 1892 on lamp (g) was also commemorative. The large colored lamp catalogue of the United States Glass Company, which has many examples of "World's Fair Lamps" made for the 1893 Exhibition, does not include coin lamps. It would therefore seem that there was a rapid rise and decline in the popularity of these lamps, and that production was limited to a period of a few years. Revi, in the Spinning Wheel's Antiques Book, reports that union problems caused the Central Glass factory to remain inactive from 1893 to 1895, and this might have had some bearing on the production of this pattern.

All U. S. Coin lamps have coins on the stem. According to Lindsay, the Clear Square font lamps, with U. S. coins, and the Panelled Round fonts without coins, each come in four sizes. She illustrates also a footed hand lamp, with U. S. coins pressed on the underside. The opaque white glass lamp (g) apparently was made only with the Columbian Coin pattern. This has four medallions with portraits. Two of Columbus and the 1492 and 1892 dates, and two of Vespucci, with the lettering Americus Vespucius surrounding the head. According to Lindsay the two others are medallions derived from the Coat-of-Arms of the United States, and the Coat-of-Arms of Spain. The font and stem of this lamp apparently unscrew, although the example pictured will not yield to light pressure. Inside the font can be seen a flattened round protrusion, but I cannot determine if metal is involved in this connection. Sizes are: (a) left 8″ and right 4-3/8″, (b) 7-7/8″, (c) 8-3/8″, (d) 7-1/2″, (e) 9-5/8″, (f) 9-3/8″, and (g) 8-1/2″.

e. Coin Blank with Owen Base

f. U.S. Coin

g. Columbian Coin

Henry & Nathan Russell

"Supplement to our illustrated catalogue, no. 11, issued October, 1884. Henry and Nathan Russell, no. 42 Barclay Street, New York. Manufacturers and dealers, glassware, kerosene lamps & fixtures, English & American crockery, and silver plated ware. New York, 1885." This information from the catalogue provides the date and description of the company. Catalogues such as this are of value in dating a particular lamp or a type of lamp. In addition to this the wholesale price of lamps at that time is interesting.

The lower left lamp, made by Adams & Company, has the Thousand Eye base and the Beaded Lattice font frequently seen combined with this base. Beside this is the lamp Aquarius, with a fine cut pattern that very closely resembles the fine cut detail of the Adams & Company, Wildflower pattern. The band around the goblet in this pattern is like that around the lower part of this lamp font. The lamp colors

are also those of the Wildflower pattern. The third lamp with the plain font was a Central Glass Company product. The stem and base may be compared with the Coin Blank lamp in the preceding section. In Lamps & Other Lighting Devices 1850-1906, lamps with this stem and base appear with other fonts, and this font is shown on a footed hand lamp. These appear under the Bellaire Goblet Company heading, but are also attributable to the Central Glass Company for reasons stated in that section.

The hanging lamp is one of a number of hall and hanging lamps in this catalogue, ranging in price from $72.00 to $168.00 per dozen. The latter, with fancy brass, prisms around font and shade, and a flowered shade which they described as "Plain Dome Shade". The hall lamp shades have frosted, or frosted and cut designs.

The three vase lamps opposite, with detachable fonts, have shades which are generally considered to be gas shades, or those

Catalogue reproductions courtesy of the Corning Museum of Glass, Corning, N. Y.

8789..In Blue and Amber, with B Hinge
Cone Burner, Illuminator,
7 inch Shade. 12¼ inches High.
$18.00 per dozen.
Lamp only, $10.00 per dozen.

ALL GLASS LAMP—OIL GUARD.

In Blue, Amber, Green and Canary.

					PER DOZ.
8785..	7½ in. high, A Bur. and Chim.,				$5.00
8786..	8	"	"	"	6.00
8787..	9	"	"	"	7.00
8788..10		"	B Bur.	"	10.00
8785..Lamp only					3.00
8786..	"				4.00
8787..	"				5.00
8788 .	"				7.00

ALL GLASS LAMP—OIL GUARD.

					PER DOZ.
New 650..	8 in. high, A Bur. and Chim.,				$4.50
" 692..	8½	"	"		5.50
" 693..	9¼	"	"		6.00
" 694..10¼		"	B Bur.		9.50
" 650..Lamp only					2.50
" 692..	"				3.50
" 693..	"				4.00
" 694..	"				6.50

5866..With 14 inch Plain Cone Shade and
B Burner, Length Closed, 43 inches, Extended, 60 inches,
$50.00 per dozen.

used with imported banquet lamps. It is therefore established that any such lamps discovered today would be appropriate outfitted in such a manner. The description, "Oil Guard Lamp", applied to any lamp with a drip depression, is surprising. Since this was the registered trade mark obtained by George Lomax in 1871, this clearly indicates an infringement. In the group of hand lamps, the left one appears to be that of the Dillaway patent, manufactured by Sandwich. The far right footed hand lamp is the Aquarius pattern again. Many examples of the composite lamps in the bottom row are seen today, although they frequently are in need of minor restoration. Other lamps in the catalogue are similar to the vase or composite lamps illustrated here.

9952..Hand Painted Centre, Assorted Tints, Brass Mountings, Detachable Fount, 7½ inches high with B Unique Burner, and 4 inch Etched Globe.
$72.00 per dozen.   Lamp only, $5.00.

9951..Hand Painted Vase, Hammered Trimmings, Brass Feet, Detachable Fount, 7 inches high with B Unique Burner, 4 inch Etched Globe.
$80.00 per dozen.   Lamp only, $6.00.

9956..Metal Lamp, Mammoth Collar, Bronze Finish, Detachable Fount, 7½ inches high, with Duplex Burner, and Extinguisher, and 4 inch Etched Globe.
$120.00 per dozen.   Lamp only, $8.00.

11132..O Burner and Chimney in Blue, Old Gold and Green.
$4.00 per dozen.
Lamp only, $2.00.

'125..A Burner and Chimney, Oil Guard.
$4.50 per dozen.
Lamp only, $2.50.

11128..A Burner and Chimney, Oil Guard, very heavy.
$5.00 per dozen.
Lamp only, $3.00.

11134..A Burner and Chimney. Oil Guard in Blue, Green, Old Gold and Canary.
$5.50 per dozen.
Lamp only, $3.50.

11133..O Burner and Chimney.
$3.80 per dozen.
Lamp only, $1.80.

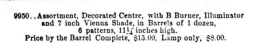

9978..Hammered Brass Centre and Trimmings. Blue and Amber Founts, 11¾ inches high, with B Burner and B Parlor Decorated Chimney.
$20.00 per dozen.   Lamp only, 12.00.

9950½..Decorated Centre, Roughed Fount, 11¼ inches high, with B Hinge Cone Burner and B Parlor Decorated Chimney.
$17.00 per dozen.   Lamp only, $10.00.
By the Barrel of 1½ dozen Complete, 15.50.
Lamp only, 9.00.

9950..Assortment, Decorated Centre, with B Burner, Illuminator and 7 inch Vienna Shade, in Barrels of 1 dozen, 6 patterns, 11¼ inches high.
Price by the Barrel Complete, $15.00, Lamp only, $8.00.

Composite Lamps

While any lamp having more than one part or material is really a composite lamp, this term when used by many collectors and dealers, refers to those with glass, china or pottery stems. A wide variety of color and decoration maintained the popularity of these lamps from the mid 1870's to the early part of this century.

The rusted tin stem of lamp (a) responded well to the rub-on dull silver finish which appears to be similar to the original one. The flower and leaves are Britannia metal or pewter. The Andrew font is very good quality, and the frosting is very smooth. Fonts of (b), (c), and (d) and the lamp opposite are all rated good. The collar of lamp (b) Privet Leaf is dated Aug. 67, June 73 and Mar. 75. Flaking or deteriorated paint is a common occurrence inside clear glass stems such as these. It is sometimes possible to remove this and repaint, leaving the transfer intact.

The Diamond in Line font (c) is combined with a lovely opaque blue glass stem. The striking lamp (d) has a bold purple slag base. The

a. Andrew Font

b. Privet Leaf

c. Diamond in Line

d. Juno

smooth band on the font has a faint yellow stain over which is painted a blue flower design. The glass pattern on the font is similar to Adams Appolo pattern. At the Ford Museum, this base is combined with a font having a clear four point snow-flake type design on a frosted background, and the collar has a wide brass shoulder. This lamp is probably a product of the 1880's.

It is interesting that both lamps in photograph (e) have patent dated collars. The small one has the 1875 and 76 dates referring to the stamped collar, and the large one has the dates Aug. 67, June 73, Mar. 75. The font and stem of the miniature and the stem of the larger one, have painted designs on opaque white glass. The miniature may have had a matching shade, and the large lamp with the Dunbar font might have had the Ives combination shade and chimney. Sizes are: (a) 10-5/8″, (b) 11″, (c) 12-1/2″, and (d) 12″. The miniature in (e) is 6-1/8″ to the top of the collar and the large lamp is 12-1/8″.

e. *Dunbar Font*

a. Sears

b. Zig Zag and Diamond

c. Feather Duster with Sawtooth Band

d. Morning Glory

The Sears, Roebuck & Co. 1897 catalogue shows lamp (a) with a combination Ives shade and chimney and a center draft burner. This one has a yellow stem with the same fancy transfer as in the catalogue illustration. Also of the nineties, lamp (b) with the Zig Zag and Diamond font has an opaque white glass stem painted blue, and a hand painted flower design. Feather Duster with Sawtooth Band (c) was a popular composite lamp font. The stem on this lamp has been repainted. Lamp (d) has a Morning Glory font with a threaded glass peg.

This is screwed into a socket which holds a nut attached to a threaded rod. The rod runs through the stem and is attached to another nut in the base.

The lamp opposite is described in Belknap as a favorite, so I think the name Belknap would be appropriate. This lamp has an opaque pink glass stem, and is reported to have been seen in blue, green and yellow. The one in the Belknap book has an opaque white font with a blue stem. Sizes are: (a) 11-1/8″, (b) 13″, (c) 12-1/8″, (d) 12-1/4″, and opposite 12-3/8″.

Belknap ▷

Mix and Match

a. Feather Duster

b. Opalescent Swirl

This is the largest and most interesting group of lamps to have had parts used in various combinations. Twenty of these lamps are clearly related and six are closely or casually related. Some are relatively plentiful, and others scarce in the areas I have investigated. In addition to clear or colorless glass, some of these came in amber, blue, turquoise, and apple green. Sometimes only the fonts or bases are colored. Opalescent coin dot or striped fonts are reported in blue and cranberry.

Presently only a few scraps of information are available regarding these lamps, but with so many designs involved, future prospects for attribution are good. In Lamps & Lighting Devices, 1850-1906, Feather Duster (a) is shown on a reproduced catalogue page. These pages, attributed to King Glass Co. circa 1890, were included in an early United States Glass Company catalogue compiled of catalogues from member companies. A Feather Duster footed hand lamp is illustrated with a handle and base like that shown in picture (c). The later United States Glass Company catalogue circa 1893, shows Feather Duster in stand, flat and footed hand lamps, available in flint, amber and blue.

Shards or fragments of the Dewdrop base were found at the site of the Burlington Glass Works, Hamilton, Ontario. In that regard it should be kept in mind that the majority of patterns found at Burlington on various digs are patterns known to have been made in the United States. To my knowledge the digs at Burlington did not yield fragments of any other lamps illustrated in this section. I am told the report on the most recent dig in 1969 is soon to be published, and that this will include information on lamps.

The glass quality of these lamps is generally good. Some fonts are dimpled, but the majority are smooth, clear and seldom tinted. Most have the common stamped collars with two deep annular grooves, and some of these have the 1875-76 patent dates. There are collars with the oval band, the fluted band and one with the hatched band. The fonts in this group are identified by the names Daisy and Button, Feather Duster, Flared Rib Panels, Inverted Swirl, Plain #1 and 2, Maple Leaf, Opalescent Coin Dot, Opalescent Swirl, Rayed Diamond Flat Band, and Rayed Diamond Rounded. Stems are Chevron, Plain and Eight Panel, and the stem-base is the Daisy and Button Trumpet Base. The bases are Dewdrop, Inverted Saucer, Round Ribbed, Square Cross, Square Fine Cut, Square Maple Leaf and Square Rayed. Because a full description of each part would be very lengthy, the lamps are captioned by their font pattern only.

c. Plain No. 1

d. Feather Duster

The font molding technique is common to all but two of these twenty related lamps. A four-part mold was used with the part below the shoulder in two parts, and the shoulder in two parts. The mold marks indicating the division between the upper and lower parts of the mold, occur under or on the roll at the shoulder. In the Plain #2 fonts, the seams of the upper two parts and the lower two parts line up, but in the others they do not. One exception is the Inverted Swirl which has two vertical seams, and no indication of horizontal lines, and the other exception is the Maple Leaf font (e) which has been made in a five-part mold. The lower part, with the maple leaves has three vertical seams, and the shoulder has two.

Lamp (a) has a Feather Duster font, Chevron stem and Round Ribbed base, 7-7/8". The Opalescent Stripe font (b) is pale blue, and the Chevron stem and Round Ribbed base are light turquoise, 7-1/8". On the Plain #1 font (c) there is a variation in texture near the handle. This starts at the junction of the top of the handle, and widens to about one inch either side of the second junction, 5-3/8". (d) Feather Duster Flat Hand Lamp is 3-1/2". Lamp (e) has a Maple Leaf font, Chevron stem and Square Maple Leaf base, 10-1/2".

e. Maple Leaf

The general description of these lamps is at the beginning of this section. The descriptions here, are of the parts and sizes.

(a) Plain #1 font, Chevron stem, Round Ribbed base, 8-3/4″.

(b) Rayed Diamond Flat Band font, Chevron stem, Round Ribbed base, 8-3/4″.

(c) Rayed Diamond Flat Band font, Chevron stem, Square Cross base, 7-1/4″.

(d) Rayed Diamond Rounded font, Chevron stem, Square Cross base, 10″.

(e) Plain #1 font, Chevron stem, Square Cross base, 7-7/8″.

(f) Daisy and Button font, Plain stem, Dewdrop base, 9-1/4″.

(g) Rayed Diamond Rounded font, Chevron stem, Round Ribbed base, 9″.

(h) Inverted Swirl font, Chevron stem, Square Cross base, 7″.

(i) Daisy and Button font, Plain stem, Fine Cut base, 10-1/8″.

(j) Plain #2 font, Plain stem, Fine Cut base, 7-1/4″.

(k) Plain #2 font, Plain stem, Dewdrop base. This base pattern is essentially the same as used on the 1876 patented Atterbury Pressed Boss lamps, and also that of the pattern known as Dewdrop & Star, which was patented by Jenkins Jones of Campbell Jones & Co. This lamp also has the 1875 and 76 dated collar 7-1/8″.

(l) Plain #2 font, Daisy and Button Trumpet stem-base, 7-3/8″.

(m) Daisy and Button font, Daisy and Button Trumpet stem-base, 9-1/4″.

(n) Daisy and Button font, Eight Panel stem, Inverted Saucer base, 8-3/4″.

(o) Flared Rib Panel font, Eight Panel stem, Inverted Saucer base, 7-1/8″.

a. Plain

b. Rayed Diamond Flat Band

f. Daisy and Button

g. Rayed Diamond Rounded

k. Plain No. 2

l. Plain No. 2

c. *Rayed Diamond Flat Band*

d. *Rayed Diamond Rounded*

e. *Plain No. 1*

h. *Inverted Swirl*

i. *Daisy and Button*

j. *Plain No. 2*

m. *Daisy and Button*

n. *Daisy and Button*

o. *Flared Rib Panel*

The lamps on this page relate to those on the preceding pages, or to each other. Lamp (a) Daisy and Button Panel can be compared to the Daisy and Button patterns of the Mix and Match lamps. It may also be compared to the Stars and Bars pattern illustrated in Don Smith's book on Findlay Glass, and in the United States Glass Company catalogue circa 1893. The flipped-up applied handle popped on the side, adds to the personality of this lamp, but it is not much help in relating it to others.

Gerald Stevens, in "Canadian Glass, 1825-1925" shows a Dominion Glass Company catalogue illustration circa 1913 of lamps (b) and (c). It was their No. 101 lamp and a 1902 Diamond Glass Company catalogue price list, shows it was manufactured at that time. Although this lamp is often described as the 101, I prefer the name, Dominion Panel, to distinguish it from the other 101 patterns, which incorporate those numbers in their design. The reason for the inclusion of these lamps here is that the square bases have been pressed in a mold of the same design and size as Mix and Match square bases. The stem sections of the lamp closely resemble the Dalzell, Gilmore & Leighton Co. Crown lamp, illustrated in the section on Findlay lamps.

The Wavy font and screw socket of the Nickel Plate 101 lamp (d) have been cemented onto this Chevron stem. The Royal Ontario Museum has a lamp on display with this same Chevron stem, a brass connector and the Feather Duster with Sawtooth Band font (e) below. It is difficult to say how these fonts happen to be combined with a stem usually used in all-glass lamps. This explains the reason for including the Feather Duster with Sawtooth Band here. Feather Duster with Star Base (f) resembles lamp (e). The sizes are: (a) 3-1/4″, (b) 4-1/2″, (c) 7″, (d) 10-1/4″, (e) 8-1/2″, and (f) 8″.

a. Daisy and Button Panel

b. Dominion Panel

c. Dominion Panel

d. Nickel Plate Wavy

e. Feather Duster with Sawtooth Band

f. Feather Duster with Star Base

preceding page

Coin Dot lamps shown on the preceding page were made by the Hobbs Glass Company, circa 1885. Advertised as "sewing lamps," they are shown here on a cherry and mahogany washstand, with needlework and sewing accessories of the period. The pretty fonts were also made in blue, gold or clear opalescent, and the bases have a design pressed on the underside, which refracts the light in such a manner as to create a sparkle effect. Other forms of this lamp are shown in the Hobbs, Brockunier & Company section.

opposite

The first two lamps on the left are overlay cut to clear. The tall Cranberry lamp has a matching font and stem design, a double marble base, and brass fittings with ormolu finish. A larger shade with an engraved design, would be more appropriate than the replacement shade used here. An interesting aspect of the design on the font is that if viewed directly, in each leaf of the quatrefoil is seen another quatrefoil from the reverse side. Few lamps can be traced to their original owners, however, this very special lamp has a recorded past. The head of a prominent shipping family who settled in Nova Scotia in the early 1800's, brought the lamp from Boston in one of their ships. This information is confirmed in a letter from the grandson of the original owner. Perhaps the same company also transported some of the thousands of the New England area lamps that were imported into Nova Scotia, and used throughout the Maritime Provinces.

The second lamp, with a double overlay of white and blue has traces of gold in the stars, and a well-preserved gold design and banding on the base. The shade holder is patent dated 1877 which suggests it is a later addition. These three lamps are considered to be products of the 1860's. The third lamp, with a white overlay stem cut to green opaline has a free-blown font with two bands of cut ovals, and a finely engraved vintage pattern on the shoulder. The lamp on the left was probably made by the Boston & Sandwich Glass Company, and the other two can be considered Sandwich or New England type. See the Atterbury section for a lamp with a similar stem and base. Size to the top of the collars are: left 21″, center 13″, and right 13-1/2″.

European elegance! Perhaps the counterpart of Sandwich, but of a later date. Foreign design in kerosene lamps is easily recognized in most examples. Both these lamps are china, and bear famous markings. The 9-1/2″ Limoges lamp on the left has a dainty floral swag and gilt design in mint condition. The 17-1/2″ Dresden lamp from the attic of a home in Buffalo, N.Y., contained kerosene when discovered. Many lamps have been imported in recent years but I believe these two were imported in the days of kerosene.

In the past few years, many lamps have been imported into Canada from England, Scotland and Ireland. These are primarily colored flat hand lamps, or beautiful tall banquet lamps with a variety of colored fonts and shades. The glass designs and patterns, and the stems and bases are quite different from American lamps.

The Princess Feather lamp, circa 1890 is shown in a setting of the period. Set on a sewing-machine cabinet, patent dated 1890, this lamp was frequently advertised as a sewing lamp. It was manufactured for several decades in a variety of colors, and is currently being reproduced in some versions. This squat style with the pink cased glass font, is said to have also been made with a blue font. Other squat Princess Feather lamps were made in opaque white, opaque green with slightly different detail on the font, and opaque turquoise with a wide matching shade. The more slender version was made in clear, green, and in cobalt blue. In the 1920's, the slender lamp was gilded, tinted, and sold with a fancy pressed and painted chimney. Some of the colors were made in footed hand lamps, like the clear glass one shown in the section on lamps 1880-1900.

This 9-1/2″ lamp was purchased in New York State. All the solid color ones described, have been seen in Ontario.

The lamp on the left is the Dalzell Oval Window lamp. Several related lamps are shown in the section on Findlay Lamps. The center lamp is the Two Panel pattern, said by Revi to be the product of the Richards & Hartley Flint Glass Company, circa 1880. While the Two Panel pattern may have two panels in the tableware pieces, the lamp has in fact, three panels. The temptation to call this a Three Panel lamp, is ruled out by the fact that the same company made another pattern which is known as "Three Panel." Perhaps the Three Panelled Two Panel lamp is most accurate. In addition to vaseline, this lamp is seen in amber, apple green, and blue, and was possibly made in other colors.

The third lamp was advertised in 1898 by the manufacturer, Dalzell, Gilmore & Leighton Company. They called it the Queen Lamp, and the same lamp with a plain font was referred to as the King Lamp. The names Queen Heart and King Heart provide easier identification, and retain the original names. This lamp, also known as Sweetheart or Beaded Heart, is further described in the section on Findlay lamps.

These lamps are left 9″, center 7-3/4″, and right 8″.

Opalescent banquet lamps and a turkey foot vase. The 12″ Nickel Plate 101 lamp on the left, is named after the Nickel Plate Glass Company, who manufactured this pattern in tableware. This distinquishes it from other patterns which appear to have the numbers 101 in their design. Lamps in this pattern were shown in the United States Glass Company catalogue circa 1893. The Nickel Plate Glass Company was a member of the United States Glass Company merger, and could have made the lamps at that time. It is not known if these lamps were made before the merger in 1891. The Atwood collar dated Oct. 31, 1876, and the threaded screw socket which appeared circa 1890, are used on this lamp. Other examples are seen in the United States Glass Company section.

The 12-3/4″ lamp on the right, has diagonal opalescent stripes on clear glass. It has been reported that this lamp was also made in blue and in cranberry glass. The Taplin-Brown collar dated April 13, 1875 and March 21, 1876 is used on this lamp, which was probably made in the 1880's.

In the top picture, the first four lamps are of the 1860's, and the second four would have been made after 1880.

No. 1. The font of Chenoa has also been seen in the same shape as one shown on a lamp in the Hobbs Glass section. The glass has a ruby stain with the pattern areas left clear. Color was applied to the inside, and presumably fired, because there isn't any deterioration. The white bird, blue branch and green leaves were outlined in gold.

No. 2. A handsome lamp with a metal base, and a ruby font without mold marks.

No. 3. This Sandwich lamp from Ogdensburg, New York, has a white overlay cut to a fuchsia-toned cranberry.

No. 4. The Sandwich-type threaded font was also made with white and blue threads of varying widths.

No. 5. Made by the Hobbs Glass Company, this Snowflake lamp is also seen in clear and in blue opalescent glass.

No. 6. This lamp was also made in blue in hand and stand lamps, and with a yellow font that has a different pattern pressed on the underside of the base.

No. 7. Stained Petals was also made in a larger size.

No. 8. Feathered Cartouche was made in a smaller size, and in a footed hand lamp. The cartouche was also made in blue.

Sizes are: (1) 11-1/2", (2) 11-3/4", (3) 10-1/4", (4) 9-3/4", (5) 5", (6) 5-3/4", (7) 10-1/2", (8) 9-3/4".

Blue and amber lamps of the 1880's and 90's.

No. 1. Americus is the name given to this lamp in the United States Glass Company catalogue, circa 1893.

No. 2. In the same catalogue, this lamp is called Pride. The design is based on lamps made earlier by the Central Glass Company.

No. 3. Moon and Star was made over a long period of time by different companies, however, Adams & Company probably made this lamp.

No. 4. This lamp was also made with a black base, and a ruby and silver font.

No. 5. The Eight Point Star lamp has a rayed rib shoulder, and an applied handle.

No. 6. The small cylinders in this design suggest the name Muff. It is seen in combinations of amber, blue and clear.

No. 7. Cathedral is the local name for this lamp. It was also made in clear, blue and amber combinations.

Sizes are: (1) 16", (2) 10-3/4", (3) 11-1/2", (4) 9", (5) 3-5/8", (6) 9-1/2", (7) 12-1/2".

1. A rather unusual lamp with a double black marble base, and brass parts which still retain their gold ormolu finish. About 80% of the gold design remains on the blue opaline stem and base, and the shade is original. Purchased in the United States, this lamp is 16″ to the top of the collar and might easily have been made before 1860. It is reported to have also been made in pink opaline.

2. Typical library or hanging lamp of the 1880's and 90's, this lamp has a September 20th, 1870 patent-dated Lomax font. The shade is clear opalescent, mold blown. The prisms and brass frame cast shadow patterns which are an important part of the atmosphere created by the use of these lamps.

Riverside Lamps

Lamps made by the Riverside Glass Company of Wellsburg, West Virginia, are unique in that they have an instantly recognizable patented collar. Unfortunately, from the standpoint of easy authentication, this collar was also used by others after the company closed down. I am indebted to Nancy Caldwell of Wellsburg, West Virginia for providing information on local glass houses. The glass industry was so vast that there is still much rewarding material to be dug out of the ground, and out of records. Individuals, historical societies and research groups play a large part in fitting each piece of information more accurately into the total picture. The Caldwell book, soon to to be published by McClain Publishing Company, Parsons, West Va., is titled, "A History of Brooke County." An excerpt regarding the Riverside Company states "This factory was incorporated September 17, 1879 by: John Dornan, formerly with the Buckeye Glass Company of Martins Ferry, Ohio; Charles Brady and J. E. Ratcliffe, former employees of Hobbs-Brockunier Glass Company of Wheeling, West Virginia; J. Flannagan and A. McGrail," and also, "Riverside was the first glass house in our area to utilize natural gas and Mr. Dornan had the first patent for this process."

Many Riverside collars have the dates Sept. 19, 1882 and Dec. 4, 1883 stamped on the shoulder. I felt information on this patent was "high priority," but unfortunately the search for this and two other patents of the same years was unfruitful. The collar with its flared sides can easily be spotted. The neck of the font was molded so that this collar could be clinched on without cement, and a notch at the edge of the collar was designed to fit into a corresponding notch in the glass. Presumably this was to prevent the collar turning when the burner was screwed in, but judging by the examples here, it was not very effective. Advertisements of the Riverside Glass Works appeared regularly in the China Glass and Lamps trade journal. The two advertisements, right, appeared in 1906, and although they show the words "the original Riverside Clinch-On Collar" stamped around the sides, and say "see mark on every lamp," I have not come across a collar so marked. Both tableware and lamps were advertised, but the lamp patterns were different from the tableware patterns. The lamp patterns show a considerable variation, and would be impossible to relate without their distinctive collars.

Ms. Caldwell also notes that "on October 23, 1899, Riverside joined the National Glass Company, a syndicate established in 1899 to help keep the glass industry in our country alive due to the importation of the foreign glass."

"In 1907, Riverside shut down and their molds were sold to the Cambridge Glass Company at Cambridge, Ohio. In 1911, the furnaces and buildings were sold to the Rithner family and Ellery Worthen." There is information at the end of this section on lamps made with the Riverside collar after that time.

a. *Frosted Panel*

b. *Genie*

The Frosted Panel lamp (a) is one of Riverside's most handsome lamps. The shade is a recent addition. Genie (b) is an interesting shape with an applied handle. Both these lamps have undated collars. Sizes are: (a) 10″ and (b) 2-3/4″.

a. Riverside Almond

b. Riverside Plain

c. Riverside Rose

The next 15 lamps shown here were probably made at the Riverside Glass Works at Wellsburg, West Va. Two of these lamps are green, and probably others were made in colored glass. Lamp (a) Riverside Almond is an attractive pattern with the font design repeated on the base. Variations of this lamp were advertised in the trade journal China Glass and Lamps in 1894. A footed hand lamp, and squat stand lamps with square and with round bases were also illustrated. Lamp (b), Riverside Plain, has a handle similar to others made in the 1890's. The pattern Riverside Rose (c), has also been seen in a green stand lamp.

Sizes are: (a) 8″, (b) 5-1/8″, and (c) 5-5/8″.

d. Riverside Swag

Riverside Swag (d) with traces of gold in the pattern, has an Art Nouveau character. Riverside Rib and Plain Band (e) was advertised in an 1894 issue of China Glass and Lamps. It was shown with a plain stem and round base, and also with a square base. The Riverside Plain lamp (f) was made in other proportions and sizes.

The collars on (a), (c) and (e) are dated. Sizes are: (d) 8-7/8″, (e) 8-7/8″, and (f) 8-1/2″.

e. Riverside Rib and Plain Band

f. Riverside Plain

a. *Riverside Fern*

b. *Scroll and Fern*

c. *Empress*

The Riverside Fern lamp (a) has a fancy design pressed on the underside of the base. It was advertised in 1898, and was shown also with a round Almond base, and in a footed hand lamp with a beaded base. Riverside Scroll and Fern (b) is a very attractive lamp that is possibly of the 1880's.

Empress (c) is the only Riverside lamp that I have seen named in an advertisement. It was advertised in 1899 and shown in a regular and squat stand lamp, and in a footed hand lamp, all with round bases with a single row of beading. This base is the same as that of lamp (a). Either side of the name was the word Emerald indicating it was possibly made only in green. This lamp is an unusual dark olive green. The font of Riverside Panel (d) is a light green. This lamp has been seen also in the footed hand form with a green font and a clear base. Riverside Beaded Bands (e) and Riverside Rib Band (f) were included in the same advertisement in 1893, and footed hand lamps in these patterns were also shown. The flowers on the base of Star-Grass Flower (g) are painted gold. This suggests probable manufacture in this century. The bases of (h) Regal Plain Font and (i) Regal Fancy Panel, have the same design.

d. *Riverside Panel*

e. *Riverside Beaded Bands*

f. *Riverside Rib Band*

g. *Star-Grass Flower*

The following lamps have collars stamped with the patent dates Sept. 19, 1882 and Dec. 4, 1883: (a), (b), (d) and (f). The first patent would have expired in 1899 and it appears that they stopped dating them after that time. All those advertised before this date have the dated collars. Sizes are: (a) 8″, (b) 9″, (c) 9-1/8″, (d) 9-1/8″, (e) 8-3/4″, (f) 8-1/4″, (g) 9-3/8″, (h) 7-7/8″ and (i) 8-1/2″.

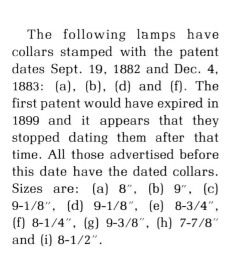

h. *Riverside Regal Plain Font*

i. *Riverside Regal Fancy Panel*

a. Riverside Ladies

Closing the company in 1907 and selling the molds to Cambridge Glass Company, did not spell the end of the Riverside Clinch-On Collar. In Marcella Bond's book on Albany Glass, catalogue pages of the Indiana Glass Company at Dunkirk, Indiana show a Six Panel lamp, a Princess Feather, a Massive Sewing lamp (c) and a Mammoth Sewing lamp ((c) with a plain font), and describe them as being available with both No. 2 Riverside special clinch collar, or a common clinch collar. The illustrations are said to be from 1907 through the depression years. In the Sears, Roebuck & Co. 1927 catalogue, a Princess Feather lamp is shown with a fancy chimney, and a Riverside collar. Hopefully the gaps will be filled in one day, and that information will be available on such lamps as the Riverside Ladies (a) and the Riverside Wild Rose (b). Both designs are pressed on the underside and the words Riverside Clinch On Collar are embossed on the outside. Each of the Ladies is different. They are painted gold, and the flowers between are red. Sizes are: (a) 8-5/8″, and (b) 8-3/8″.

b. Riverside Wild Rose

As mentioned, the Massive Sewing lamp (c) was made with the regular or Riverside Clinch On Collar. It was made in a flat hand lamp and in a tall slender version; all with matching chimneys.

My first introduction to the Riverside Clinch Collar was the left lamp, Riverside Rondo (d). It has the patented collar. The right hand lamp discovered some months later, has an undated collar, but the words Riverside Clinch On Collar were embossed on the top of the base. Thereafter I began to watch for these collars. The hollow stem on one is quite apparent in the picture.

The King Heart lamp with the Riverside Clinch Collar gives rise to some speculation. A tall stand lamp in this pattern also has a Riverside Collar, and both have poorly molded bases. Dalzell, Gilmore and Leighton Company originally made this lamp in Findlay, Ohio. They went out of business about 1902, and it is quite possible that Riverside acquired some of their molds and produced these lamps. Sizes are: (a) 9-1/2″, (b) left 8″ and right 8-1/8″ and (c) 6″.

c. Massive Sewing Lamp

d. Riverside Rondo

e. King Heart

Findlay Lamps

a. Findlay Onyx

b. Findlay Chimney

c. Two Post Lamp

If a large quantity of related lamps found in a particular area was an indication of local manufacture, the lamps in this section would be said to have been made in Southwestern Ontario. They are however, Findlay Ohio products, well documented in the book Findlay Glass Patterns by Don Smith. The abundance of these lamps is explained by records of lamps having been shipped by the carload.

With the exception of the Currier and Ives and Pillow Encircled, all lamps in this section are in patterns made by the Dalzell, Gilmore and Leighton Co. Perhaps the best known glass of this area is Findlay Onyx, patented by George W. Leighton in 1889 and manufactured by Dalzell, Gilmore and Leighton. An example of this glass is the Sugar Shaker (a), which is ivory with silver flowers, and shows its inner layer of vibrant orange-red when back-lit. The rectangular base chimney (b) with its original wrapper is a type made in the 1880's. This one, made by the Globe and Chimney Glass Works at Findlay, claims to have lead content, but does not have any ring when tapped. Extravagant claims of lead content in chimneys were common. The Two Post lamp (c) is related to an outstanding lamp shown in the Smith book. It shows a Two Post stem in black, set diagonally on a fancy square base. The font is Findlay Onyx, and the base is screwed into a socket recessed in the font. According to Smith, this lamp was combined with different patterned fonts.

Like those in the Mix and Match section, many of these lamps are found in different combinations, and therefore, require names for their various parts. I have used the names given by Mr. Smith, and have chosen names for those not identified. One exception is where I have used the original names of King and Queen and added the word Heart, for the lamp called Sweetheart by Smith. This is because I have discovered two other heart lamps known in other areas as Sweetheart. In a collection at Findlay, I have seen Cross Lens (d) combined with the stem and base (h). The Triple Rib font combined with the Ellipse Stem (e) is the footed hand form of lamp (h). The Feathered Arch font (f) on the Triple Stem lamp may be frosted or clear. Another Triple Rib font is combined here with a Rib Base in (g). This base and that of (h) were used with cake plates of various patterns. Currier and Ives, a pattern made by Bellaire, is very attractive in the lamp form (i).

Bullseye with Diamond Point (j), known in Canada as Pointed Bullseye, is a well-known Findlay pattern. Shortly after this pattern was advertised in the trade journal, China Glass and Lamps by Dalzell in 1892, there was published a list of buyers in town (Pittsburgh, Pa.). These included J.A.C. Poole of the T. Eaton Company, Toronto. Perhaps he ordered the many examples of this pattern seen in Canada. With so many examples of Findlay lamps in Canada, it is indeed probable that they also exported much of their tableware. Eyewinker (k) with the Bubble Base is a pattern which is well suited to lamps. The Bubble Base (l) is combined with a plain font. Both (k) and (l) come in footed hand lamps with the Bubble Base and two handles as in (e). Sizes are: (c) 9-1/2″, (d) 3-3/4″, (e) 5-1/2″, (f) 6-1/2″, (g) 8-1/4″, (h) 7-3/4″, (i) 7-3/8″, (j) 7-3/4″, (k) 7-5/8″, and (l) 7-7/8″.

d. Cross Lens

e. Triple Rib Font—Ellipse Base

f. Feathered Arch Font—Triple Stem

g. Triple Rib Font—Rib Base

h. Triple Rib Font—Ellipse Base

i. Currier and Ives

j. Bullseye with Diamond Point

k. Eyewinker

l. Plain Font with Bubble Base

a. Six Panel Fine Cut

b. Fishscale with Panelled Font

Lamp (a), Six Panel Fine Cut appears to be the same pattern as that of a goblet pictured in the Findlay Pattern Glass book, however, there is not any mention of a lamp, or shards of a lamp in this pattern. Fishscale with Panelled Font (b) is a very heavy lamp, often seen in green with the Cable Font. This lamp and Eyewinker with a plain font (c) or Plume Font (d) were made on a semi-automatic machine. According to Smith, Phillip Ebling, foreman of the Dalzell mold shop patented a lamp-making machine in 1899. Lamps made on this machine are of one piece with the inside of the font extending down into the stem. Lamp (e) Eyewinker with Oval Window font is also seen in green in the color section.

c. Teardrop with Eyewinker with Plain Font

d. Teardrop with Eyewinker with Plume Font

The King Heart lamps (f) and (g) with plain fonts, and the Queen Heart lamp (h), were advertised by Dalzell, Gilmore and Leighton in Glass and Pottery World August, 1898. Lamp (f) and (g), which are also shown in the Riverside section, have Riverside Clinch Collars. It may be pointed out here that while the handle of lamp (g) differs from those of the other footed hand lamps on the

e. Eyewinker Thumbprint with Oval Window Font

f. King Heart Lamp

g. King Heart Lamp

following pages, it is the same as the shard of a Crown hand lamp shown in the Findlay Pattern Glass book. These lamp bases (f) and (g), are poorly molded, which may indicate they were made from worn molds purchased after Dalzell, Gilmore and Leighton went out of business towards the end of 1901. Green Queen Heart lamps with the **Krys-Tol** trademark have been reported. Dr. Peterson points out that this trademark was never registered, and that it was coined in 1906 by Benjamin Jacobs when he was with the Ohio Flint Glass Company, and that he took the trademark with him to the Jefferson Glass Co. where he became General Manager in 1908.

The Heart lamps have combinations of green and clear as shown in the color section, and many of these lamps have hand-painted designs. A particularly attractive Queen Heart lamp has frosted hearts with hand-painted flowers. Sizes are: (a) 9-3/8″, (b) 10-1/4″, (c) 10-1/4″, (d) 9-3/4″, (e) 9-3/4″, (f) 10″, (g) 6″, and (h) 10-3/4″. The Queen lamp came in five sizes of stand lamps, one size sewing lamp, one size footed hand lamp, one size flat hand lamp and one size night lamp "complete".

h. *Queen Heart Lamp*

a. Oval Window

b. Queen Heart

All the flat hand lamps shown here have molded handles of the same design; and the footed hand lamp handles have their own distinctive shape. A patented collar was used on all these lamps. According to Smith, Phillip Ebling of the Dalzell, Gilmore and Leighton Company obtained a patent for a clinch collar, first used in May, 1894. This collar was clinched on while the glass was still hot, thus obviating the need for cement. It has the same appearance as the undecorated 1876 patent clinch collars which required cement. If Dalzell was the only company to use this collar it would provide easy identification for their lamps. It is possible however, that when they joined The National Glass Company in 1899, other member companies used this collar.

Lamp (a) is Oval Window, (b) Queen Heart, and (c) Cable. The font of Plume (d) has been molded with a protrusion at the side to accommodate the molded handle. Lamp (e), Crown is the flat hand lamp form of those pictured opposite.

Lamp (f), Fishscale with Cable Font, and (g) Teardrop with Eyewinker and Plume Font are well molded with bright clear glass. Fishscale with Panelled Font (h) is poorly molded and has a gray tint. The stem is shallow with fewer scales, and the base does not have the double step as in (f). Sizes are: (a) 3-5/8″, (b) 3-5/8″, (c) 3-5/8″, (d) 3-5/8″, (e) 3-3/4″, (f) 6-1/4″, (g) 6-3/8″, and (h) 6-3/8″.

c. Cable

d. Plume

e. Crown

f. Fishscale with Cable Font

g. Teardrop with Eyewinker and Plume Font

h. Fishscale with Panelled Font

The Crown lamps (i) have separately molded fonts. These lamps advertised in Glass and Pottery World, November, 1897 were called Crystal lamps. The advertisement states: "We make five styles of decorated lamps: Crystal lamp, decorated bowl. Crystal lamp, decorated foot, plain bowl. Crystal lamp, ruby stem. Crystal lamp, ebony foot with decorated bowl. Crystal lamp with decorated ebony foot." The latter are in collections in Findlay, Ohio. Many of the Dalzell, Gilmore and Leighton lamps came in several sizes, including the miniature or as they called them, the "night lamps". Sizes are to the top of the collars, left 5-1/4″ and right 10″.

i. Crown Lamps

Dalzell, Gilmore and Leighton Co. became a member of The National Glass Company merger in 1899. According to Don Smith in his book, Findlay Pattern Glass, Dalzell was founded in Wellsburg, West Va. in 1883, and moved to Findlay in 1888. All lamps in this section are shown or related to lamps or cake plate bases illustrated in the Smith book. This book also provides many statistics on the five companies which manufactured tableware patterns in Findlay.

Pillow Encircled (a) is a pattern attributed to the Model Flint Glass Company, although there isn't any reference to lamps or lamp shards in the Smith book. This lamp was also made in green. The Ball Base lamp with the Swirl Font (b) is very feminine and charming. A real "Belle of the Ball". Shards of this lamp are shown in the Smith book. Sizes are: (a) 11″ and (b) 9-3/4″.

a. *Pillow Encircled*

b. *Ball Base Lamp*

Gone with the Wind or Vase Lamps

The graceful limestone Möbius Strip by sculptor E.B. Cox, and the turn of the century lamp, present contrasts in time and materials, which heighten our awareness and appreciation of each object. This 12-1/2" opaque white glass lamp, with foliage and red flowers, was also made in a miniature.

The frequently deplored situation which has renamed parlor and vase lamps, has been described in many books and articles. This type of lamp, made from the mid-seventies on, was inappropriate in the Civil War setting of the movie Gone With The Wind. The result of this choice has been to make the name of the movie synonymous with lamps having fonts with matching chimneys or shades. Perhaps it is now time to accept it as the most famous anachronism of the movies, and to let it serve to illustrate how difficult it is to reverse an anachronism or an incorrect attribution. These lamps which generally combine glass and metal parts were made in miniatures, semi-miniatures and full size up to 3 feet or more. They may be grand or grotesque; garish or delicately decorated. In Kenneth Wilson's book, the advertisement showing the wares of the Smith Brothers Company in 1878 would attest to the fine quality decoration on some of these lamps. A sampling of the tremendous variety available is shown here. Reproductions of mail order catalogues show many more examples.

The western migration of the Midwest factories in the search for a new supply of fuel, was during a time when these lamps were very popular, and therefore, produced in great quantities. A study of these lamps and their history will no doubt be undertaken one day.

The bases of some of these lamps have separate metal or glass oil containers. For lamps with translucent glass, this would avoid discoloration caused by dirty oil. Many fragments of lamp (a) were found at the site of the Burlington Glass Works, Hamilton, Ontario. This lamp, purchased in the United States, has a few traces of brown decoration. The quality of the frosted Beaded Crinkle lamp (b) is superior to a similar frosted Beaded Drape that I have seen. I am not certain if the Owl lamp (c) had a matching chimney or shade. In Lamps and Other Lighting Devices, 1850-1906, lamps of this size and type are seen with big bulge chimneys. The red satin-finish lamp opposite has been converted to electricity. This lamp was photographed at an antique shop, and measurements were not taken. Lamp (a) is 13″ to the top of the shade, lamp (b) is 18-3/4″ overall, and lamp (c) is 8-1/4″.

a. Vase lamp

b. Beaded Crinkle

c. Owl lamp

Late Related Lamps—After 1880

When two or more related lamps are found, there is a good possibility that other related ones will be discovered. The name St. Lawrence Hand Lamp has been chosen for this first group. Lamp (a) and the dark brown one opposite, are also found in blue and green. The unusual shape of the handle is common to all examples I have seen, and appears to have been the work of one glass house, or possibly one glass worker. These lamps are the same size and shape as lamp (e). Lamp (e), smooth on the outside and ribbed inside, like (c) and (d), also has a distinctive bold handle which is seen on other examples of this lamp. Lamps (b), (c) and (d) are all slightly shorter. Handles of (b) and (c) were first applied at the bottom and curved around to the top. All lamps have a rayed pattern on the base, with 20 rays. Lamp (d) has a depressed button in the center, and on the others this button is raised. Lamps (a), (e), (d) and opposite have the type of stamped collars used from 1876 on. The collar on (b) is the Oval Band type and (e) has the Fluted Band type. These collars are seen on lamps made in the 1880's and 90's in the United States. The lamps are attributed to the Quebec glass houses in the Hudson-Como area, but according to Canadian Glass books, the companies went out of business before their later collars were made. The details of these lamps are given here in the hope that some day convincing evidence will link them to their origin. Sizes are: (a) 3-3/8″, (b) 3-1/4″, (c) 3-1/8″, (d) 3-1/4″, (e) 3-1/2″, and opposite 3-1/2″.

a.

b.

c.

All Hand Lamps—St. Lawrence Hand Lamp ◁ ▷

d.

e.

The Heart lamp (a) has the same molded handle as lamp (b) Dorothy. There are two sizes of Heart footed hand lamps, and a flat hand lamp also. The stand lamp (c) is an opaque pale green, and this lamp has also been seen in a custard color. The mold marks on all fonts (a), (b), (c), and (d) indicate that they were made in a five-piece mold. A horizontal seam just below the shoulder divides the three lower mold seams from the upper two. One of the lower seams lines up with a shoulder seam.

Lamp (d) has the same stem and base as the Heart lamp, but with a plain font. The Heart lamp has been referred to as American, and as Canadian, but I have not heard of any convincing basis of authentication. Perhaps the key to attribution will be in the molded handles of the footed hand lamps, or in the fonts with their many mold seams. In the Mix and Match section, the Maple Leaf Font was molded in this manner. Sizes are: (a) 5-1/2", (b) 4-3/4", (c) 10-1/2", and (d) 8".

a. Heart Lamp

b. Dorothy

c. Heart Lamp

d. Heart Lamp Base

The stem (e) of the Egyptian lamp (f) is very attractive and well detailed when viewed from any angle. In comparing this with the Duncan & Miller Three Face lamp, pictured in Lamps 1880 to 1900, I would say the frosted surface of the latter is finer and smoother. There is more intricate detail in the Egyptian head, and the composition is perhaps more interesting than that of the Three Face lamp.

Although it is not easily discernible in the photographs, in actual examination the bases of the Egyptian lamp (f) and the Three Face Medallion (g) appear to be of the same design. Sizes are: (f) 12″ and (g) 9-1/4″.

e. Egyptian Stem

f. Egyptian

g. Three Face Medallion

a. Harmony with Panelled font

b. Harmony with Round font

c. Thousand Eye

d. Bradford

e. Apollo

f. Apollo

The two lamps, Harmony with Panelled Font (a) and Harmony with Round Font (b), have bases of the same design. Both lamps have a primitive quality and the three-mold round font has a dimpled surface from the chisel marks in the mold. The two-mold Panelled Font is similar to the Dominion Panel font. These lamps appear to be circa 1880.

Lamps (c), (d), (e), and (f) were all made by Adams & Company of Pittsburgh, Pa. The well-known Thousand Eye pattern (c) is also shown in the 1885 Henry & Nathan Russell catalogue with a Beaded Lattice Font. The Russell advertisement notes the lamp came with an illuminator and 7″ shade. This refers to the Ives combination chimney shade. The plain font of Bradford (d) is the same shape as the Thousand Eye, and the bases have the same design.

Lamps (e) and (f) include the Adams Apollo design, and both are essentially the same shape. They were made in blue, amber and canary, now known as vaseline. The frosted surface of (e) often had a hand-painted design. Both Thousand Eye and Apollo are well-known tableware patterns. Sizes are: (a) 8″, (b) 8-3/4″, (c) 12-3/8″, (d) 7-1/2″, (e) 11-7/8″, and (f) 7-3/8″.

The lamps on this page relate from top to bottom. The missing links to connect the top two lamps (g) and (i) to the bottom one (k) are in the Ford Museum. Because each lamp involves many designs, I have chosen the name Carlisle for all, and a number for each. The footed hand lamp (g) and the stand lamp (i) are both Carlisle 1. At the Ford Museum is a lamp Carlisle 2, with an unusual patterned amber hollow square stem, and the Carlisle 1 font. The Carlisle 3 lamp has the patterned amber square hollow stem, and the font of (k), Carlisle 4. It is quite possible that parts of these busy patterns will one day relate these lamps to other lamps, or patterned glass.

The Co-Operative Flint Glass Company, Limited, of Beaver Falls, Pa. 1894 advertisement illustrated in Kamm 6 shows lamp (j) Flute and Block with Beaded Diamond Base. A plain font stand lamp and footed hand lamp are also shown with the Beaded Diamond Base. The stand lamps were made in five sizes.

The Flute and Block lamp (h) and the Ava Font with Diamond Base (l) are clearly related to lamp (j). Sizes are: (g) 4-7/8", (h) 9-1/4", (i) 7-1/2", (j) 8-1/2", (k) 7-3/8", and (l) 9-3/4".

g. Carlisle 1

h. Flute and Block

i. Carlisle 1

j. Flute and Block with Beaded Diamond Base

k. Carlisle 4

l. Ava Font with Diamond Base

a. Eyebrow

b. Torch and Wreath

c. Eclipse Patterned

d. Eclipse Plain

e. Claudia

f. Claude

Lamps (a) and (b) have interesting fonts, and their bases have the same pattern. The original collar of Eyebrow (a) has been replaced. It may have been the 1894 patented clinch type like that on Torch and Wreath (b).

Eclipse Patterned (c) and Eclipse Plain (d) were made on an automatic, or semi-automatic lamp-making machine. Claudia (e) and Claude (f) have had their stems pressed in a mold of the same design. The plunger used with (f) has pressed a design on the underside of the base. Sizes are: (a) 9″, (b) 8-1/8″, (c) 10-1/8″, (d) 10-1/8″, (e) 9-5/8″, and (f) 9-7/8″.

The stand lamp bases shown on this page are all the same design. Lamp (h) Sharon Panel is really the squat form of lamp (k). The fonts of these two lamps were made in a two-part mold. The lower part of the Rib Font (l) has a mold seam at each corner, from the beading at the shoulder to the stem. The shoulder itself has two mold seams from the collar to the beaded edge.

The flat hand lamp (i) appears to match the Sharon stand lamps, and the lamp (j) with the high shoulder is a variation, probably made by another company. These lamps appear to be circa 1900. Sizes are: (h) 8-1/8″, (i) 3″, (j) 3-1/4″, (k) 10″, and (l) 8-7/8″.

h. Sharon Panel

i. Sharon Panel

j. Sharon Panel

k. Sharon Panel

l. Sharon Panel Base with Rib Font

a. L Buttons and Bows 1.
   R Buttons and Bows 2.

The left lamp in the picture (a) has been given the name Buttons and Bows in the Nova Scotia Museum book on Nova Scotia Glass. It is shown beside one referred to as Nova Scotia Diamond, which is the same lamp as the one called Tudor shown in the section on La Belle and Central Glass. The molds were probably made in the United States. The glass quality of the lamps Buttons and Bows is only fair, and that of the Tudor lamp is very good.

In picture (b) the left lamp is Saturn and the right one is Saturn Ribbed. The Saturn footed hand lamp (c) has an unusual handle. Sizes are: (a) left 8-3/4″, right 9-3/8″, (b) both lamps are 7-1/4″ and (c) 4-3/4″.

b. L Saturn
   R Saturn Ribbed

c. Saturn

Both Dunlop lamps in picture (d) are attractive. The shoulder of the left lamp rises sharply to the collar. The right lamp, Dunlop with Frame and Sprig has mold seams at each corner from the collar to the stem.

The stem and base of Humber (e) has the plain basic shape of many lamps. Two of these are shown in picture (f). The left one is Humber with Plus Base and Rose Font, and the right one is Humber with Plus Base and Quatrefoil Font. I have seen the latter with the area around the quatrefoils frosted. Other Humber lamps have been seen in larger sizes with clear designs on a frosted font. Sizes are: (d) left 9″, right 9-5/8″, (e) 7-1/8″, and (f) left 8″ and right 7-7/8″.

d. L Dunlop
   R Dunlop with Frame and Sprig

e. Humber

f. L Humber with Plus Base and Rose Font   R Humber with Plus Base and Quatrefoil Font

Lamps 1880-1900

Craig ▷

In placing lamps into a limited time slot, the margin of error is greater at the termination dates. In most instances, design characteristics and quality are the sole basis for the decision to assign a date. With those clustered around the chosen termination date, the decision as to which side of these dates to place each lamp becomes guesswork. Future research will necessitate moving lamps in and out of their placement of time and relationship.

Lamp (a) Hanson is simple and graceful with an 1894 patent clinch collar. Opaque fonts have the advantage of hiding dirty oil, and the disadvantage of not indicating when it is necessary to refill. Gay Opalescent (b) has a pale yellow font, and a collar with the 1875 and 76 patent date. The combination of an art glass font with a frosted base is unusual.

The embossed flower design on the base of Primrose (c) is repeated on the white opalescent font. Joining the font and stem has been accomplished by unusual means. Inside the font there is a raised knob about half an inch high in the opalescent patterned glass. This is nearly obscure, but there does appear to be metal underneath. It would appear that the stem is threaded or cemented to a metal socket or thimble, however it may have to wait for a broken specimen to provide the answer. Like (a) the collar is clinched on without cement. Occasionally a photograph accentuates details which have previously escaped notice. The line down the stem of lamp (d) Gaiety, prompted further examination which revealed a wisp of opalescent glass in the center. The pressed design of the base, and the light, free-flowing opalescent design rather casually applied, contribute to making this a dainty little lamp.

Opposite, the pine whatnot with original brown paint and leather trim from Quebec, creates a dramatic background for the small opalescent lamp without a handle. The glass thickness varies greatly from collar to mid-font giving an unusual effect against strong light. Sizes are: (a) 9″ to the collar, (b) 8-1/4″, (c) 10-1/4″, (d) 7-1/4″, and opposite 4-1/2″.

a. Hanson

b. Gay Opalescent

c. Primrose

d. Gaiety

The most recent information on the Bullseye lamp is contained in an article by Janet Holmes of the Royal Ontario Museum, included in The Book of Canadian Antiques. This states lamps with clear fonts and blue opaque glass stems were from the Diamond Glass Company, Montreal, 1890 to 1902, and that all-colorless glass Bullseye lamps were made by the Dominion Glass Company, Montreal, from 1913 to about 1925. Catalogue pages in Gerald Stevens' book show these lamps as being available from the Diamond Glass Company with an Opal foot and with an Emerald foot. There is also an illustration from the Dominion Glass catalogue showing three sizes of stand lamps, a flat hand lamp and a footed hand lamp, like lamp (f).

My observations on Bullseye lamps include, the fine sharp detail on lamps with rows of V's on the stem, on the footed hand lamps (d) and (e), on all-green or opaque-base lamps, and on many all-clear glass lamps. Soft or rounded pattern detail appears only on clear glass lamps. There is an abundance of the attractive all-green Bullseye lamps in types (a), (b), and (d), and one like (e) with a green base and handle, and a colorless font is at the Royal Ontario Museum. Possibly the fine detailed and colored Bullseyes are the earlier types. It is not known if this pattern was also made in the United States, or why three types of handles were made. Variations exist in the proportions of the stems, and in some fonts. Sizes are: (a) 3-1/8″, (b) 9″, (c) 8″, (d) 5-3/8″, (e) 5-3/4″, and (f) 5-3/4″.

a. Bullseye Flat Hand

b. Bullseye Fine Detail

c. Bullseye Soft Detail

d. Bullseye Safety Handle

e. Bullseye Loop Handle

f. Bullseye Base Handle

Gerald Stevens and Janet Holmes both describe lamps (g), (i), and (k) as Canadian Drape, a product of the Burlington Glass Company, Hamilton, Ontario. Fragments of this lamp have been found at the site of this factory, and the custom-molded font for a Canadian patent in 1885 was made with this base. (See the Patent Lamps section.) Current opinion is that molds used at Burlington were designed and made elsewhere, probably in the United States. Variations exist in the glass quality and in the drape itself. On some, the drape is smooth, and on others tiny flowers are shown against a fine scale-like background. On some examples a cable design is on the underside of the four base scallops which are slightly above the four scallops of the feet.

Lamp (h) Squirrel is a pattern which is similar to, but not exactly like the many other squirrel patterns on goblets. Alva Rib Band (j) with a dated 1875 and 76 collar was made with a light blue font with opalescent stripes.

Fragments of the Butterfly and Anchor lamp (l) were also found at the Burlington site. The font is sometimes frosted, and a frosted stem and base have been seen with a plain font. Sizes are: (g) 9-1/2", (h) 8-3/4", (i) 9", (j) 7-3/8", (k) 12-1/4", and (l) 11-5/8".

g. Canadian Drape Etched

h. Squirrel

i. Canadian Drape

j. Alva Rib Band

k. Canadian Drape

l. Butterfly and Anchor

a. Rib Band and Ladder

The pattern, Rib Band and Ladder (a), is very unusual. It bears no relationship or similarity to any other lamps in this book. The glass is very good quality and heavy, and the lamps appear to have been made by an automatic process. It is possible a flat hand lamp was also made. Hackle (b), has a plain font which combines well with the fancy base. The unusual stem pattern here is carried to the font in the stand lamp form.

Lamp (c), Cox is a type which was made in the 90's, and in this century. These inexpensive lamps were sold in general stores and catalogues. The handle on lamp (d), Nita is attached to the font and base. The top of handle (e), Lisa is attached to a thin strip of glass which continues to the base. This is another form of safety handle, in which the handle and base are a single unit providing a holder for the font. Sizes are: (a) left 8-1/8″, right 6-5/8″, (b) 4-5/8″, (c) 4-3/4″, (d) 4-5/8″, and (e) 4-1/8″.

b. Hackle

c. Cox

d. Nita

e. Lisa

Columbia (f) is a pattern made in a wide range of tableware pieces. Ruby stain or gold often decorated the tableware, and perhaps some lamps were finished this way too. Erskine Rib (g) is an amusing example of an attempt to fuse together a font and handle whose dimensions were not compatible. The profile of each indicates they were intended for each other, and a little coaxing in the plastic state produced this lopsided result. The collar has been adjusted to compensate for the angle of the font.

Lamp (h) Angela has a yellow opalescent font and a molded handle. This is essentially the same lamp as shown in the color section, although the pattern pressed on the underside is different. Snowdon (i) has an applied handle with an attractive toolmark. This lamp is from the Boston area. The collar is the patented 1876 clinch type with the design on the shoulder.

Lowell Loop (j) is an exceptionally large hand lamp in good quality glass. It is reported to have been made in colored glass also. Sizes are: (f) 5-3/4″, (g) 4-1/8″, (h) 4-3/4″, (i) 4-1/2″, and (j) 6-1/4″.

f. Columbia

g. Erskine Rib

h. Angela

i. Snowdon

j. Lowell Loop

a. Erin Fan

b. Raglan Rib

c. Erin Fan

d. Raglan Rib

e. Octavia

f. One Piece Swirl Band

Erin Fan, (a) in clear, and (c) in green, is a design with characteristics which have been compared with three other patterns. One is Whitten, shown in Metz II, one is Feather Duster shown in Revi and the other is the Bullseye lamp included in this section. The latter two are made in a green color which closely resembles the Erin Fan green. Raglan Rib (b) and (d) is a pleasantly proportioned lamp. The continuity of patterns repeated on font, stem and base, almost always results in an attractive lamp. Adapting a single pattern to each part of the lamp suggests a more carefully thought out total product. This is evident in Octavia (e) a later lamp made apparently by a completely automated process.

One Piece Swirl Band (f) is another "one piece" lamp. This pattern of the 90's is similar to goblets of that period. Sizes are: (a) 3″, (b) 5-1/4″, (c) 9-5/8″, (d) 9″, (e) 8-1/2″, and (f) 8-1/2″.

Cinderella (g) and Grace (h) are examples of glass patterns made to simulate cut glass. Although cut glass certainly requires more skill, pressed glass imitations of this 1890 to 1910 period are often in greater demand. It is more in keeping with today's casual living to relate to glassware of everyday use from the past, than to desire the precision of crystal skillfully made by craftsmen for the elite. Collars on these two lamps have a band of dots around the middle.

Lamps (i) Logan and (j) Bolton, are similar types having plain fonts and rather elaborate stembases. The collar on lamp (k) Allenby is the same collar as on (g) and (h). The diamond design pressed on the underside gives interest to the simple shape and smooth exterior. Calumet (l) is another simple but well-proportioned lamp. It may be that all of these lamps were made in the 90's, although (i), (j), and (l) could have been made in the 80's. Sizes are: (g) 8-3/8″, (h) 9-1/4″, (i) 8-1/2″, (j) 10″, (k) 8-3/8″, and (l) 8-3/4″.

g. Cinderella

h. Grace

i. Logan

j. Bolton

k. Allenby

l. Calumet

a. Poppy

b. Stipple and Leaf

c. Arms Akimbo

d. Convex Window

e. Plain Six Panel

f. Eileen

(a). Leaves and flowers swirl around this lamp from collar to base. The Poppy pattern in high relief on heavy glass is perhaps more suggestive of products of the 1920's, but the design seems to be better thought out. The collar is clinched on without cement. Stipple and Leaf (b) has the pattern pressed on the outside of the font and the underside of the base.

Arms Akimbo (c) may be easily passed from hand to hand. To carry the lamp I find four fingers will fit comfortably inside the handle. The number three collar is rarely seen on glass lamps, particularly ones as small as this. The Convex Window lamp (d) comes in a taller size with more slender proportions.

(e) Plain Six Panel is shown in Marcelle Bond's book on Albany Glass. Catalogue pages of the Indiana Glass Factory at Dunkirk, which are said to be from 1907 through the depression years, show this lamp with a matching chimney. It is shown beside a Princess Feather lamp which was known to have been produced in the 90's, so presumably this was also an earlier design. Eileen (f) is an unsophisticated cottage or farm type lamp that is difficult to date.

Opposite, Leaf and Jewel at first glance appears to have an upside down font. The jewel however is also at the bottom of the pattern on the stem, and no doubt the font is in the right position. The font of the footed hand lamp is ribbed inside, and a stippled flower and leaf pattern is pressed on the underside of the base. Sizes are: (a) 8-1/8″, (b) 7-5/8″, (c) 8-5/8″, (d) 8-1/8″, (e) 10-1/4″, and (f) 8″. Opposite left 9″ and right 5-1/2″.

Leaf and Jewel ▷

a. Picture Frame

This group presents an assortment of rather unique lamps. The Picture Frame lamp (a) has a thin sheet of glass in the oval. A picture could be pasted on either side of this, although nothing would protect it from spilled oil. The Lighthouse lamp (b) is complete with windows, door, and a rope ladder.

Hand and Torch (c) is one of two hand stem lamps seen by the author. The other hand lamp has a stem which is also seen on a cake plate. The Stippled Fishscale and Rib lamp (d) has a font which is smooth on the outside and ribbed inside. Sizes are: (a) 9-1/8″, (b) 9″, (c) 8-3/4″, and (d) 9-1/4″.

b. Lighthouse

c. Hand and Torch

d. Stippled Fishscale and Rib

Princess Feather (e), (f), and (i) was one of the fanciest lamps produced. This name is widely accepted for this lamp, as well as for the entirely different tableware pattern. One of the most popular lamps today, it was no doubt a "best seller" from the beginning. The finely detailed and deeply embossed pattern has an almost frothy look, particularly in clear glass. In Kamm 6 an 1894 catalogue page from the Consolidated Lamp and Glass Co., Coraopolis, Pa. advertised this lamp. In Bond's book on Albany Glass, catalogue pages ranging from 1907 through the depression years, of the Indiana Glass Factory at Dunkirk, show a heavy squat version of this lamp. Recent, and perhaps current reproductions, have been seen in the large size in clear and colors, and in the squat size in blue and perhaps other colors. The latter are easily recognized by a coarse appearance, and by the presence of a flower on the font. The early varieties were made in clear and opaque green, in the squat form like the opaque white (i), and in the clear base with a pink cased font shown in the color section. The cased font is reported to have come in blue, and possibly yellow.

e. Princess Feather

The tall form (f) was made in clear, pale green, cobalt blue, and probably other colors. The cobalt blue commands a high price and a potential purchase should be examined carefully. I am told the reproductions are difficult to distinguish. I have seen only one example of the opaque turquoise Princess Feather lamp, with the wide matching shade. I hope one day to be able to examine it further, and perhaps photograph it. It is possible the well-defined detail on it is the same as on the squat pale green lamp. This has a small scroll extending from the reversed ram's horn part of the design on the font.

Prince Edward (g) and (h) is similar to Princess Feather in design, and in the colors available. They both have a squat form in opaque white and both come with clear bases and cased fonts. Sizes are: (e) 5-3/4″, (f) 8″, (g) 9-5/8″, (h) left 3-5/8″, right 9″, and (i) 9-1/2″. The author has a 10-3/8″ cobalt blue Princess Feather and a 10-3/8″ green Prince Edward.

f. Princess Feather

g. Prince Edward

h. Prince Edward

i. Princess Feather

a. Coolidge Drape

b. Beaded 101

c. Clustered Fans

d. Broad Inverted Flute

e. Grange Twelve Panel

f. Sunlight

g. Allover Herringbone

h. Markham Swirl Band

i. Flat Oval Window

j. Florence

Coolidge Drape (a) is the flat hand form of those pictured opposite. The circular flipped up applied handle is like that on the Fishscale flat hand lamp. According to Metz, this lamp is named because of its presence on a table in a photograph, taken on the occasion of President Coolidge taking the oath of office. This was at his grandfather's farm, after President Harding's sudden death. It was made in cobalt blue. The lamps opposite are pale amber, and a pale green was also made.

Beaded 101 (b) was also made in a stand lamp, and in tableware pieces. The pointed handle on Clustered Fans (c) and on many other flat hand lamps provides a more secure grip. Broad Inverted Flute (d), with excellent quality glass, has a clinched collar cemented on. The smooth interior and pontil mark on the bottom suggest it was pressed upside down. The Grange Twelve Panel (e) is similar to many lamps of the 90's. The base of the Sunlight font (f) screws into the tin saucer holder, which has traces of blue paint.

Allover Herringbone (g) with a reeded handle is a light cranberry, but has been seen in a deeper color. The Markham Swirl Band (h) has a collar with an oval band. Flat Oval Window (i) like others on this page may also have been made in a stand lamp. The gold decorated Florence (j) is white, shading to deep blue cased glass, with a reeded handle. The Coolidge Drape lamps opposite are described above. Sizes are: (a) 3-1/4″, (b) 3-3/8″, (c) 3″, (d) 3-1/8″, (e) 3-1/8″, (f) 2-7/8″, (g) 3-1/4″, (h) 3-1/2″, (i) 3-1/2″, (j) 4-3/8″, opposite left 10-1/4″, right 5-7/8″.

Coolidge Drape ▷

a. Rosette and Diamond Band

b. Peacock Feather

All the lamps on this page have fonts fused to the stems. Rosette and Diamond Band (a) has an unusual base, in that the stem pattern is molded on the outside, and the base pattern is molded on the underside. Revi notes the Peacock Feather pattern (b) originally called Georgia, was made circa 1895. It was manufactured by the United States Glass Company until 1907. Blue lamps were also made. Fandango (c) is a busy pattern with the base and stem pattern pressed on the underside. Fan Band (d) also has the base pattern pressed on the underside.

Pearl Loop (e) and Pearl Panel (f) have bead patterns which continue from the top of the fonts to the bottom of the bases. Sizes are: (a) 7-3/8", (b) 8-1/4", (c) 7-1/4", (d) 9-5/8", (e) 7-3/8", and (f) 8-1/8".

c. Fandango

d. Fan Band

e. Pearl Loop

f. Pearl Panel

In lamp (g) Dogtooth, a serrated line and the dogtooth design appear on the font and base. The base pattern on the underside also has a circle of beads. Scalloped Panel (h) repeats the design in an interesting manner on the stem. Match Holder Base (i) has two indentations on the base for holding matches, and a roughened surface adjacent to it. This serves as a match striker. The same stem and base has been seen in blue, combined with a plain font having a few horizontal rings. The glass quality of (j) Epaulet is excellent but not leaded. This is typical of the mid 1890's.

The unusual pattern Bat and Fan (k) has an appropriate, pleasantly proportioned stem and base. Garfield (l) is so named because the stem and base are the same as seen with the Garfield Drape cake plate. The font was made in a two-part mold. Sizes are: (g) 7-1/4″, (h) 7-1/2″, (i) 8″, (j) 7-3/4″, (k) 7-3/4″, and (l) 8-1/2″.

g. Dogtooth

h. Scalloped Panel

i. Match Holder Base

j. Epaulet

k. Bat and Fan

l. Garfield

a. Fancy Panel

b. Fickle Block

c. Britannic

d. Fostoria Swirl

e. Plain Footed Saucer

The top three lamps on this page are typical of designs popular in the 1890's. Their handles are also typical of those used at that time. Fancy Panel (a) has the pattern continued on the underside of the base. This provides a smooth surface upon which to perch the rather large handle. Fickle Block (b) most closely resembles the goblet pictured in Metz II. This is said to have been made in Pennsylvania in 1893. Similar patterns are shown in Millard and Kamm, but they appear to be slightly different. In Kamm 6 Plate 98, the pattern (c) Britannic is shown on a page of an 1894 trade catalogue of the McKee Glass Company. The patterns they show are described as "prescut" glass. This referred to the popular pressed patterns which imitated cut lead glass. Fostoria Swirl (d) is named for the manufacturer. This pattern was featured on the cover of the trade journal China Glass & Lamps on May 4th, 1892. Flat hand lamps and stand lamps were also made in this pattern. The practical Plain Footed Saucer lamp (e) has a simple shape and very pleasing proportions.

The two lamps opposite are further examples of pressed glass patterns designed to imitate cut glass. Both these lamps have patterns deeply impressed in excellent quality glass, and both have clinch collars cemented on. Like Fickle Block above, many patterns of the 1890's closely resemble the left lamp, Diamond Sawtooth and Sheaf. The collar on the large banquet lamp, Clarissa, is patent dated 1876, and has a design stamped on its shoulder to help it adhere to the cement. Sizes are: (a) 5-1/8″, (b) 5-1/4″, (c) 4-7/8″, (d) 5-3/8″, (e) 5-7/8″, and opposite left 3-1/4″ and right 14-3/4″.

Left—Diamond Sawtooth and Sheaf ▷
Right—Clarissa

a. Inverted Thumbprint and Prism Stem

b. Sawtooth and Bar Panel

c. Herringbone Band

d. Waffle Cubes

e. Vera

f. Stanbury

The Inverted Thumbprint and Prism Stem (a) is a lovely deep blue color. Sawtooth Bar and Panel (b) is a well-proportioned lamp with very good quality glass. Lamp (c) Herringbone Band has a grey tint which makes the bold pattern appear even more pronounced. The pattern of Waffle Cubes (d) suggests the square candies in the Christmas hard candy mixes. Vera (e) is a green glass lamp with an attractive stem, and Stanbury (f) is amber. Opposite are Sheldon Swirl lamps. The left one has a colorless font and a black stem with a leaf pattern. The right lamp has a pale yellow font with opalescent stripes. Other colors were likely made. Sizes are: (a) 9-1/2", (b) 9", (c) 9", (d) 9", (e) 7-5/8", (f) 10", and opposite the left lamp is 8-3/4" and the right lamp 5-3/4".

Sheldon Swirl ▷

a. Belmont

b. Rounded Hobnail Band

c. Corner Windows

d. Three Panelled Two Panel

e. Rib and Bubble Stem

f. Bubble Stem

An advertisement for Belmont Glass Works of Bellaire, Ohio, in Kamm 6 shows the foot on Belmont (a) combined with pieces of their No. 100 ware. The plain font allows the attractive base to dominate, whereas it is almost lost with the other exceptionally busy pieces. This lamp was amber. With every collection involving quantities of glass, accidents are inevitable. It was the cat.

The hobnails on Rounded Hobnail Band (b) are separated and staggered as opposed to the arrangement of those on the Thousand Eye lamp. This creates a different effect with perhaps more sparkle in this lamp. The base is amber and the font clear. Corner Window (c) is a deep amber color. The Three Panelled Two Panel lamp (d) is shown in vaseline in the color section. This lamp, so named because it has three panels of the Adams & Company Two Panel pattern, is also seen in pale green, blue and amber, and in other sizes.

Hollow stems were often intended to contain dried flowers. The knop on Rib and Bubble Stem (e) is stained yellow, and that of Bubble Stem (f) is clear. Sizes are: (a) 8-7/8″, (b) 8-1/2″, (c) 9″, (d) 8-3/4″, (e) 8″, and (f) 9-1/2″.

The font of Salem Swirl Band (g) is similar to Fostoria Swirl except for the width of the center plain section. Heavy excellent quality glass is compatible with the simple design of Rib and Bead Rings (h). This type of pattern enhances the quality of the glass, and vice-versa. The pattern Diamond Pendants (i) has pointed diamonds.

Hatched Window (j) has a hatched design repeated on the base. This is pressed on the underside. The glass of Frosted Birds (k) has a charcoal tint. In addition to the font, the stem and base of this lamp were also blown. While this type of lamp is generally associated with European manufacture, it is quite certain some were made in North America. Reproduction lamps of this type abound, with primitive quality glass in a variety of colors.

The Morning Glory font (l) was often combined with composite lamps. It has a threaded peg which screws into a metal socket, which in this case was cemented into the metal stem section. This rusted stem advertised spices, and perhaps the lamp was given to merchants for advertising purposes. The glass stem and base have been seen with all-glass lamps having a different font. Sizes are: (g) 9-1/8″, (h) 9-1/4″, (i) 9-7/8″, (j) 9-5/8″, (k) 9-1/4″, and (l) 12-1/4″.

g. Salem Swirl Band

h. Rib and Bead Rings

i. Diamond Pendants

j. Hatched Window

k. Frosted Birds

l. Morning Glory Font

a. Scalloped Ribbon Band

b. Stained Petals

c. Famous

d. Inverted Thumbprint and Fan Base

e. Margo

f. Royal Rib

Scalloped Ribbon Band (a) has a band of blue painted on the surface. The pattern resembles the Scalloped Tape pattern in Kamm 2. Stained Petals (b) has been seen in two sizes, and with blue or red stain. The stain is usually thin and worn. The Co-Operative Flint Glass Company Ltd. of Beaver Falls, Pennsylvania, advertised the pattern (c), which they called Famous, in 1899. The advertisement noted that the design was patented January 18th, 1898.

Inverted Thumbprint and Fan Base (d) is a lamp with a busy design, made in good quality glass. The 12 panelled lamp Margo (e) has a base with four large scallops, and a pattern pressed on the underside. Royal Rib (f) has a rather small base, but the ribbed stem and font are a good combination.

Torpedo, opposite, is a pattern well suited to lamps, and handsome in other pieces of very good quality tableware. An advertisement of 1899, reproduced in Kamm 6, Plate 17, shows this pattern was made by Thompson Glass Co. Limited, Union Town, Pa. Sizes are: (a) 7-1/4″, (b) 8-1/4″, (c) 7-3/4″, (d) 8-1/8″, (e) 8-1/2″, and (f) 7-3/4″. Opposite, left to right 3-1/4″, 5-7/8″, and 5-1/2″.

Torpedo ▷

a. Poppy Band

b. Pickard

c. Nosegay

d. Oakleaf Bubble

e. Wild Rose and Bowknot

f. Gavotte

Poppy Band (a) has a geometric pattern pressed on the underside of the base. This pattern was also made in a stand lamp. The collar on lamp (b) Pickard, is clinched on without cement. This lamp has a stippled leaf and flower design pressed on the underside, and the flat hand lamp in this pattern has an applied handle. The pattern on the base of Nosegay (c) is pressed on the underside. Oakleaf Bubble (d) has the design pressed on the outside of the font, and the underside of the base. This base has also been seen combined with another font.

The Boyd book on Greentown Glass illustrates three Wild Rose & Bowknot lamps (e). Made in Indiana, these lamps are shown in what is described as chocolate, (a very light chocolate), opaque glass, and in colorless glass combined with a chocolate base. Gavotte (f) has a pattern pressed on the underside of the base. This unusual design bears no relationship to the stem or font.

Opposite are two lamps in the attractive pattern Janice. A larger stand lamp, and blue lamp have also been seen. Sizes are: (a) 6-1/4″, (b) 6″, (c) 8-1/2″, (d) 7-7/8″, (e) 8-1/4″, and (f) 8-1/4″. Opposite, left 5-5/8″ and right 8-3/8″.

Janice ▷

The pink lamp Florette (a) is a pattern that was made in cased glass by the Consolidated Lamp & Glass Company of Pittsburgh, Pa. Kamm 6, Plate 81, shows an advertisement from an 1894 issue of the trade journal China Glass and Lamps. The lamp shown with others of similar elongated proportions, has the adornment of a large silk and lace flounced shade. Saltshakers and miniature lamps were made in various colors in this pattern. All-glass lamps, of broader proportion, have been seen with clear bases, and with pink or yellow cased fonts. The Diamond Triumph lamp (b) has similar proportions to Florette and was probably decked out with a silk shade also.

Opposite, the lamp Paula, has a blown font, stem and base, of opalescent white glass. The collar, with the oval band, is most frequently seen on lamps made in the 80's and 90's. The lower portion of the Ives shade has a pattern similar to the Canadian pattern. Sizes are: (a) 11-1/4″, (b) approx. 11″, and opposite, 9-5/8″ to the top of the collar.

a. Florette   b. Diamond Triumph   Paula ▷

a. Carleton Medallion

b. Ladybug

c. Heavy Bullseye Band

d. Beaded Drape Panel and Francis Base

e. Swirled Rosettes

f. Pinwheel

The adaptation of the Carleton Medallion pattern (a) to the stem, has produced an interesting triangular stem. This attractive lamp has very good quality glass. Ladybug (b) repeats the design on font, stem and base. The Heavy Bullseye Band (c) banquet lamp is indeed very thick and heavy with fair quality glass.

The 1894 patented clinch collar on Beaded Drape Panel and Francis Base (d) places its manufacture after that date. The charcoal tint and thin stippled glass font are inclined to give it the appearance of an earlier lamp. Belknap shows a squat version in opaque white glass with a poppy on the font, and another pattern on a clear glass font has been seen combined with the base illustrated here.

Swirled Rosettes (e) has a base which is like that shown with Diamond Pendants. Pinwheel (f) is a bold distinctive pattern with the design pressed on the underside of the base. Sizes are: (a) 10-5/8″, (b) 9-7/8″, (c) 13″, (d) 10″, (e) 8-1/2″, and (f) 10″.

The all-glass lamps on this page are the "one piece" type, without horizontal mold marks from shoulder to base, and without any mold marks on the shoulder itself. Pioneer's Victoria (g) was a tableware pattern manufactured by the Pioneer Glass Company Ltd. of Pittsburgh, Pa. This design was patented on November 24th, 1891 by Julius Proeger of Greensburgh, Pa., for a period of three and a half years. Lamp (h) is Depressed Jewel Band and lamp (i) is Center Medallion with the vertical mold marks cleverly concealed in the pattern, at the corners of the stem and base. This pattern is shown in Metz II. The Daisy and Button One Piece (j) is a handsome clearly molded version of this popular pattern. Excellent quality glass is found in lamps (h), (i), and (j).

Cantata (k) has a slight pink tint. Lamp (l) is a factory conversion to electricity. This One Piece Flute lamp, in black opaque glass, had the hole for an electric cord molded when manufactured, rather than drilled later. This lamp was also made for kerosene in clear glass without the hole.

It is difficult to determine whether the shoulders of these lamps were drawn into the collar, or whether they were pressed separately and fused on. Sizes are: (g) 8″, (h) 8-1/2″, (i) 8-3/8″, (j) 10-1/8″, (k) 8-7/8″, and (l) 8-7/8″.

g. Pioneer's Victoria

h. Depressed Jewel Band

i. Center Medallion

j. Daisy and Button One Piece

k. Cantata

l. One Piece Flute

a. *Pointed Panel One Piece*

b. *Thumbprint One Piece*

c. *Dart*

d. *One Piece Ruby*

e. *Duncan Bar Rayed Panel*

f. *Duncan Bar Panel*

Pointed Panel One Piece (a) is another lamp of this type with very good to excellent quality glass. The Thumbprint One Piece (b) has been seen tagged as a Lomax lamp by dealers. A pointed bubble clearly indicates the top was drawn into the collar, and the flange is tooled upwards as in the 1870 patent. On the other hand the indentations on this lamp are round, and on the Lomax Vienna lamp they are clearly ovoidal. Lomax also made pressed lamps with continuous seams from base to shoulder but these were always dated. I think Lomax type is a safe description.

The Dart pattern (c) is illustrated in Metz I and Kamm 3 and 4. The simple design repeated four times on the font closely resembles One Piece Ruby (d). La Belle's Ruby, designed by Andrew Baggs, was patented in 1878 and its significant motif is the same as on this lamp.

Duncan Bar Rayed Panel (e) and Duncan Bar Panel (f) are lamps made by Geo. Duncan's Sons and Company, Washington, Pa., in 1893. All lamps on this page and those opposite are the "one piece" type.

The group opposite illustrates four sizes in the Quartered Block pattern. At least three other sizes were made. Sizes are: (a) 8-7/8″, (b) 9-3/8″, (c) 9-5/8″, (d) 9-1/8″, (e) 7-1/2″, (f) 9″, and opposite, left to right 6″, 8″, 3-3/8″, and 7-1/2″.

Quartered Block ▷

Three Face (a) is a well-known popular pattern, and the lamp is quite spectacular. The design was patented by John Ernest Miller in 1878, and it was made by George Duncan & Sons of Pittsburgh, Pa. Several glass books have descriptions of this pattern and its manufacturer. Ruth Webb Lee notes the lamp was made with the patterned font illustrated here, and with a plain round font. She mentions also that the lamp was made in amethyst.

Several references have been made regarding reproductions of Three Face lamps, but they do not state which type was reproduced or whether they both were. The glass quality of this lamp, with its minor flaws and striations, and a silky smooth frosting are not likely to be found in a reproduction. In addition, this lamp has the 1876 patent dated collar with the design on the shoulder. Perhaps that was the only one used on this lamp. The interesting flat hand lamp Ida (b) has a streak of olive green glass in the font. Sizes are: 11-3/4″ and (b) 3-3/4″.

The Conglomerate lamp (c) is shown as it was acquired by a picker. I believe it is an honest attempt to continue the use of a lamp that started out in the early 1860's. The beautiful clear lead

a. Duncan Three Face

b. Ida

glass font has a Honeycomb with Scallop pattern, and the slate base is painted black. These two parts are characteristic of the early 1860's. The font has a small opening to take a No. 1 collar and the larger No. 2 replacement collar made after 1876 was likely used to be more in keeping with the proportions of the stem. The original stem would have been a short brass one, and this later addition was the type used on composite lamps of the 1880's, with an iron base. The Ives shade was a type used from the late 70's on. The total effect is much more pleasing than is usually the case when parts made at different periods of time are combined. It is 22-1/2″ to the top of the shade.

The strange Tube Lamp (d) has a tin sleeve which fits over the iron post on the base. This was connected to the tin tube which fits inside the glass tube in the font. The glass tube is open beside the collar, and at the bottom of the font. The vertical iron prongs secured the base inside the stem which was completely filled with plaster. Although it is not apparent in the photograph the fancy cast iron base rests on a spring attached to a plain base, which is connected to the prongs. This lamp, from Des Moines, Iowa, is a puzzle in every respect.

c. Conglomerate

d. Tube Lamp

Lamps 1900-

a. *Eagle Container Base*

b. *Deanna*

c. *Colonial*

d. *Ella*

e. *Rib and Plume*

f. *Irene*

g. *Greek Key*

Most of the lamps in this section may be positively attributed to this century, although some designs may have been manufactured in the late 1890's. Lamp (a) has a container base, presumably for an extra supply of oil. This is topped with a metal combination cap and font holder. The Fleur-de-lis pattern is on both the font and base, and the words Eagle, Made in U.S.A. are embossed on the base. The footed hand lamp Deanna (b) is circa 1905. The next four lamps were all made in a lamp-making machine. In Gerald Stevens' book, Canadian Glass 1825-1925, reproduced catalogue pages show the pattern called Colonial (c) was made from 1913 on by the Dominion Glass Company Limited, Montreal.

The glass collars with a metal thread inside date from 1910 on. Lamp (d) is Ella and (e) is Rib and Plume. Irene (f) with a transfer design of dancing damsels, has been seen also with dancing oriental figures. The clinched collar is the 1876 patent type.

Greek Key was a popular motif for lamps throughout the kerosene period. The lamp (g) with the rakish handle is one of several of this period which used the key design. Sizes for these lamps are: (a) 9-1/8″, (b) 5-1/2″, (c) 8″, (d) 7-3/4″, (e) 8-3/8″, (f) 9-1/2″, and (g) 4-7/8″.

Bead and Petal

Bead and Petal is an attractive lamp of this century with the character of earlier lamps. The pages reproduced in Stevens' book show this mold-blown lamp was included in both the Dominion Glass Company catalogue circa 1913, and in a Jefferson Glass Company Limited of Toronto catalogue. The latter had its parent company in the United States, and perhaps catalogues from its Follansbee, West Va., or Millersburg, Ohio factories will be located one day. Lamps are left to right 9-7/8″, 5-1/2″, 9-3/8″, 3-3/8″, 11-1/4″, and 8-1/4″.

a. Peanut

All the stand lamps on this and the opposite page are the so-called "one piece" lamps made on an automatic machine. Possibly made also in the 1890's, the Peanut lamps (a) are quite plentiful today. The Ruffled Bullseye (b) and Dewdrop and Petal (c) and (d), have the collars that place their date of manufacture after 1910. The amethyst tint which occurs frequently in lamps of this period, is particularly pronounced in the thick stem of lamp (c).

Fishscale opposite is an example of a lovely pattern made on an automatic machine. Collars on these lamps are the 1894 patent clinched-on type, and the applied handle of the flat hand lamp is typical of this period. Like the Peanut, this lamp may have been made in the 1890's. Sizes for these lamps are: (a) left 3″, right 10-1/8″, (b) 7-5/8″, (c) 9-5/8″, (d) 4-1/4″, and opposite, the left lamp is 3-3/8″ and the right lamp 9-1/4″.

b. Ruffled Bullseye   c. Dewdrop and Petal   d. Dewdrop and Petal   Fishscale ▷

a. Zipper Loop

Zipper Loop Carnival glass lamps found in smoky blue and marigold, place manufacture of these lamps in this century, however they were possibly made earlier in clear glass. This is a common and popular design patterned after the Atterbury Ribbed Loop. Reproductions are now made in Marigold Carnival and possibly clear glass. Sizes for these lamps are: left 8″, right 5-1/8″.

b. Belsize

The United States Glass Company advertised the lamp (b) Belsize as one of their new lamps for 1906. This lamp, made on a lamp-making machine, has very good quality glass. The wine colored flowers which appear to have been stencilled on, show little sign of wear, although the frosted surface of the font is worn.

Hawkeye (c) was advertised by the National Glass Company in 1900 as being a product of the Ohio Flint Glass Works, at Lancaster, Ohio. Revi states this company's output was over a million lamps that year. Two other lamps with the same bases were also advertised. One with a plain font was called Badger, and one with the beading on the base repeated in an interwoven design on the font, was called Empire.

Sizes are: (b) 10-1/2″ and (c) 10-1/4″.

c. Hawkeye

United States Glass Company

The economic conditions of the time lead to the development of a merger of 18 glass companies, to form the United States Glass Company in 1891. The first catalogues of the United States Glass Company, were simply a compilation of catalogues used by member companies before the merger.

Lamps & Other Lighting Devices 1850-1906, attributes a number of lamps to the Bellaire Goblet Company on the basis of a United States Glass Company catalogue supplement. The majority of these lamp designs indicate however, that they were made earlier by Central Glass Company. The Bellaire Goblet Company was formed in 1876, whereas Central Glass Company was a much earlier company, and these particular lamps were made by them prior to 1876. Because so many of these lamps are known to have been made by Central Glass and at an earlier date, they are included with Central Glass lamps. One possible explanation for this circumstance is that the Central Glass Company had an arrangement with the Bellaire Goblet Company whereby Bellaire was allowed to include these illustrations in their catalogue, and production could have been by Central Glass or Bellaire at that time.

Through catalogue or advertisement illustrations of lamps, or of patterns used in lamps, we are able to attribute many of these lamps included here to a particular company, either when involved in the merger, or prior to that time. In these pages we see the screw socket originally patented by Atterbury in 1868. After the expiration of that patent, Hobbs Glass Company in 1891, and the United States Glass Company catalogue circa 1893, advertised lamps with a threaded screw socket connection. Other lamps illustrated here and in the section on Lamps 1880-1900, show characteristics of earlier patented manufacturing techniques of Joseph Magoun, Atterbury and George Lomax. Each of these methods produced a font without a mold mark on the shoulder. Many of these designs are bold and attractive, and indicate that the initial response to the revival of these manufacturing techniques was that of good original design and not imitation.

Towards the end of the century the use of semi-automatic blowing machines, and later fully automatic machines, produced lamps with a great range of quality. A few designs had very attractive proportions, a few showed considerable imagination, and a number of designs would probably be considered very good. Some designs were heavy and coarse and yet still with some interest and appeal. At the bottom of the scale as we approach the close of the first decade of this century, design was undeniably coarse and heavy. In the early years of this century, frosting or acid etching the surface of the lamps, and then finishing with hand painted flowers was a very popular technique. These lamps, many of which had matching painted chimneys, introduced a new and different appearance and was no doubt an attempt to conceal a coarse lamp. Throughout the entire kerosene era, there was little attempt to imitate the design, patterns or shape of lamps of preceding years. Kerosene lamps throughout this period were unique in that they were a product of the age, and rarely an imitation of any other earlier period of time. Throughout the history of electricity, how many lamps are imitations of the kerosene era, and how few are statements of the quality of the light and the tremendous range of natural and man-made materials available.

The merger to form The United States Glass Company included the following companies:

Adams & Company, Pittsburgh, Pennsylvania
Bryce Brothers, Pittsburgh, Pennsylvania
Challinor, Taylor & Co. Ltd., Tarentum, Pennsylvania
George Duncan & Sons, Pittsburgh, Pennsylvania
Richards & Hartley, Tarentum, Pennsylvania
Ripley & Company, Pittsburgh, Pennsylvania
Gillinder & Sons, Greensburg, Pennsylvania
Hobbs Glass Company, Wheeling, West Virginia
Columbia Glass Company, Findlay, Ohio
King Glass Company, Pittsburgh, Pennsylvania
O'Hara Glass Company, Pittsburgh, Pennsylvania
Bellaire Goblet Company, Findlay, Ohio
Nickel Plate Glass Company, Fostoria, Ohio
Central Glass Company, Wheeling, West Virginia
Doyle & Company, Pittsburgh, Pennsylvania
A. J. Beatty & Sons, Tiffin, Ohio
A. J. Beatty & Sons, Steubenville, Ohio
Novelty Glass Company, Fostoria, Ohio

World's Fair lamps named for the Chicago World's Fair in 1893, are advertised in the large colorful United States Glass Company lamp catalogue at the Corning Glass Museum, Corning, New York. Although the catalogue is not dated, it is reasonable to assume it to be a catalogue of 1893. Lamps pictured on this page are named in the catalogue, (a) Chicago, (b) New York, and (c) St. Louis. The name always refers to the font in the various font and base combinations in the catalogue. Colors advertised are crystal (colorless), Opal (white), blue, and amber. Lamp (a) is amber, (b) is blue, and (c) has an amber font and white base. Sizes are: (a) 11-3/8″, (b) 10-1/2″, and (c) 8-7/8″.

a. Chicago

b. New York

c. St. Louis

The Hobbs Glass Company advertised screw sockets like those on (a) and (b) just before they joined the United States Glass Co. in 1891. Lamp (a) Inverted Thumbprint in spatter glass, with the Detroit Base in end of day glass, was possibly made by them about that time.

Kings Crown (b) is shown in the circa 1893 catalogue in several sizes of footed and stand lamps. This pattern was originally made by Adams & Company. The container stem lamps (c) and (d) hold an extra supply of oil. Both top and bottom of the stem are threaded, and of course the bottom is solid. These stems are often seen in amethyst. The fonts are (c) Chicago and (d) Bent Bars.

The Chicago font opposite is screwed onto a threaded tin base. This painted base is pink, shading to a deep rose. Green, black, or copper flash are sometimes seen. Bases which have lost their paint may be buffed up with fine steel wool and waxed to give them the attractive patina of toleware. Sizes are: (a) 10-1/8″, (b) 9-1/8″, (c) 11-1/8″, (d) 11-1/8″, and opposite 8-5/8″.

a. Inverted Thumbprint font—Detroit Base

Chicago with tin base ▷

b. Kings Crown

c. Chicago with container stem

d. Bent Bars with container stem

A Tumbler in the 101 pattern is attributed by Revi to the Nickel Plate Glass Company, Fostoria, Ohio. This celery dish (a), and fruit nappies which have the same intricate design pressed on the underside of the dish, suggest there were probably other tableware pieces made. The lamps (b), (c) and (d) represent a few of the sizes. The font or base threaded pegs, are usually marked with a letter indicating a size. Lamp (b) is marked A on font and base, lamp (c) is marked D on the font, and lamp (d) is marked C on the base. This font is the Chicago font shown combined with other bases in the same catalogue. It is often seen with tin bases, but the threaded pegs on these are slightly smaller. Combinations of U.S. Glass Company fonts and bases other than those illustrated in the catalogue, may have been made at the time they were sold originally, or they may have been made later as a matter of choice, or to combine spare parts.

The pair opposite have Wavy fonts which are marked E. These lamps were often made without a frosted finish, and sometimes have an Opalescent font as shown in the color section. The old shades are a recent addition to these lamps, which have had nightly use on our dinner table for the past several months. A catalogue illustration of these lamps with a shade of the day, is shown towards the end of this section. All these lamps have the decorated dated clinch collars of the 1876 patent. Sizes are: (b) 9-1/2″, (c) 9-1/4″, (d) 11-3/8″ and opposite 15″ to the top of the collars.

a. Nickel Plate 101 Celery

b. Plain Font, Nickel Plate 101 Base

c. Plain Font, Nickel Plate 101 Base

d. Chicago Font, Nickel Plate 101 Base

Wavy Font, Frosted Nickel Plate, 101 Base ▷

a. L. Basketweave
   R.Cube and Diamond

d. Mammoth with Rose Base

b. King Melon

c. King Comet

In picture (a) Basketweave left, and Cube and Diamond right, have the same slender swirl stems. The United States Glass Company catalogue c. 1893 shows a hobnail font on the same stem and base. A footed hand lamp in the Cube and Diamond pattern is shown in the catalogue pages following. Both footed hand lamps, King Melon (b) and King Comet (c), are attributed to the King Glass Company of Pittsburgh, Pa., in the book Lamps & Other Lighting Devices, 1850-1906. Both came in different forms and sizes, including a 13″ banquet lamp. The King Melon stand lamp has a ribbed stem, and the flat hand lamp is shown with a coin dot opalescent font.

The King Comet is shown in the catalogue pages of this section, in a banquet size with a pleated and fringed shade.

The Mammoth Sewing lamp with Rose Base (d) is illustrated in a squat form in the 1909 catalogue pages following. Sizes are: (a) left 7-5/8″, right 7-1/2″, (b) 5-1/2″, (c) 5-1/8″ and (d) 11″.

Aquarius (e) and Ambrose (f) are shown on the same page of the catalogue circa 1893, and they are both described as having grove tops, and heavy feet. They do have a drip depression at the top of the font, so perhaps this should have read "groove tops." Aquarius came in amber, blue and vaseline glass. There were six sizes of stand lamps, and two sizes of footed hand lamps made. In the Henry & Nathan Russell section, the possible attribution to the Adams Glass Company is described, and the footed hand lamp is shown in the catalogue pages following. The lamp Ambrose was made in five sizes of stand lamps.

According to Kamm, the pattern Fleur-de-lis and Tassel of lamp (g), was made by the United States Glass Co. in the factory of the former Adams & Company at Pittsburgh. It was a tableware pattern made in clear and opaque white glass.

The Cross Diamond Band lamp (h) was made in different sizes in clear, blue and amber. Sizes are: (e) 8-1/8″, (f) 9″, (g) 8-1/2″ and (h) 8-3/4″.

e. Aquarius

f. Ambrose

g. Fleur-de-lis and Tassel

h. Cross Diamond Band

a. Duncan Ribbed Band

The Duncan Ribbed Band lamp (a), is typical of the lamps described as "one piece heavy" in the catalogue circa 1893. They show this lamp and the two-handled footed hand lamp form. The design on the font is the same as on a Three Face biscuit jar illustrated in the Victorian Glass Book by Lee. The Three Face lamp made by George Duncan & Sons of Pittsburgh, Pa., and the Duncan Ribbed Band lamp both have the 1876 patent dated clinch collars. Like the Westmoreland stand lamp opposite, this lamp has three mold marks from shoulder to base. The shoulder must then have been molded and fused on separately, or drawn into the collar.

The Double Arch lamp (b) is a pattern named by Kamm. Revi attributes this pattern to both the King Glass Company and to the O'Hara Glass Company. The lamp shown in the catalogue circa 1893 has three mold seams from the base to the top of the pattern on the font. It appears to have been drawn into the collar in the manner of the Joseph Magoun patents of 1847. The design, the thickness and the quality of the glass, give this lamp the appearance of those made in the 1860's.

The Thumbprint Panel lamp (c) is shown in three forms in the catalogue pages following. Removing these thick-stemmed lamps from the molds too quickly, resulted in their having a list to one side.

b. Double Arch

c. Thumbprint Panel

d. Westmoreland

Shown in the catalogue circa 1893, Westmoreland (d) is an example of the excellent quality heavy glass lamps made in the mid 90's. According to Revi, this pattern was patented by Thomas W. Mellor in 1889, and was first made by Gillinder & Sons, Philadelphia, Pa. Made in a full line of tableware, it was advertised by the United States Glass Company for many years. It was also made in a variety of night lamps with matching patterned shades. Sizes are (a) 10″, (b) 7-7/8″, (c) 10-1/8″, and (d) right 3-1/4″ and left 9″.

a. Icicle

b. Late Petal

c. Moon

d. Late Petal

e. Serrated Loop

f. Serrated Loop

The Icicle hand lamp (a) is shown in the catalogue circa 1893 in this form only. The Late Petal flat hand lamp (b) and footed hand lamp (d) may be seen with the lamps reproduced from the 1909 catalogue. It is interesting to compare the catalogue illustrations and photographs with the actual lamps to see how readily identifiable they are. These are machine-made lamps which closely resemble those made by the Dominion Glass Company in Montreal, Quebec. The latter have knops between the font and stem.

The Moon lamp (c) is shown in the 1909 catalogue as a night lamp. Reproductions of these small lamps are seen in many colors. This lamp is sometimes seen with alternate moons on the base stained red. The dark moons in the photographs are merely the effect of lighting on what is actually a clear-glass lamp. These Serrated Loop lamps (e) and (f) circa 1905 have the frosted and hand-painted treatment popular at that time, and their clinch collars are applied without cement.

The Turkey Foot lamps opposite were called Plume in the 1909 catalogue. The stems of the stand lamps are unusually smooth. These attractive machine-made lamps are often seen with an amethyst tint, and have been reported in blue. Sizes are: (a) 3-3/8″, (b) 3″, (c) 6-5/8″, (d) 6-3/8″, (e) left 9-7/8″ and right 3-3/8″, (f) 11″, and opposite left to right 3-5/8″, 8-1/2″, and 6-1/2″.   Turkey Foot ▷

The illustrations from the United States Glass Company catalogues, circa 1893 and 1909, are reproduced with the permission of the Corning Glass Museum, Corning, N.Y. In instances where only a name is given, there is currently no additional information.

1. & 2. — Foster

3. & 4. — Kings Crown Variant

These lamps closely resemble the Kings Crown tableware pattern, but differ considerably from the Kings Crown stand lamp.

5. — Kings Crown, Excelsior or Ruby Thumbprint

6. — Ava — see Late Related Lamps

7. — Fleur-de-lis and Tassel — see photographs in this section.

8. & 9. — Rowena

10. & 11. — Nail

According to Revi, this pattern was produced by Bryce Bros. before 1891, and by Ripley & Co. after 1892.

1. *Foster*

2. *Foster*

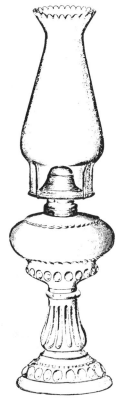

3. *Kings Crown Variant*

4. *Kings Crown Variant*

5. Kings Crown

6. Ava

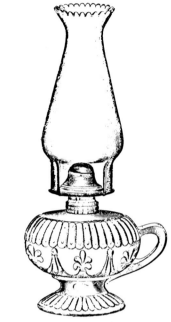

7. Fleur-de-lis and Tassel

8. Rowena

9. Rowena

10. Nail

11. Nail

1. King Comet—see photographs in this section.
2. Pinwheel Button—This lamp was made in different forms and several sizes.
3. Aquarius—see photograph in this section.
4. Banbury—see matching stand lamp opposite.
5. Rib Scallop—Font.
6. Radford—Font.
7. Palmetto—This lamp has the following catalogue description: "These lamps are made with the Pegs or Founts Crystal while the Feet are Assorted Jet, Gold, Blue, and Crystal. Equally making a Handsome Contrast and Variety." The generous use of capitals was probably for emphasis.
8. Optic—Made in many forms and sizes including a night lamp with a ribbed shade. Ruby stems and etched fonts were available.
9. Ainslie Block.
10. Diagonal Bar.
11. Daisy and Button with Crossbar—This pattern is shown on a goblet in Metz I.
12. Richmond—This lamp, shown in four sizes, was advertised in 1891 by the Richards & Hartley Glass Company, Tarentum, Pa. They were described as being available in crystal or colored glass. Revi calls this pattern Richmond.
13. Block and Bar Band.
14. Crystal Wedding—This pattern, shown in Metz I, is said to have been made originally by Adams & Co.
15. Pinwheel Buttons.
16. Banbury—This lamp was also made with a shell or ribbed pattern at the bottom of the font.
17. Merton.
18. Whirlpool with Shell Font—

1. King Comet.

2. Pinwheel Button

3. Aquarius

4. Banbury

5. Rib Scallop

6. Radford

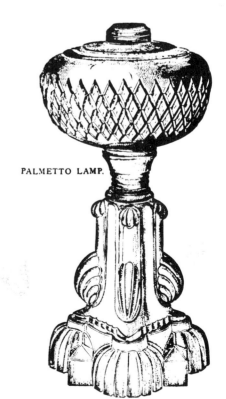

PALMETTO LAMP.

7. Palmetto

Originally made by the Central Glass Company.
19. Owen.

8. Optic

9. Ainslie Block

10. Diagonal Bar

11. Daisy and
Button with Crossbar

12. Richmond

13. Block and Bar Band

14. Crystal Wedding

15. Pinwheel Button

16. Banbury

17. Merton

18. Whirlpool with Shell Font

19. Owen

1. *Otis*   2. *Otis*   3. *Otis*

1., 2. & 3. — Otis—These lamps illustrated in Lamps & Other Lighting Devices, 1850-1906 are attributed to the King Glass Company, Pittsburgh, Pa.

4. — Sunken Window—One of the "one piece heavy pressed lamps."

5. & 6. — Leland

7. & 8. — Zippered Block (7) and Barred Oval (8) — Both these patterns are said by Revi to have been made by George Duncan & Sons, Pittsburgh, Pa.

9. & 10. — Expanded Prism—The stand lamps in this pattern have the screw socket connection.

11. — Whirlpool — Originally made by the Central Glass Company, Wheeling, West Va.

12. — Kings Crown Variant — Shown here in a banquet size with a screw socket.

13. — Nickel Plate 101 — This illustrates the type of shade used at the time the lamp was manufactured. See photograph in this section.

14. — King Comet — Banquet size lamp with shade. See photographs of a footed hand lamp in this section.

4. *Sunken Window*

5. *Leland*

6. *Leland*

NO.90 PATTERN
—ONE PIECE—
HEAVY·PRESSED·LAMP

7. *Zippered Block*

8. *Barred Oval*

9. Expanded Prism

10. Expanded Prism

11. Whirlpool

No. 9805—OPTIC SCREW SOCKET LAMPS.

The Bowl and Foot of these Lamps are screwed firmly together by a metal socket, which obviates excessive breakage in transit. The socket is covered by a pressed glass sleeve, which completely conceals the metal, producing a brilliant effect and making practically an all glass Lamp. Sold also without the glass sleeve.

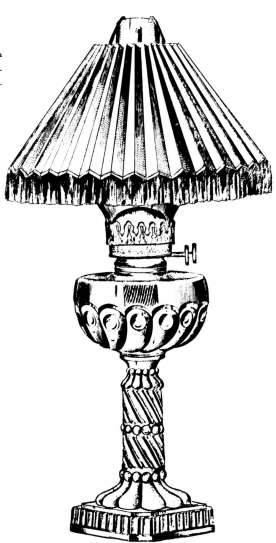

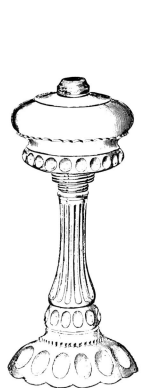

12. Kings Crown Variant—
    Banquet Lamp

13. Nickel Plate 101

14. King Comet

1. Banbury
2. Double Bar Band
3. No. 20 Footed hand lamp
4. Plain Rayed Base
5. King Melon — There is a photograph of the footed hand lamp in this section.
6. Central Beaded Panel — This pattern was made by the Central Glass Company, Wheeling, West Va.
7. Plain Rayed Base
8. Owen
9. Shell
10. Cube and Diamond — A photograph of the stand lamp in this pattern is shown in this section.
11. Pinwheel Button — This lamp has the same font as that used on the Pinwheel Button stand lamp.
12. Saucer Base night lamp
13. Stars and Bars Cigar Lighter — This pattern is attributed to the Bellaire Goblet Company in Findlay Pattern Glass by Smith. Kamm feels it was a pattern made in the 1870's. The cylinders surrounding the font contained little wire brushes on metal stems. These were held in the flame until they became sufficiently hot to light a cigar.
14. Stars and Bars night lamp
15. Remington night lamp
16. Vivian night lamp
17. Ellipse Band
18. Kings Crown Vase Lamp

1. Banbury   *2. Double Bar Band*   *3. No. 20 Footed Hand Lamp*

4. Plain Rayed Base   *5. King Melon*   *6. Central Beaded Panel*

7. Plain Rayed Base   *8. Owen*   *9. Shell*

10. Cube and Diamond   *11. Pinwheel Button*   *12. Saucer Base Night Lamp*

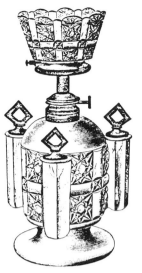

13. *Stars and Bars Cigar Lighter*　　14. *Stars and Bars Night Lamp*　　15. *Remington Night Lamp*　　16. *Vivian Night Lamp*

17. *Ellipse Band*

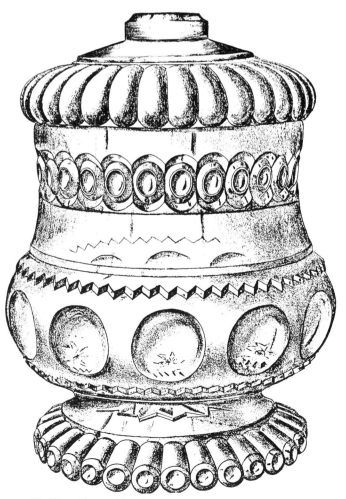

18. *Kings Crown Vase Lamp*

Lamps on these and the following pages are from the 1909 United States Glass Company catalogue. They clearly show the dramatic change in design, with the sharp decline of interest in pressed glass tableware and in the use of kerosene as an illuminant.

1., 2. & 3.   Late Petal — Photographs of these lamps are shown in this section.

4., 5. & 6. — Heavy Plain Band Opposite — Many of the night lamps illustrated are miniature forms of other lamps in this section. The Mammoth Rose Base lamp is included with the photographs in this section.

A Flat Hand   No. 1 Collar, $1.20 per doz.
Also make ¼ A Size, $1.10 per doz.

1. *Late Petal*

One Piece
Won't Break

½ A Footed Hand   No. 1 Collar
Also make ¼ A Size
½ A, $1.60 per doz.
¼ A, 1.40   "

2. *Late Petal*

One Piece
Won't Break

¼ A Stand   No. 1 Collar
$1.40 per doz.

3. *Late Petal*

½ A Flat Hand   No. 1 Collar
$1.40 per doz.

4. *Heavy Plain Band*

One Piece
Won't Break

¼ A Footed Hand   No. 1 Collar
$1.70 per doz.

5. *Heavy Plain Band*

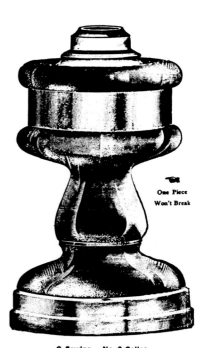

One Piece
Won't Break

C Sewing   No. 2 Collar
$3.50 per doz.

6. *Heavy Plain Band*

Lamps (Miscellaneous.)

ILLUSTRATIONS ONE-THIRD SIZE, EXCEPT AS NOTED.

No. 4 Fount and Filler, Handled, $2.00 per doz.
Also make without Handle, $1.30 per doz.

Drip Fount with Filler
$1.30 per doz.
With Handle, $2.00 per doz.

No. 7—½ Flat Hand Lamp, $1.20 per doz

Kitchen Fount, No. 2 Collar
$7.50 per gro.

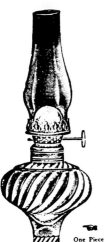

One Piece
Won't Break

9919 Night Lamp
Complete with Burner and
Chimney
$2.20 per doz.

Oxley Hand Lamp, No. 1 Collar
$1.20 per doz.

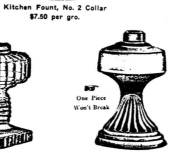

9873 Night Lamp
Complete with Burner and
Chimney
$2.20 per doz.

338 Night Lamp
Complete with Burner and
Chimney
$2.20 per doz.

One Piece
Won't Break

9920 Night Lamp
Complete with Burner and
Chimney
$2.20 per doz.

One Piece
Won't Break

9918 Night Lamp
Complete with Burner and
Chimney
$2.20 per doz.

Standard Sewing Lamp, 2 Collar
$5.00 per doz.
Also make with Filler, 2 Collar
$5.30 per doz.
With No. 3 Collar, 20c per doz.
additional

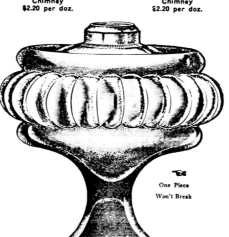

One Piece
Won't Break

9929 Mammoth Library Lamp
One dozen in barrel. Gross weight, 90 pounds
Height, 10 in. Base, 7¾ in. Bowl, 7¼ in.
(Illustration ½ Size)
Decorated, $8.00 per doz.
Plain,   6.00   "

Saucer Foot Hand Lamp
$1.60 per doz.

The thickness and weight of these lamps appeared to be a selling point. Perhaps at this late stage of the kerosene era, practicality was the only real concern.

1., 2. & 3. — Albion

4., 5. & 6. — Marlee. Similar to Serrated Loop. See photograph in this section.

7. — Stockton

8. — Appleton Plain

9. — Craven

10. — Appleton Patterned

The collars of Stockton, Appleton and Craven appear to have a narrow patterned band stamped in the center.

¼ A Flat Hand, No. 1 Collar
$1.10 per doz.

1. *Albion*

¼ A Footed Hand, No. 1 Collar
$1.40 per doz.

2. *Albion*

C Sewing, No. 2 Collar
$3.00 per doz.

3. *Albion*

½ A Flat Hand Lamp   No. 1 Collar
$1.40 per doz.

4. *Marlee*

½ A Footed Hand Lamp   No. 1 Collar
$2.10 per doz.

5. *Marlee*

C Stand   No. 2 Collar
$3.80 per doz.

6. *Marlee*

504 Immense Sewing Lamp Assortment.

Every lamp dealer knows it—The best assortment of lamps that was ever made up.   Extra large and heavy.   Fitted with brass clinched on collars.

ILLUSTRATIONS SCALE HALF SIZE

ASSORTMENT CONTAINS—

½ Dozen 9903 C Size Sewing Lamp
½ " 9904 C " " "
½ " 9905 C " " "
½ " 9906 C " " "
—
2 Dozen Glass, $7.50
Package. 50c net

One Piece
Won't Break

9903 Sewing Lamp   No. 2 Collar

7. Stockton

One Piece
Won't Break

9904 Sewing Lamp   No. 2 Collar

8. Appleton Plain

One Piece
Won't Break

9906 Sewing Lamp   No. 2 Collar

9. Craven

One Piece
Won't Break

9905 Sewing Lamp   No. 2 Collar

10. Appleton Patterned

Frosting and hand-painting generally improved these otherwise coarse lamps.

1. & 2. — Moore with Daisies — These lamps called the "decorated daisy assortment" were described as "a magnificent line of solid one piece pressed and fitted with our famous patent clinched on brass collars and handsomely decorated. The decoration is burnt into the glass". This lamp was also made with a sailing ship and lighthouse in a cartouche.

3., 4. & 5. — Chilton — These lamps were available with two different types of decoration. One consisted of tiny flowers or berries on the stem and base only, and the other had an apple blossom design on the font, stem and matching chimney.

6., 7. & 8. — The Long Loop pattern is more like the Thumbprint Panel to the right of it, or like the Turkey Foot pattern shown with the photographs in this section, and advertised in both the 1893 and 1909 catalogues. Long Loop and Thumbprint Panel lamps may have been made years before the 1909 catalogue.

9. & 10. — Thumbprint Panel — see above.

11. — Moore Plain — see No. 1.

12. — Long Loop — see No. 6.

13. — Moore Plain — see No. 1.

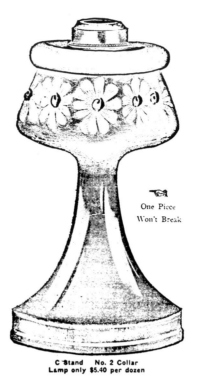

One Piece
Won't Break

C Stand   No. 2 Collar
Lamp only $5.40 per dozen

1. Moore with Daisies

No. 2 Chimney
No. 1 Chimney $1.40 per dozen
" 2 "   1.80 "   "

2. Moore with Daisies,
Matching Chimney

½ A Flat Hand   No. 1 Collar
$1.40 per doz.

3. Chilton

One Piece
Won't Break

¼ A Footed Hand   No. 1 Collar
$1.70 per doz.

4. Chilton

One Piece
Won't Break

¼ A Stand   No. 1 Collar
$1.70 per doz.

5. Chilton

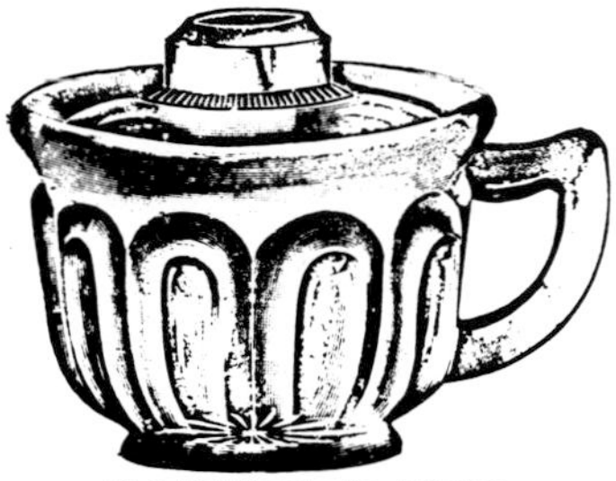

½ A Flat Hand No. 1 Collar
$1.40 per doz.

6. *Long Loop*

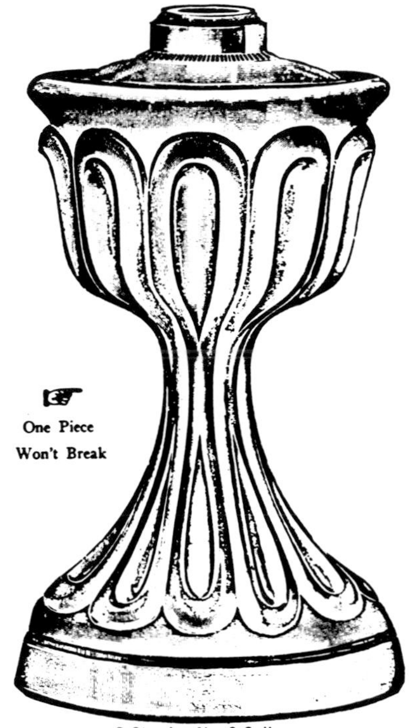
One Piece
Won't Break

C Stand No. 2 Collar
$3.80 per doz.

8. *Long Loop*

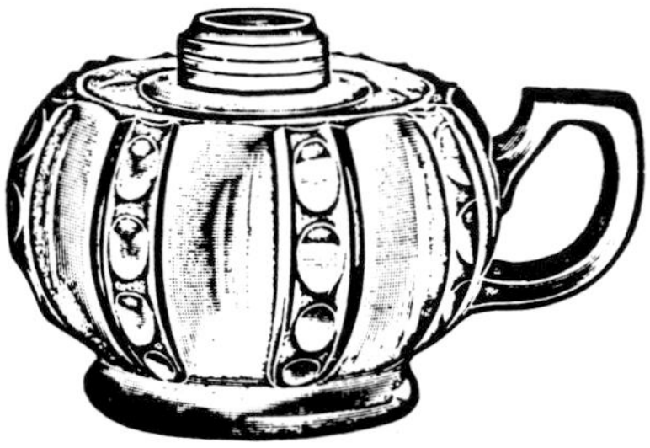

½ A Flat Hand No. 1 Collar
$1.20 per doz.

9. *Thumbprint Panel*

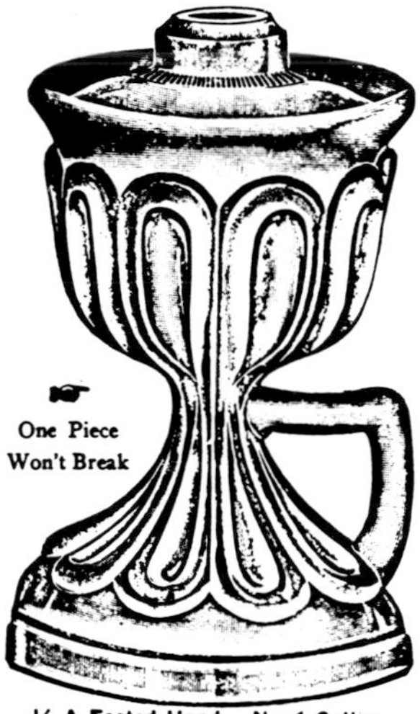
One Piece
Won't Break

¼ A Footed Hand No. 1 Collar
$1.70 per doz.

7. *Long Loop*

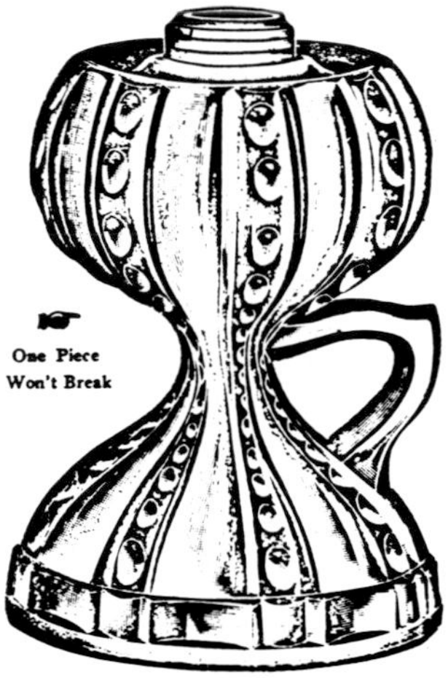
One Piece
Won't Break

¼ A Footed Hand No. 1 Collar
$1.40 per doz.

10. *Thumbprint Panel*

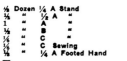

⅓	Dozen	¼ A	Stand
⅓	"	½ A	"
1	"	A	"
⅓	"	B	"
⅙	"	C	"
⅙	"	C	Sewing
⅓	"	¼ A	Footed Hand

3 Dozen Glass, $7.90 Package 50c net

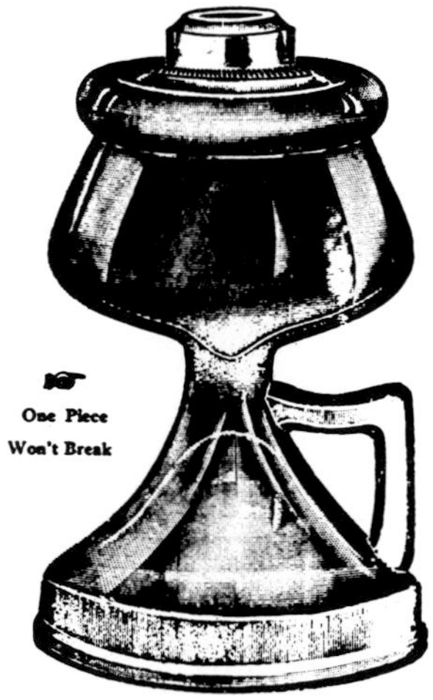
One Piece
Won't Break

¼ A Footed Hand No. 1 Collar

11. *Moore Plain—Footed Hand Lamp*

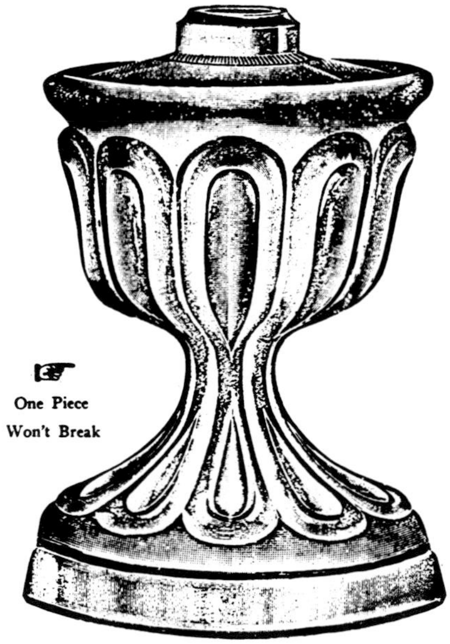
One Piece
Won't Break

C Sewing No. 2 Collar

12. *Long Loop*

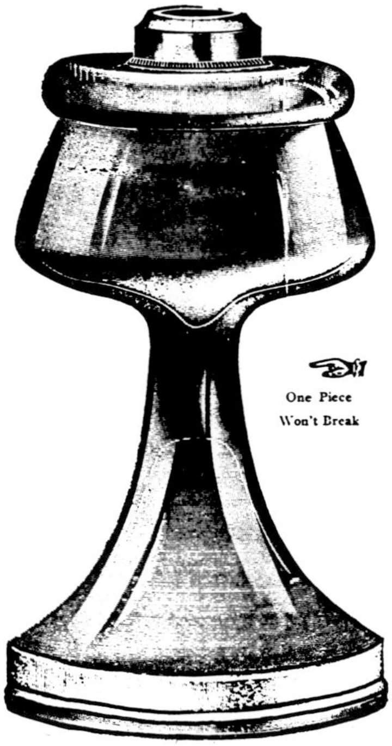
One Piece
Won't Break

C Stand No. 2 Collar

13. *Moore Plain*

China Glass & Lamps

The trade journal, China, Glass and Lamps, was published weekly from December, 1890 until 1920. The editorials, articles and advertisements give an insight into the decor and design of the times. Illustrated here are a few pages which describe this in the language of the day. These pages are from the first decade of the paper, because they show the enthusiasm for Victorian eclecticism which was running rampant. After the turn of the century, this enthusiasm for bizarre design began to wane, and the rapid increase in domestic use of electricity sounded the death knell for the era of tremendous production of kerosene lamps. Some examples of the wide variety of art glass techniques developed in the 90's, and which continued into this century, are seen in the glass vase lamps, and in some glass stand lamps. These include Art Nouveau and Tiffany type styles. Evidence today however, suggests that quantity and quality in this area was reserved for electric lamp shades.

A glance at these pages from the 90's will quickly establish the character of popular design of the times. There were relatively few new and interesting designs after 1900. Production dwindled as the word lamp lost its kerosene connotation, and the era of the electric light was established.

This news item on the Metric System from a 1906 issue, is a departure from the kerosene scene, but timely and topical today.

METRIC SYSTEM IN CANADA.

Consul Seyfert, of Stratford, Ont., reports an active movement in Canada that has for its object the adoption of the metric system of weights and measures. Active propaganda is at work to have the question properly presented to the Canadian people. The consul writes: With a view of adopting the metric system in weights and measures at an early day the Canadian government is preparing and educating the people for the change. Prof. J. C. McLennan, of the University of Toronto, has been engaged by the Dominion government to devote the next year to explaining the system in a series of lectures in all the leading cities from Halifax to Vancouver. The professor delivered his first lecture on the subect at Stratford, February 7, before the board of trade. According to his explanation it is the object of the Canadian government to secure a uniform standard of weights and measures throughout the entire British Empire, and thus to advance trade relations among the different colonies of the Empire. The board of trade at Stratford unanimously adopted resolutions, urging the adoption of the system.

VOL. 1. PITTSBURGH, DECEMBER 17, 1890. NO. 1.

Peerless Lead Glass Lamp Chimneys

THEY WILL NOT BREAK FROM HEAT.

THE LAMP TRADE.

NEW YORK.

[A portion of the appended lamp notes are from the columns of our observant contemporary, the New York Press.]

UNABATED is the rage for ornamental lamps. It began four or five years ago and speedily reached such a point that every bride hoped to obtain among her wedding gifts a lamp for every room in her new home. Since that time designers have almost exhausted their ingenuity in devising lamps of various forms and materials. Half a dozen metals, all sorts of pottery, malachite, marble and a dozen other materials have been pressed into service, while ingenuity has run riot in the matter of design.

Pottery and metal are the commonest materials in use. When a handsome and costly lamp is to be made a rich and unique vase of Japanese or American manufacture is selected and a designer is set to work to decide upon the style of metallic work to accompany the pottery. The two are made so thoroughly harmonious that one does not at first realize that the parts of the lamp were made in widely sundered places. The handsomest lamps have for foundation vases that cannot easily be duplicated. The design for the metallic work and the shade is made to correspond with the general style of the vase, and the result is a lamp that is the only one of its kind.

A peculiarly rich lamp is made of a white and gold vase, shaped somewhat like the capstan of a ship, ornamented with gold bronze, Russian in design. The shade is a globe of faded yellow glass, especially made for the purpose. A coronet of bronze, with crosses mounted upon tiny balls, surmounts the globe. These crosses are repeated at various points in the bronze work. Such a lamp costs $325.

Standing lamps of Mexican onyx, some in antique form, cost from $150 to $250. A tall standing lamp of black iron and red clay pottery costs $90. One of black iron, representing a rose tree with gilded roses, brings the same price. A lamp of richly painted Sevres pottery and gold bronze costs $450.

Cut glass lamps for the dinner table are now fashionable. They are ornamented with rich silk and lace shades and some have around the base small detachable cups for holding buttonhole bouquets. Small cut glass lamps are now made with a short glass spike, which, with the aid of a spring, fits snugly any candlestick. These lamps, mounted upon silver candlesticks, are used to light the dinner table. In lamps, as in everything else, crude and vulgar designs are seen. The object of the designer is originality, if not novelty, and knowing that he must attract many who have wealth without taste, he is sometimes content with novelty alone. The result of working on these lines is costly but hideous things that find their way into unlovely drawing rooms and go to increase the confusion of ugliness there reigning. The contrast between such designs and the simplicity of things copied from the antique is very striking. A table lamp consisting of a Corinthian column of cut glass upholding a simple globe of the same material is beautiful by comparison with a hideous gilded affair of modern design costing five times as much.

Along with costly lamps have developed expensive shades. These are made of silk, satin, lace, artificial flowers and what not. The handsomest cost from $15 to $30 each. Some are made over frames shaped not unlike parasols. Many of these shades are the work of ladies in moderate circumstances, who take this means of increasing their incomes. Sometimes the design and the material are furnished by the shopkeeper. At others both are furnished by the person doing the work. The materials are costly and the work is tedious. The cleverest workers find the business profitable, but it must make them heartsick to see the prices marked on their product in the shop and contrast them with the wages earned. In some cases this work is done in small shops established by milliners. Two or three assistants work with the proprietress of this shop. This work has not yet developed large factories, partly because it depends for its success upon individual taste and skill. Fashionable ladies change the style and trimming of their lamp shades quite as religiously as their headwear. Gold and other metal fringes are just now the proper thing, while jewels and moths and butterflies are a novelty. In colors, those liked best for millinery purposes are the ones chosen for the parlor pet.

Lamps still continue to be favored as wedding presents. This is the one gift that cannot be duplicated too often. Two or three handsome drawing room lamps, several for the dinner table, a standard lamp for the hall, at least one such for the library and a small one for each bedroom are none too many for the ambition of the young housekeeper. It is a considerable tax to live to such a collection of lamps, for shades do not last forever, and they are a costly luxury to renew. The black iron lamp is perhaps the favorite with people of moderate means. It requires no very elaborate shade, yet it is handsome and artistic. The New York workers in black iron turn out as good work as can be found except among antiques.

Lamp manufacturers and dealers are not doing a very lively business just now, yet their hopes for the future are sanguine and they expect big things to happen towards the middle of August. In the lamp trade there is tremendous competition and prices tend to run down all the time. No remedy seems possible, for the lamp manufacturers will not attempt to form a trust or combination, and everything must be left to individual effort. So much the better for the purchasing public.

The Plume & Atwood Mfg. Co., make a handsome lamp, a first class illuminator, brilliant and steady in its flame, easy to handle, cleanly, suited particularly for household purposes—in all respects an excellent lamp and one that is bound to live and flourish. The company sell their goods at most moderate prices and their customers have no reason ever to complain.

The Rochester Lamp Co. exhibit a vast collection of lamps, all goods of the highest order of excellence, finished in first class style, affording a superb light, and in every detail to be praised and admired. For the fall trade the Rochester Co. are making big preparations and will be found as usual ahead when the busy season arrives.

Messrs. Swann & Whitehead, Trenton, N. J., exhibit at their New York salesrooms, 96 Church street, corner Barclay street, some of the finest decorations in the metropolis. Their lamps and shades are among the handsomest of their kind in existence. Considering the beautiful manner in which these wares are ornamented it is wonderful the low price at which they are offered.

The Haida Lamp & China Co., 53 Warren street, have placed on the market one of the most attractive, useful and popular articles known to the trade. The Haida lamp furnishes a splendid light and has met with a most gratifying measure of success.

Mr. B. B. Schneider is one of the most experienced lamp manufacturers in the world. What this veteran in the lamp business does not know about the trade is not worth knowing. Mr. Schneider has always on hand full lines of the most popular lamps on the market, and his prices are invariably reasonable.

Lamps continued on page 24.

HOBBS ✧ GLASS ✧ COMPANY,
WHEELING, W. VA.

Patent Applied For.

Made in Crystal, Crystal Opalescent, Sapphire, Opalescent and Ruby Opalescent.

The Bowl and Foot of these Lamps are screwed firmly together by a metal socket, which entirely obviates the excessive breakage attending all blown Lamps. The socket is covered by a pressed glass sleeve, which completely conceals the metal, producing a brilliant effect and making practically an all glass Lamp. The saving in breakage will make the dealer a handsome profit. Patent applied for.

HAIDA LAMP & CHINA CO.,
MANUFACTURERS,

HAIDA

✻ PIANO LAMPS, BANQUET LAMPS, LIBRARY LAMPS, ✻
DECORATED VASE LAMPS,
53 and 55 Warren St., New York.

THE LANE MANUFACTURING CO.,
MANUFACTURERS OF
The Aurora Central Draft Burners, the Improved Magnum, Cleveland Student Lamp, and Perkins & House's Non-Explosive Lamps.

FACTORIES AT KENOSHA, WIS.

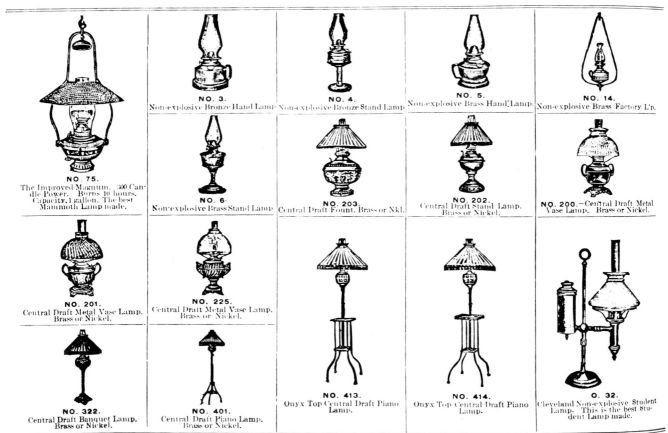

NO. 75. The Improved Magnum, 300 Candle Power. Burns 10 hours. Capacity, 1 gallon. The best Mammoth Lamp made.

NO. 3. Non-explosive Bronze Hand Lamp.

NO. 4. Non-explosive Bronze Stand Lamp.

NO. 5. Non-explosive Brass Hand Lamp.

NO. 14. Non-explosive Brass Factory L'p.

NO. 6. Non-explosive Brass Stand Lamp.

NO. 203. Central Draft Fount. Brass or Nkl.

NO. 202. Central Draft Stand Lamp. Brass or Nickel.

NO. 200.—Central Draft Metal Vase Lamp. Brass or Nickel.

NO. 201. Central Draft Metal Vase Lamp. Brass or Nickel.

NO. 225. Central Draft Metal Vase Lamp. Brass or Nickel.

NO. 413. Onyx Top Central Draft Piano Lamp.

NO. 414. Onyx Top Central Draft Piano Lamp.

O. 32. Cleveland Non-explosive Student Lamp. This is the best Student Lamp made.

NO. 322. Central Draft Banquet Lamp. Brass or Nickel.

NO. 401. Central Draft Piano Lamp. Brass or Nickel.

VOL. III. NO. 21. PITTSBURGH, MAY 4, 1892. $2.00 PER ANNUM.

Fostoria Glass Co.,
Moundsville, W. Va.

Hollenden Egg Cup—⅓ size.

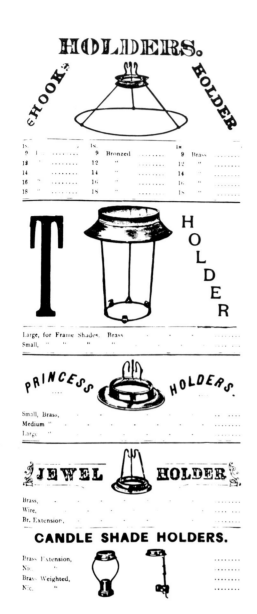

HOLDERS.

HOOK HOLDER

Is.			Is.			In		
9		....	9	Bronzed	....	9	Brass	....
12		....	12	''	....	12	''	....
14		....	14	''	....	14	''	....
16		....	16	''	....	16	''	....
18		....	18	''	....	18	''	....

T HOLDER

Large, for Frame Shades. Brass	.	.	.	....
Small, ''	.	.	.	....

PRINCESS HOLDERS.

Small, Brass,	.	.	.	....
Medium ''	.	.	.	....
Large ''	.	.	.	....

JEWEL HOLDER

Brass,	.	.	.	....
Wire,	.	.	.	....
Br. Extension,	.	.	.	....

CANDLE SHADE HOLDERS.

Brass Extension,				....
Nic. ''				....
Brass Weighted,				....
Nic. ''				....

C.G.&L. 1891

Simplest, Cheapest and Cleanest Method of Heating Rooms.

The Patent Falls Heater.

By application of a scientific principle, the heat of the lamp is increased and distributed evenly throughout the room, making it comfortable in the coldest weather. Can be used over any lamp.

NO ODOR.

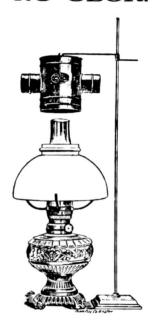

In successful use for two years. Best of references furnished from all sections of the country.

Dealers find it one of their most popular and profitable household articles. LIBERAL TERMS.

Enterprise Mfg. Co.,

C.G.&L. 1892

Height, 6 inches.

ILLUMINATED CLOCK.

NEW. NEAT. NOVEL. SAFE. SIMPLE. SATISFACTORY.
——COMBINING——

A DAY CLOCK,   A NURSERY LAMP,   A NIGHT CLOCK,   A MEDICINE CLOCK.

A PRACTICAL AND USEFUL INVENTION.

This Clock is a good time-keeper; not liable to get out of order; invaluable in the sick room, useful in the nursery, and indispensable in every family.

Farmers, mechanics and business men, whose duty calls them up before daylight, will find it a great convenience to be able to ascertain the hour at a glance without rising.

As a night lamp in the nursery or sick room, where a soft light is needed, which is pleasant to the eye and yet sufficient to make objects distinct, this illuminated clock furnishes the light and gives the correct time.

In the sick room it is the watchful nurse, and by its medicine indicator, which can be set to point to any hour, tells the exact time when the next dose is to be taken.

The globe revolves once every twelve hours, passing the index hand or pointer. Inside is placed a lamp which contains oil enough to give a light for twenty-four hours at a cost of about one cent or a ha'f penny.

No unpleasant odor arises from the lamp, the globe being so constructed that the combustion is perfect. Alcohol or wax tapers may be used in place of oil if so desired.

Each clock is securely packed in a wooden box.

Price per dozen, $17.50; for orders of 6 dozen, $16.25; for orders of 12 dozen or over, $15.00.

MANUFACTURED EXCLUSIVELY BY

F. H. LOVELL & CO., 118 John and 231 & 233 Pearl Sts., New York.

C.G.&L. 1892

THE NEW "UNIVERSAL
✦~wwww~ MAMMOTH. ~wwww~✦

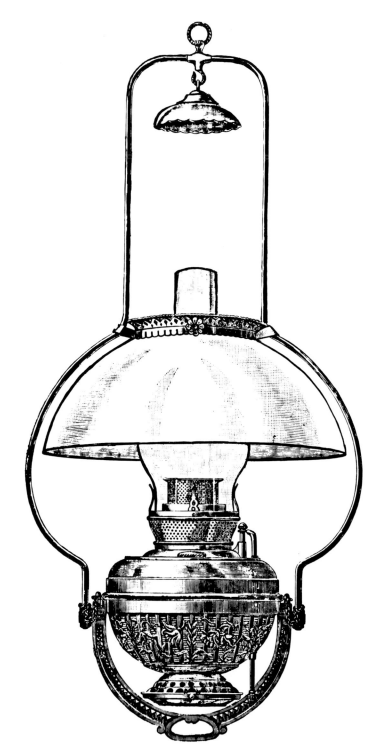

NO. 09—WITH CROWN.
Diameter of Fount, Nine Inches. Burns Nine Hours. This lamp without Crown takes a Tin Reflector.
We can furnish either Spring Balance or a Ball Weight Balance for this Lamp.

THE ANSONIA BRASS & COPPER CO
19 and 21 Cliff Street, **NEW YORK, U. S. A.**

No. 10 Mammoth Rochester Fount and 162   No. 2 Rochester Fount.
Harp.

No 391.
Rochester
Banquet.

No. 2 Rochester Parlor.

No. 354 Rochester
Piano Lamp.

"The Rochester"

Within the reach of all!

All prices are withdrawn, and a new list is now ready.
It is an eye-opener.

If any lamp dealer in America, Europe or Asia wants
to see what the best lamp in the world can now be bought
for, send to us.

The Rochester Lamp Co.,

42 PARK PLACE.   **NEW YORK.**
37 BARCLAY STREET,

LARGER VARIETY THAN ANY OTHER HOUSE IN THE WORLD.

No. 283 Rochester Piano Lamp.

No. 422 Rochester Piano L

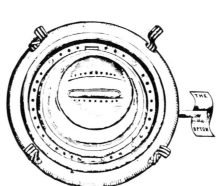

Jr. Rochester Hotel Lamp.   Jr. Rochester Parlor.   The Upton Burner.   Upton Hand Lamp

C.G.&L. 1893

FORT PITT BANQUET LAMP.

ASSORTED DECORATIONS.

——Best and showiest lamp for the price ever offered.——

►ARTISTIC AND BEAUTIFUL.◄
—— WRITE FOR PRICES. ——

DITHRIDGE & CO.,

Fort Pitt Glass Works, • Pittsburgh, Pa.

Architectural Glass Co.,

No. 7 D, No. 2 Collar.   No. 7 C, No. 1 or 2 Collar.   No. 7 B, 1 or 2 Collar.   No. 7 A.   No. 7 O.   No. 7, O or A Hand.

No. 9 O or A Hand.   No. 9 O.   No. 9 A.   No. 9 B, No. 1 or 2 Collar.   No. 9 C, No. 1 or 2 Collar.   No. 9 D, No. 2 Collar.

No. 14 D, No. 2 Collar.   No. 14 C, No. 1 or 2 Collar.   No. 14 B, No. 1 or 2 Collar.   11 A, No. 1 Collar.   No. 110, No. 1 Collar.   No. 11 O or A Hand.

No. 11 O or A Hand.   No. 11 O, No. 1 Col.   No. 11 A, No. 1 Col.   No. 11 B, No. 1 or 2 Col.   No. 11 C, No. 1 or 2 Col.   No. 11 D, No. 2 Col.

We wish to impress upon the trade that we can always give prompt shipment on lamps, and as we steadily carry a loose stock can pack them as desired at any time.

Rooms 525 & 526 Standard Building, 531 WOOD, ST., PITTSBURGH, PA.

"No, that's not the way. You pull a little latch, and the lantern OPENS ITSELF. It's the slickest lantern I ever saw. Each tube is made of ONE PIECE of metal with the turns round and smooth, not like the old patched-up ugly elbows. I believe that makes her draft so fine. I tell you she's a daisy right through; had her along that night of the blizzard. That's the time to get ACQUAINTED with a lantern. Hadn't been for the "Surprise Tubular" that night I wouldn't be here now."

OHIO LANTERN CO.,
TIFFIN, OHIO.

SURPRISE TUBULAR.

C.G.&L. 1893

NATIONAL GLASS COMPANY,

OPERATING

RIVERSIDE GLASS WORKS,

WELLSBURG, W. VA.

No. 15 515.   No. 15 514.   No. 15 516.

ON THIS PAGE ARE SHOWN SOME OF OUR NEW STYLES AND DESIGNS OF THE CELEBRATED RIVERSIDE CLINCH COLLAR LAMPS. THE DESIGN SHOWS FOR ITSELF IT IS THE PRETTIEST LAMP IN PROPORTION AND STYLE THAT YOU WILL FIND ON THE MARKET THIS YEAR. ORDERS WILL BE FILLED PROMPTLY, AND PRICE AND ILLUSTRATED CATALOGUE OF THESE GOODS MAILED ON APPLICATION.

The New Rochester

THE NEW ROCHESTER
No. 534 WITH
No. 616 BENT GLASS GLOBE

Line for Spring 1898 ready. We are showing some Striking New Shapes and Decorations in Reception Lamps.

The Rochester Lamp Co.

Eagle Glass & Mfg. Co.
WELLSBURG, W. Va.

367.

650.

602.

625.

Eagle Night Lamp.

600.

615.

AGENTS—Doctor & Co., 48 Park Place, New York.   H. B. Foster, cor. 6th & Arch Sts., Philadelphia.   Green & Seeman, 23 S. Charles St., Baltimore

C.G.&L. 1898

Bibliography

American Historical Catalog Collection. Lamps & Other Lighting Devices 1850-1906. Princeton, The Pyne Press, 1972.

_____ Pennsylvania Glassware, 1870-1904. Princeton, The Pyne Press, 1972.

Barret, Richard Carter. A Collectors Handbook of Blown and Pressed American Glass. Manchester, Vermont, Forward's Color Productions, Inc., 1971.

_____ Blown and Pressed American Glass. Manchester, Vermont, Forward's Color Productions, Inc., 1966.

Belknap, E. McCamby. Milk Glass. New York, Crown Publishers, 1949.

Blount, Bernice and Henry. French Cameo Glass. Des Moines, Iowa, Dr. and Mrs. Henry C. Blount, Jr., 1968.

Bond, Marcelle. The Beauty of Albany Glass (1893 to 1902). Berne, Indiana, Publishers Printing House, 1972.

Boyd, Ralph and Louise. Greentown, Second Edition. Lagro, Indiana, Commercial Printing, 1970.

Christensen, Erwin O. The Index of American Design. New York, The Macmillan Company, 1950.

Courter, J.W. Aladdin the Magic Name in Lamps. Simpson, Illinois. J.W. Courter, 1971.

Delmore, Mrs. Edward J. Victorian Miniature Oil Lamps. Manchester, Vermont, Forward's Color Reproductions, Inc., 1968.

Drepperd, Carl W. ABC's of Old Glass. New York, Award Books, 1966.

Freeman, Dr. Larry. New Light on Old Lamps. Watkins Glen, New York, Century House, 1968.

Hammond, Dorothy. Confusing Collectibles. Des Moines, Iowa, Wallace-Homestead Book Company, 1969.

Hayward, Arthur H. Colonial and Early American Lighting, Third Enlarged Edition. New York, Dover Publications Inc., 1962.

Kamm, Minnie Watson. Pattern Glass Books, Volume 1 to 8 inclusive. Grosse Pointe, Michigan, Kamm Publications, 1939 to 1954.

Kampher, Fritz and Beyer, Klaus G. Glass, A World History. The Story of 4000 Years of fine Glass-Making translated and revised by Dr. Edmund Launert. London, Studio Vista Ltd.

Knittle, Rhea Mansfield. Early American Glass. New York, The Century Co., 1927.

Lee, Robert W. Boston & Sandwich Glass Co. Boston, 1874 Catalogue. Wellesley Hills, Massachusetts. Lee Publications, 1968.

Lee, Ruth Webb. Antique Fakes and Reproductions, Enlarged and Revised. Wellesley Hills, Massachusetts, Lee Publications, 1966.

_____ Handbook of Early American Pressed Glass Patterns. Wellesley Hills, Massachusetts, Lee Publications, 1936.

_____ Early American Pressed Glass, Enlarged and Revised, 36th ed. Wellesley Hills, Massachusetts, Lee Publications, 1960.

_____ Sandwich Glass, The History of the Boston & Sandwich Glass Company, Enlarged and Revised. Wellesley Hills, Massachusetts, Lee Publications, 1966.

_____ Victorian Glass. Wellesley Hills, Massachusetts, Lee Publications, 1927.

Lindsey, Bessie M. American Historical Glass. Rutland, Vermont, Charles E. Tuttle Company, 1967.

MacLaren, George. Nova Scotia Glass, Occasional Paper No. 4 Historical Series, No. 1 (Revised). Halifax, Nova Scotia, Nova Scotia Museum, 1968.

McKearin, George S. and Helen. American Glass. New York, Crown Publishers, Inc., 1941.

Metz, Alice Hulett. Early American Pattern Glass, Twelfth Printing, 1971. Beverton, Oregon, Charles Metz, 1958.

_____ Much More Early American Pattern Glass, Book II. Beverton, Oregon, Charles Metz, 1965.

Millard, S.T. Goblets, The Fifth Edition, 1947. Topeka, Kansas, S. T. Millard, 1938.

_____ Goblets II, Second Edition. Topeka, Kansas, S. T. Millard, 1940.

Lafferty, James R., Sr. "The Phoenix". James R. Lafferty, Sr., M.A., 1969.

Papert, Emma. The Illustrated Guide to American Glass. New York, Hawthorn Books, Inc., 1972.

Peterson, Arthur G. Glass Patents and Patterns. DeBary, Florida, A. G. Peterson, 1973.

_____ 400 Trademarks on Glass. DeBary, Florida, A. G. Peterson, 1968.

The Plume & Atwood Manufacturing Company Illustrated Catalogue of Kerosene Oil Burners, Gas and Oil Lamp Trimmings, Lamps, Oil Heaters, etc. Simpson, Illinois, J. W. Courter Enterprises.

Rogers, Frances, and Beard, Alice. 5000 Years of Glass. New York, Frederick A. Stokes Company, 1937.

The Rushlight Club. Early Lighting, A Pictorial Guide. Boston, Massachusetts, The Rushlight Club, 1972.

Russell, Loris S. A Heritage of Light, Lamps and lighting in the early Canadian home. Toronto, University of Toronto Press, 1968.

_____ Lighting the Pioneer Ontario Home. Toronto, Royal Ontario Museum, 1966.

Revi, Albert Christian. American Pressed Glass and Figure Bottles. New York, Thomas Nelson Inc., 1964.

_____ Nineteenth Century Glass, Its Genesis and Development. New York, Thomas Nelson Inc., 1967.

_____ The Spinning Wheel's Complete Book of Antiques. New York, Grosset & Dunlap, 1972.

The Sandwich Historical Society presents Glass. Exhibited in the Sandwich Glass Museum. Sandwich, Massachusetts, Sandwich Glass Museum, 1969.

Savage, George. Glass. London, Weidenfeld and Nicholson, 1965.

Smith, Don E. Findlay Pattern Glass. Findlay, Ohio, Privately Printed, 1970.

Smith, Frank R. and Ruth E. Miniature Lamps. New York, Thomas Nelson & Sons, 1968.

Spence, Hilda and Kelvin. A Guide to Early Canadian Glass. Don Mills, Ontario, Longmans Canada Limited, 1966.

Stevens, Gerald. In a Canadian Attic. Toronto, McGraw-Hill Ryerson Limited, 1963.

_____ Early Canadian Glass. Toronto, The Ryerson Press, 1961.

_____ Canadian Glass, c. 1825-1925. Toronto, The Ryerson Press, 1967.

Thwing, Leroy. Flickering Flames: A History of Domestic Lighting through the Ages. Rutland, Vermont, Charles E. Tuttle Company, 1958.

Unitt, Doris and Peter. American and Canadian Goblets. Peterborough, Ontario, Clock House, 1970.

_____ American and Canadian Goblets, Volume II. Peterborough, Ontario, Clock House, 1974.

_____ Treasury of Canadian Glass. Peterborough, Ontario, Clock House, 1969.

Watkins, Lura Woodside. Cambridge Glass 1818 to 1888 The Story of the New England Glass Company. New York, Bramhall House, 1930.

Webster, Donald Blake—Edited by: The Book of Canadian Antiques, Toronto, McGraw-Hill Ryerson Limited, 1974.

Wilson, Kenneth M. Glass in New England, Second Edition. Sturbridge, Massachusetts, Old Sturbridge Village, 1969.

_____ New England Glass and Glassmaking. New York, Thomas Y. Crowell Company, 1972.

Wills, Geoffrey. Glass (Orbis Connoisseur's Library). London, Orbis Publishing, 1972.

RESOURCE CENTERS

Canadian Patent Office—Ottawa, Canada.
Carnegie Institute, Pittsburgh, Pa.
Corning Museum of Glass, Corning, N.Y.
Henry Ford Museum, Dearborn, Mich.
Historical Society of Western Pennsylvania, Pittsburgh, Pa.
Library of Congress, Washington, D.C.
Oglebay Institute, Wheeling, West Va.
Ohio Historical Society, Columbus, Ohio
Ontario Archives, Toronto, Ont.
Royal Ontario Museum, Toronto, Ont.
Sandwich Glass Museum, Sandwich, Mass.
Toronto Public Libraries, Toronto, Ont.
United States Patent Office, Alexandria, Va.

Index

Named Lamps or Patterns in Italics
* indicates section.